THE PILGRIMAGE TO RUSSIA

THE SOVIET UNION AND THE

THE
PILGRIMAGE
TO RUSSIA

TREATMENT OF FOREIGNERS, 1924-1937

Sylvia R. Margulies

THE UNIVERSITY OF WISCONSIN PRESS
Madison, Milwaukee, and London, 1968

Published by the
University of Wisconsin Press
Madison, Milwaukee, and London

U.S.A.: Box 1379, Madison, Wisconsin 53701
U.K.: 27–29 Whitfield Street, London, W.1

Printed in the United States of America
by Kingsport Press, Inc., Kingsport, Tennessee

Library of Congress
Catalog Card Number 68–16062

Preface

The word "pilgrimage" was chosen for the title of this study because it suggests more than an ordinary journey to a foreign country. For many, a trip to Russia was a journey to worship at the shrine of a new civilization seemingly based on the ideal of social justice. For others, it was a trip to a land of opportunity which promised work for the unemployed and training for the unskilled. For the majority, the curious, it was an expedition to a country which challenged the world by claiming to repudiate the Western political, economic, and social ethic. A pilgrimage may be filled with risks, its outcome uncertain, the expectations associated with it high. The pilgrimage to Russia was no exception.

While there were a number of foreigners in Russia at the time of the Revolution, and a number of visitors during the period following 1917, it was not until very late in 1924 that the USSR began actively to attract foreign labor delegations. Its first success was the visit of the British Trades Union Congress delegation in December, 1924. Invitations designed to serve Soviet policy goals were issued to individual workers, engineers, and intellectuals as well as to other labor delegations and to ordinary tourists in the next five years. This continued, with changing emphases on different groups, until late 1937, when increasing Soviet preoccupation with major problems of diplomatic and military strategy, combined with the uneasy atmosphere generated internally by the purges, served both to reduce Soviet interest in foreign visitors and to influence foreigners to travel elsewhere for adventure. In addition, by 1937, the Soviet regime was producing its own technical intelligentsia and no longer had need of major foreign technical assistance. Thus, I believe that the dates 1924–37 encompass the major period of the pilgrimage to Russia.

The Pilgrimage to Russia is a study of conditions in one definite society at one definite period, but it is hoped that the framework can apply to the Soviet Union today or to any other closed society which fears contact with the rest of the world. It is primarily a study of communication between foreigners and natives within a context where all contacts are susceptible to political control.

The study first tries to answer the following questions about motives and techniques. Under what circumstances and for what purposes does a totalitarian society encourage the presence of foreign visitors and residents? How does the society try to incorporate people from an open society into its structure? To what extent does such a system manipulate visitors in order to promote an image of the country which it wishes disseminated to the outside world? What techniques and mechanisms are used to accomplish this aim?

Secondly, the study examines the impact of Soviet manipulation on foreign visitors and residents. Under what circumstances are these efforts successful? To what extent are initial preconceptions crucially important? What happens to visitors when their particular view of reality is tested against the hard facts of reality itself? Does the image change? Finally, what is the overall effect of the experiences within a closed society on people's attitudes after they leave the country?

Sources for a study of the pilgrimage to Russia are extremely varied. A major source consists of memoirs written by people who visited or lived in the Soviet Union during the period under study. Although many of the memoirs proved to be quite valuable, others were less so because of their extreme bias, or because they dealt primarily with the operation of the Soviet system rather than with the author's personal experience within the country.

A second important nucleus of material is to be found within the Decimal Files of the Department of State, several hundred items of which, generally diplomatic dispatches, contributed immeasurably to the study. Before as well as after the recognition of the Soviet Union by the United States, the State Department was much interested in finding out from Americans and Europeans who had visited or worked in Soviet Russia many of the same things that interested me. Diplomatic personnel stationed in Berlin, Riga, Helsinki, and Warsaw were authorized to question individuals who had just left the Soviet Union about their experiences within the country. Although the responses were too varied to lend themselves to statistical treatment, often the answers of a number of people who had shared the same working location or the same type of experience tended to agree.

A third source of material includes the publications of the Soviet Communist party, the Communist International, and the national Communist parties and Communist "front" groups in Great Britain, France, and the United States. This type of material was extremely valuable for an understanding of the entire promotional campaign of the Soviet Union and the organizational structure which supported it, as well as of the organizational division of labor within Soviet Russia.

Finally, to supplement manuscript and published material, approximately forty interviews were conducted with British and American citizens who had visited and/or lived in the Soviet Union during the period under investigation, and with other individuals (such as members of the American Communist party) who had special knowledge on the subject. Because there exists no complete listing of the people who went to the Soviet Union between 1924 and 1937, and because so many of those who went have since died, it was impossible to get a representative sample in the strictest sense. My prime objective was to locate individuals who, because of their presence in the Soviet Union or their knowledge of Soviet activities to attract foreigners, had special insight into the subject. A study of the written materials, memoirs, and other documents, supplemented by *Who's Who*, helped to locate a number of people who had been to the Soviet Union between 1924 and 1937. Talks with prominent scholars in Soviet studies and with the staffs of organizations interested in the Soviet Union helped to locate others. Many of the people who were interviewed were happy to suggest other names. It was not possible, however, to interview all those mentioned. Others who were contacted were too busy or did not want to talk about the subject. A number of interviews were held with American and British journalists who had lived in the Soviet Union for long periods of time between 1924 and 1937. Other interviews were conducted with individuals who had studied in the Soviet Union or who had worked in Soviet industry and agriculture. Nine respondents had visited the Soviet Union for shorter periods as part of a delegation or an arranged group tour. Several interviews were with diplomatic personnel stationed in Moscow with the American Embassy after 1933. Two respondents were connected with American organizations doing business with the Soviet government. A number of interviewees were former Soviet citizens who had worked at one time with foreigners in Soviet industry.

The interviews were conducted during 1962 and 1963 in the United States, Great Britain, and Germany. Because the informants had been selected on the basis of their probable ability to provide information on certain aspects of the study, a generalized questionnaire was not used. The responses to the interviews were integrated with other relevant material in the body of the study. A few of those interviewed preferred not to be identified and are referred to in the notes only by number and the date on which they were interviewed; all others are identified by name.

The interview material was chiefly valuable for filling in certain gaps of knowledge and for evaluating the written material on the subject. The interviewees who had spent a number of years within the USSR were able to discuss their observation of the parade of transient visitors and offer comparative information about the different sub-periods between 1924 and 1937.

The material in Chapter 8 is not based on a comprehensive treatment of the subject. The material was used for comparative purposes in order briefly to consider the question of continuity and change in Soviet behavior toward foreign visitors.

I wish to acknowledge the assistance of many institutions and individuals, both in the United States and Europe, who made this project possible. My gratitude goes to the staffs of the Historical Office of the Bureau of Public Affairs, Department of State; of the State Department Division of the National Archives, Washington, D.C.; of the manuscript divisions of the New York Public Library and the library of the State Historical Society of Wisconsin, in Madison; of the Bibliothèque de Documentation Internationale Contemporaine of the University of Paris; and of the Institute for International Education, New York, for furnishing needed material. I also wish to thank the staffs of the British Ethical Culture and Humanist Movement, London; the Institute for the Study of the USSR, Munich; Radio Free Europe, Munich; and Radio Liberty, Munich, for their co-operation. Lastly, a debt of gratitude must go to the many people who allowed me to question them about their experiences or who suggested individuals to interview.

Without the financial assistance of the University of Wisconsin, the research for this study would not have been possible. Above all, I am deeply grateful to John A. Armstrong, professor of political science at the University of Wisconsin, for counsel during the long period of inception and preparation of the study and to Grace Shipley, Wisconsin State University, Eau Claire, for invaluable advice in technical preparation of the study. Finally, without the encouragement of my husband, Morton Sipress, final revisions would not have been completed.

SYLVIA MARGULIES SIPRESS

Eau Claire, Wisconsin
September, 1967

Contents

THE PILGRIMAGE TO RUSSIA

1

The Closed Society and Foreign Guests

Although more than forty-three years have passed since Soviet Russia began courting foreign tourists in 1924, to most of the Western world the USSR still remains the riddle inside an enigma that Winston Churchill called it, attracting the curious, the ideological pilgrim, the adventurer, and the scholar. A state which began its history in 1917 as a challenge to the West still remains a challenge today, both in intellectual terms and in terms of power. Convinced that its knowledge of Marxism-Leninism affords it unique advantages in the modern world, the leaders of the Soviet state are extremely confident of long-range success in competition with other nations. This conviction is reinforced by the belief that the USSR is the embodiment of a social system more progressive than that of the West; thus, in the interest of progress, it must propagate its viewpoint beyond its own citizenry.

A present-day Intourist publication proclaims that a trip to the USSR is unlike any other trip, and that every tourist is an expert in his field or profession, who can see far more for himself than he can ever hope to learn by relying on the reports of others. Foreign travel to the Soviet Union today plays an important role in influencing world opinion, as well as serving to provide the Soviet state with badly needed Western currency.

Travel to the Soviet Union during the 'twenties and 'thirties played a similar role, although foreigners also contributed then to Soviet development by furnishing the regime with technical skills. Studying the experiences of foreigners within the USSR during the period 1924 to 1937 increases our understanding of contemporary Soviet behavior toward foreign visitors, as well as of the behavior of other closed societies such as Communist China and Cuba. A study of this earlier Soviet campaign to attract foreigners is especially valuable for an understanding of the development of a policy which utilized the presence of foreigners within the USSR to implement certain national and international objectives. Further, it can extend our knowledge of the techniques used by a totalitarian regime in this very specialized form of propaganda, techniques generally not so extensively used by democratic regimes which seek to educate foreign opinion rather than to manipulate it.

The importance of the late 'twenties and 'thirties in the history of the Soviet Union has long been apparent, as the many books which re-examine the tumultuous events of this period testify. The Soviet attempt to convince the world that it represented a progressive social force, the wave of the future, took place at a time when Western society was being plagued by political, economic, and social problems. Thus, the subject under study, the pilgrimage to Russia, lends itself to a fruitful examination of the interrelationship between propaganda and the international milieu.

International communication, in the special sense of the communication of ideas across national borders, is a relatively new field of study, one which has been restricted chiefly to research in mass media and psychological warfare. Only a handful of books and articles have been published concerning the exchanges of people between open societies.[1] Even fewer studies have been made of the experiences of foreigners within a closed society.

A major American study to date concerning the exchange of people deals with foreign students in the United States.[2] Researchers, through a series of interviews, tried to evaluate the effects of environmental conditions on the development of social relationships between these students and Americans, and to determine how these social relationships affected the attitudes of the students toward the United States.

Two other American studies concerning the exchange of students should be noted. One deals with the social relationships of American youth in African societies.[3] The other is an article citing the effects of certain types of intercultural experiences on individual attitudes and behavior.[4] The single attempt to explore communication between foreigners and natives in a closed society has been made by Frederick C. Barghoorn.[5] His study concentrates primarily on the contemporary period, and limits its scope to patterns of short-term cultural exchange.

Communication between a closed society and its foreign visitors deserves further investigation because the very nature of the society creates problems which differ substantially from those of an open system. Unlike open societies, which can tolerate a voluntary consensus, modern closed societies attempt to enforce their "passion for unanimity" on everyone within their borders through devices of manipulation. A monopoly of mass communication enables them to establish the one "proper" view. Friedrich and Brzezinski find this an important element of the totalitarian syndrome.[6]

The myths of a closed society rest on a picture of a hostile outer world where most people are far worse off. This image of a poorer, oppressed outer world is utilized by the regime of the closed society to help justify internal sacrifices. Even though modern aviation has made virtually every country accessible, these closed societies are often only theoretically accessible: they use visa and passport controls, and such a stark physical barrier as the Berlin Wall to limit human contact and to avoid the danger of different ideas. Despite these controls, most such regimes, for economic, psychological, and even political reasons, provide a show of welcome for foreign visitors. Thus tension often exists between factors making for greater contact among peoples and nations and those barring contacts and increasing isolation.

In its external relations, the regime has some alternatives. Like Japan prior to the mid-nineteenth century, it could try to seal itself off almost completely from the world. But this is a costly and irrational procedure in a highly interdependent world. Or, it could allow limited contacts, subject to manipulation by the political authorities. This is the alternative that modern closed societies have chosen. Such manipulation is necessary because, although the government of such a society may find it necessary to have foreigners within its borders, it may fear the repercussion if they leave with a clear vision of the actual state of affairs there.

The regime of the closed society spends considerable money, time, effort, and manpower to prevent its visitors from gaining negative impressions. Extravaganzas are provided to divert them from any opportunity of becoming acquainted with the country. Contacts between aliens and natives are screened for fear that free communications ultimately might disturb the stability of the regime. This course of activities is feasible because the people interested in visiting a closed society are rarely objective observers; although extolling their own objectivity, they have biases formed and molded by economic, psychological, and historical currents and experiences.

Why would a visitor to or foreign resident in the Soviet Union have a very different experience than he would have if he went to the United States, Great Britain, or any other Western European country? The answer, I believe, is inherent in Leninist theory, where two key ideas are manipulation and control.[7] Of vital importance also is the pessimistic view of human nature (including distrust of human capabilities) held by Communist leaders. A basic tenet of the Soviet system asserts that it is in the nature of man, at least until he is transformed under the conditions of perfect communism, to require guidance; without proper guidance, man deviates from the desirable. Truth is an officially defined and imposed "proper view of reality."[8] Soviet leaders early realized that the survival of Russian Communism depended on their skill as communicators of a controlled flow of material designed to enhance respect for a totalitarian government and to generate approval of its policies. The two tools of the party became propaganda and terror.

Contemporary studies in communication have pointed out that, although the power of the mass media has continued to grow, there is a two-step flow of communication: first, from the communication media to an individual who because of certain qualifications (e.g., his place in society and/or interest in a certain area) becomes an opinion leader; and secondly, from this individual to the part of the mass audience which comes into contact with him.[9] Approval of a statement by an influential person or organization may have a positive effect. One of the basic media of propaganda within the Soviet Union has been the use of such persons or organizations for direct personal agitation. This system of organized opinion leadership involves literally thousands of agitators who organize mass meetings, give lectures, visit families in their homes, and attempt to draw everyone into active participation in the indoctrination process.

The Soviet Union has tried to adapt to its foreign propaganda system the principle of direct personal agitation used among its own population, by inviting and/or encouraging both individuals and groups to become "personal witnesses" to a positive image of the country and then to return home and act as opinion leaders. Tamara Solonevich, a Russian girl who served as interpreter to a visiting trade union delegation, wrote: "But in order to conduct their propaganda more effectively, the Bolsheviks need in addition to the Press, the living word. It is essential that someone living should confirm that he was in the USSR and that he saw achievements." [10] The Soviet regime, then, subordinates its fears of alien influence to the more crucial consideration of winning helpers and allies among powers potentially and actually hostile toward the Soviet Union.[11]

By playing host to many different types of people, the Soviet Union hoped to utilize opinion leaders throughout the structure of Western society. While it is difficult exactly to define what makes an opinion leader, it has been hypothesized that, first of all, the individual should have an interest in a certain area.[12] That interest will often lead to expertness. Expertness is considered by psychologists and communicators as an important element of credibility, and being a personal witness is often equated with expertness.[13] The day has certainly passed when one could be an armchair expert in a regional field of interest, but the day has not yet arrived when people realize that expertness is something more than being a firsthand witness. A person who can assert, "I have seen it with my own eyes," has a *prima facie* claim, at least in the view of the unsophisticated, to expertise. The returning visitor from the USSR could plausibly assert, as did Lincoln Steffens: "I have been over into the future, and it works." [14]

But opinion leadership is not only a matter of "expert" qualification, but of access to big publics. Potential leaders returning from the Soviet Union found such large publics in the many dissatisfied sections of society whose prior interest in the Soviet experiment made them vulnerable to persuasion. Experiments with persuasion, however, have demonstrated that people are more easily influenced to change their opinions to agree with individuals they consider congenial than with individuals they consider antagonistic.[15] Ultimately, what determines social attitudes and opinions is the influence of those held in esteem, regardless of their status in society. Opinion leaders, thus, exist among all levels of society.

When a person of esteem and hence of influence visits a closed society like the Soviet Union, he is cultivated as a potential opinion leader. To allow a witness to come to his own conclusion might defeat the Soviet purpose: acceptable thinking must be politically defined, created, controlled, and enforced. Hadley Cantril writes: "If a person looks at things in a different way from that of the Soviet leaders, then that person is [according to Soviet doctrine] looking at things incorrectly. And if he is looking at things incorrectly, he must be appropriately treated until he has the proper view of reality." [16] The Soviet distrust of man's capabilities leads to the replacement of education by manipulation.

During the earlier years of the period under study, the Soviet Union was able to rely on some of the spontaneity of the Russian people in communicating an image of a regime they could still believe in. But, as the totalitarian tendencies of the regime were accelerated, the spontaneous efforts of individual Soviet citizens to influence foreigners in favor of their system declined, while the range of manipulation and the rigidity of control of contacts between foreigners and Soviet society increased.

The Soviet Union was aided in its manipulation by the favorable preconceptions of its guests. Experimental studies in human perception indicate that we don't see with our eyes alone nor hear with our ears alone. We see and hear with our whole person; and under certain conditions our eyes and ears become instruments which serve our desires, partisanships, and biases.[17] In other words, the way we see things is a combination of what is there and what we expect to find there. Walter Lippmann points out that, "for the most part we do not first see, and then define, we define first and then see." [18] If we believe that a certain condition exists, we tend to accept all concrete facts as proof of that condition and do not properly evaluate the facts.

If even carefully controlled laboratory situations indicate the intricacies of perceptions, the complications inherent in less controlled and structured situations—those situations which are unfamiliar to the senses—must be many. Visitors in the Soviet Union found themselves in such a situation. The unfamiliar scene was to them like a baby's world, one great, blooming, buzzing confusion. Yet following an important principle of perception, their minds tended to organize and to fill out their observations because, like all human beings, they strove to impose meaning on their experience. They supplied what was not there and altered what was there to build a meaningful pattern. What was ignored and what was added depended upon certain characteristics of the individual personality.[19]

Understanding these principles of perception, the Soviet leaders realized that any effective communiqué must be especially designed for the intended recipient. Their efforts to promote a particular image of the country were based on knowledge of what their guests were looking for. And this latter consideration was greatly conditioned by the historical context of the period.

By the mid-'twenties, the West once more seemed a good place to live in. The devastation of World War I was quickly receding into the background; most of the European countries had managed to stabilize their currencies, and the United States was experiencing a period of prosperity. The major powers met at the conference table and displayed a willingness to discuss issues of disarmament and international co-operation even though they showed little interest in implementing them. These conferences gave hope that war could be outlawed by the stroke of a pen.

Although peace and prosperity appeared dominant on the surface, pockets of unrest existed everywhere, early omens of economic crisis and the spread of totalitarian Fascism. In the principal Western countries, distribution of economic goods was still very unequal. In Britain, the Conservative government wrestled with the problem of unemployment, but made little headway. Many of the workers within such declining industries as coal mining came to believe that their wage rates could be maintained only if made independent of the condition of the industry. To many of the underprivileged, the only solution which remained was the abolition of capitalism. The citizenry of France was burdened with the highest tax rate in Western Europe, while German economic recovery was perched on the unstable base of inflation. Tariff walls remained unyieldingly high.

To many segments of European society, the formation in 1927 of the Heimwehr, a semi-Fascist military organization in Austria, appeared to be the first sign that in Central Europe the period of democracy and moderation was over. Despite disarmament conferences, world armament continuously increased with the growing feeling of insecurity among nations.

In 1929 the relatively favorable set of conditions in the capitalist world changed abruptly as the Great Depression began.

The Communist International's 1928 forecast of increasing con-
tradictions among capitalist countries and the onset of a more
serious economic crisis appeared correct.[20] Western capitalism
was seriously struck by the depression. Hundreds of thousands of
workers went hungry because they could not find work. The
trade unions were unable to ameliorate the situation. Britain and
France, saddled with the still unpaid war debts, found it impossible to pierce American tariff walls. Farmers ploughed their
crops under in the United States, while other goods glutted the
market. Prices continued to fall, and banks closed their doors.

A depression brings into focus ideas about economic democracy. The right to vote becomes a luxury compared to the right
to work. Powerful pressures arise to force society to assume
vast responsibilities for its members, and in particular its
industrial members, dependent upon income from regular
employment. There is no certainty that the working class
automatically becomes revolutionary during a state of unemployment and depression, but workers do begin to look around for a
savior. They leave their old organizations, partly because they
cannot afford the expenses of membership, and partly because
they feel that the organizations are powerless to help.

Also disillusioned with the existing economic system were the
intellectuals: submerged dissatisfaction over the material emphasis of the previous prosperity turned to complete disillusion
during the depression. Intellectuals became convinced that
drastic political measures were necessary to cure the human
environment of its malady. Lacking faith in society as it was then
constituted, intellectuals everywhere searched for an answer to
the world's problems, for a "belief in some ultimate reality," or
an ideal to which they could dedicate their lives. The eyes of the
world were focused on Soviet Russia, which seemed to be under-
going a dynamic economic and social transformation, while the
rest of the world appeared unable to lift itself out of the depression. Economic questions overshadowed all others in the
international relationships of the world during the early 'thirties.

The Soviet Union between 1924 and 1937, attempting to re-

main afloat in a fast-flowing sea of events, found itself forced to
alter objectives somewhat. When it first tried to break out of
isolation, external conditions were not favorable: the capitalist
world felt that it could function without substantial relations
with Russia. But the Great Depression resulted in a major
revaluation of this situation. By 1929 the Soviet Union, proclaim-
ing the policy of "socialism in one country," had embarked on a
plan of total industrialization.[21] Although the scheme was
directed toward ultimate economic autarky, the regime was
forced at the beginning to utilize technical skills, industrial machinery, and commercial credits of the West, basic resources
which the Soviet Union lacked. The West in turn became more
interested in Soviet Russia as a market for goods and a source of
ideas for the organization of society.

Fulfillment of the plan for industrialization demanded certain
specific conditions which became the primary objective of
Russian diplomacy. By the end of the 'twenties the Soviet Union
had established economic and diplomatic relations with most of
the major countries except the United States, but it was
threatened by frequent outbreaks of hostility, and the regime
wanted to improve its existing diplomatic and economic relations
and to gain recognition by the United States. Improvement in
economic relations depended on two things: Russia's image as a
peaceful nation and its position as buyer or seller on the world
market.

But short-range objectives, such as the need for peace, for
diplomatic contact, and for material aid often contradicted the
USSR's long-range plans to extend Communism. Although
secondary to the policy of "socialism in one country" at this
time, plans for the extension of Communism were not neglected.
Soviet diplomacy displayed to western countries a properly co-
operative spirit, but the Comintern (Communist International),
the vehicle of long-term Soviet objectives, was steering a sharply
leftward and revolutionary course, pursuing an irreconcilable
struggle against capitalism and what Communists considered the
capitalists' more dangerous agent, social democracy, alternatively

called social fascism. It continued the attempt to extend Soviet power throughout the world.

In 1934 the long-range objectives of the Soviet regime were almost entirely obscured by aims basic to Soviet national security, a change forced on the regime by the full-blown threat of Hitler and Nazism in the West and the extension of Japanese power in the East. The growing danger of the further rearmament of Germany finally forced Russia to seek friends elsewhere, in order to protect herself against the threat of German expansion eastward.

Paul Kecskemeti, in discussing Soviet political communication, stated that what was needed for the success of Soviet communication was "some universal trauma, some elementary revulsion against a supreme evil stalking the world. If the Soviet communicator succeeds in projecting an image of the Soviet Union as being bent upon combatting this manifest evil, he can indeed make a significant impact upon the political behavior of people beyond the boundary." [22] Fascism was one such evil, and after 1933, the Soviets embarked on a crusade against it.

The year 1935 marked the official beginning of the period of the Popular Front, when foreign Communists in countries such as France were encouraged to restrain their feuds with Socialists and to merge their efforts with those groups and other domestic elements in order to create a bulwark against Fascism. In France the Communists joined with the Radical Socialists and Socialists in an election coalition supporting the Socialist leader, Léon Blum, although the Communists later refused to enter his cabinet. The Soviet Union combined this Popular Front policy with that of collective security by issuing a call for a broad alliance of all segments of world opinion against the Fascist threat. In the interests of Soviet national security, Soviet diplomatic policy and Comintern policy were co-ordinated. This new policy brought such diplomatic successes as recognition by the United States, the Franco and Czech-Soviet Pacts, and an invitation to join the League of Nations.

Stalin valued his political relations with the West so little,

according to George Kennan, that he was always ready to sacrifice Soviet external relations to the interests of his domestic-
political position.[23] Thus, at the height of the Soviet policy of
external collective security in 1936, internal developments once
more exerted an influence on foreign relations. In the great
purges directed against his domestic opponents, Stalin implicated
foreign countries in charges of sabotage and other crimes against
the Soviet regime. The statements by former Soviet heroes at
the "show" trials gave impetus to the growing skepticism of
Western intellectuals about the entire regime. To the Western
democracies, the purges revealed the true nature of Soviet
totalitarianism, causing them to have serious doubts about any
policy of collaboration with the Soviet Union, even for the
containment of Fascism.

At the same time, the Soviets were losing faith in the policy
of collective security. The appeasement policy of the democracies
toward Germany, culminating in the Munich Pact, contributed
to the deterioration of Soviet relations with the West. During
this and the subsequent period, out of which came the German-
Soviet Nonaggression Pact, the Soviet Union was too occupied
with problems of major diplomatic and military strategy to be
concerned with attracting foreign visitors to the country.

This factor, combined with the atmosphere of intense suspicion
during the purge period, was responsible for the decrease in
foreign visitors. While no specific accusation was made during the
trials against any foreign visitor, the proceedings left a definite
impression that Soviet citizens should be on their guard against
all foreigners. Louis Fischer reported that in 1937 only a very few
Soviet citizens welcomed him back after a trip out of the
country, in contrast to the large numbers of Russian friends who
had greeted his return in previous years.[24] Americans and
Europeans who had spent long periods in the Soviet Union
hastened to obtain exit visas. Despite continued advertising by
Intourist until 1939, foreign travelers preferred to go elsewhere
where life appeared to be more predictable and less risky.[25]
Thus ended the pilgrimage to Russia: the Soviet Union became
(with some exceptions) a sealed society.

2

Objectives and the Soviet Image

In Chapter 1 the hypothesis was advanced that a closed or totalitarian society might, under certain circumstances, encourage foreign contacts. Leninist theory prescribes that "if the Party or the people are to have any contact with outside non-Communist groups, these groups must be used; otherwise Soviet citizens or groups will themselves be used to the advantage of the outside groups."[1] Obviously such contacts must promote definite objectives of the Soviet system. The objectives served by welcoming foreigners to the country after 1924 can be divided into two categories: psychological advantage and material gain. These categories, however, were not mutually exclusive; material gain often depended upon achieving psychological advantage.

Numerous objectives by means of which a psychological advantage might be gained were established by the Soviet Union. They included the prevention of capitalist intervention, the achievement of recognition and regularized diplomatic relations, and the battle for a united international labor movement under Soviet direction, an accomplishment which would also assist the extension of Communism. The first two objectives were immediate goals, and they became prerequisites for all others. The timetable for the attainment of Soviet control of labor throughout the world was more flexible; thus the Soviet regime could sub-

15

ordinate this long-term objective to the other two when the means to attaining all three were contradictory. At other times, campaigns for the long-term goal were intermixed with tactics designed to achieve objectives of more immediate importance.

It was hoped that attainment of these psychological objectives would create the climate that the Soviet regime believed necessary for achieving such material advantages as credits, foreign exchange, favorable trade agreements, and technical assistance. However, the regime intended that the duration of this assistance be as brief as possible a stopgap in the progress toward ultimate economic autarky.

The Soviet Union decided that one of the best ways it could promote these psychological objectives was to create and disseminate to the outside world a positive image of Soviet society. Potential opinion leaders were to be personally convinced after a visit or after residence in the Soviet Union of the superiority of Soviet civilization over that of the West.

The methods adopted by the Soviet leadership to create a popular image of Communist society were similar to those used in modern public relations. The regime presented half-truths, hoping that the average individual would accept them as a simplified version of the whole truth. In many cases, the image became more important than the reality, although its success depended upon its revealing some measure of truth about the real world.

The positive image which the Soviet authorities wished to disseminate was multifaceted. There was something in it to appeal to everyone. To the worker, the Soviet Union was to appear as a revolutionary fortress, a land of opportunity, the only home for the world proletariat. For the intellectual, the society became a humanitarian one, non-revolutionary, devoted to the advancement of mankind. And to the businessman, it was a thriving society, desirous of co-operating economically with the capitalist world in mutually beneficial arrangements.

The different parts of the image, however, partly contradicted each other. The Soviet regime attempted to disseminate to most people a picture consistent with its policy of "socialism in one country" in order to achieve regularized relations with the rest of the world and to obtain material aid. At the same time, however, the regime continued to impress on visiting labor delegations and radical intellectuals that they were invited to observe the functioning of the "dictatorship of the proletariat," and later to express their newly found inspiration in revolutionary work. The regime also utilized the services of intellectuals whose interests in the Soviet Union did not extend to revolutionary work. When they served as leaders of various societies devoted to Soviet-American friendship, they did not know they were mere figureheads of organizations controlled by Communist leaders which served the cause of international Communism.

A study of the various objectives of the Soviet Union must start with considerations of national security. As early as Brest-Litovsk (the signing in 1918 by the Soviet regime of a separate peace treaty with Germany), the Bolsheviks realized that the most important task of the new government was maintaining Soviet independence. Throughout the 'twenties and 'thirties, they expected every crisis in relations with the outside world to result in war and foreign invasion. The memory of the earlier foreign intervention contributed to periodic war scares which appeared after such events as the break in Anglo-Soviet relations in 1927, Japan's initial action in Manchuria in the early 'thirties, and later the Reichstag fire and acts of German expansion. The Soviet government aimed to prevent such a new attack on its territory, and to this end it tried to gain support among many different foreign groups.

Prime targets in this endeavor were the labor delegations. During the Fourteenth Congress of the Soviet Communist party in December, 1925, Stalin had commented that the world proletariat represented by the visiting delegations constituted the basic weapon against imperialism and intervention.[2] The Programme of the Communist International, adopted at the Sixth World Congress of the Comintern in September, 1928, expressed the view that, since the USSR was "the only fatherland of the

international proletariat, the principal bulwark of its achievements, and the most important factor for its international eman-
cipation," the proletariat must "defend her against the attacks
of the capitalist powers by all the means in its power." In the
event of attack by the imperialist states on the USSR, "the international proletariat must retaliate by organizing bold and
determined mass action and struggle for the overthrow of the
imperialist governments, with the slogan of: Dictatorship
of the proletariat and alliance with the USSR." [3]

The organizers of the proletariat in this endeavor, according
to Stalin, would be the workers who had already visited the
Soviet Union. Thus, as noted in a report issued by the Communist
party of Great Britain (CPGB) in 1926, a major theme for
agitation at the commencement of the campaigns to send worker
delegates to the Soviet Union was "struggle" against the threat
of Western intervention. [4] The Communist International reported
that between the Fifth and Sixth World Congresses worker
delegations of the organization played an important part in the
mass demonstrations initiated by the German Communist party
against the threat of intervention. [5] On the other hand, a 1929
report of the CPGB remarked that the "public refusal of the
Miners' Executive to send fraternal delegates to the Moscow
celebrations (October) seriously increased the isolation of the
Soviet Union and therefore the war danger." [6]

The November, 1927, Congress of Friends of the Soviet Union
(FSU), ostensibly called by British workers but in fact directed
by the Soviet Communist party, was intended to utilize "the
presence of so many delegates from all parts of the world in
Moscow in order to discuss practical measures for the defense of
the Soviet Union." [7] Subsequent meetings at both the central
and local levels of FSU paid prime attention to the danger of
war. Pledges by foreign delegations to defend the Soviet Union
continued through 1937, although by this time Germany had
replaced Great Britain as the major enemy. Thus, the Soviet
regime tried to accomplish what the Russian Communists had
failed to do at the outbreak of World War I—mobilize the world

proletariat around the cause of a specific ideological movement.

Although labor delegations constituted the main targets in campaigns to defend the Soviet Union, resident foreign workers and intellectuals were not ignored. The Soviet authorities asked visitors and foreign residents to subscribe to statements pledging support of the Soviet Union in case of intervention by the capitalist world.[8]

Soviet Russia hoped to ward off foreign intervention by achieving recognition by the United States and regularized diplomatic relations with Great Britain and other countries. She also hoped that such diplomatic relations would facilitate the granting of loans and long-term commercial credits to Soviet industry. Since businessmen had been partly responsible for America's non-recognition policy and for the rupture of relations by Great Britain in 1927, Soviet authorities began to woo visiting businessmen as persons who might be able to influence a policy change.

The Soviet regime argued that closer commercial relations afforded the best prospect of overcoming the existing political friction; at the same time it stressed to visiting business delegations that the potential of the Russian market would only reveal itself completely after the re-establishment of diplomatic relations.[9] This argument was part of a general thesis that the state of uncertainty created by non-recognition prejudiced every possibility of genuine intercourse in any direction.

Labor delegations and intellectuals were also asked by the regime to work for recognition. A delegation of American workers to the 1932 May Day celebration pledged themselves "to work to influence public opinion for the recognition of the Soviet Union by the United States." [10] According to one historian, Stalin demonstrated his interest in recognition by giving Raymond Robins, a man long engaged in a campaign to effect economic and political collaboration with Moscow, a ninety-minute interview on May 13, 1933.[11]

The Bolsheviks viewed the battle for a united labor movement under Profintern (Red Trade Union International) control as an important way both to expand Communist influence among the working classes abroad, and to undermine the strength of the Socialist International. While the Bolsheviks hoped that labor delegations would help the Soviet Union achieve its short-range objectives, their primary intention was that the delegations should serve as weapons in the long-term struggle against non-Communist labor leaders. The first labor delegation to lend itself to this goal was a group of British Labour members of Parliament and labor leaders sent by the General Council of the Trades Union Congress in December, 1924, to get acquainted with the situation in the Soviet Union and to strengthen contact with the Soviet labor movement.[12] However, since there were few signs that their example would be followed by other union leaders, the Soviet regime spent most of its energy after this visit courting the more radical elements among the rank and file, those from Communist-dominated unions, either in basic heavy industries or in declining fields of work such as mining, and those elements basically dissatisfied with their present conditions.

Later delegations of rank-and-file workers came as part of the propaganda war being waged against the more moderate labor leaders. In Denmark, campaigns against maritime unions affiliated with the Amsterdam International included the sending of delegations of union members to the Soviet Union.[13] The dispatch of a young workers' delegation to the Soviet Union (despite opposition from Socialist youth leaders) was termed by the Communist party of Great Britain "not only a victory for the [Young Communist] League but also for the Party, in its struggles against the reformist influences." [14] An article in *Labor Unity*, organ of the American section of the Profintern, called the sending of delegations "an important step in the building of the revolutionary trade unions." [15] *Trud*, the Soviet trade union paper, commented that delegations after returning home would "expose to the masses of social-democratic workers the real character of their 'leaders,' to give a public lesson to the social-fascist organizers of intervention." [16]

Although the campaigns against the Social Democratic leaders became official only at the Sixth Congress of the Communist International in 1928, there is much evidence to show that the Soviet regime used workers' delegations to undermine the authority of labor leaders as early as 1925, during a period when relations between Socialists and Communists were ostensibly friendly. In 1925 representatives of the Profintern and of the Communist International drew up a program by which delegations of German and Swedish workers agreed on their return home to work toward a united front of the trade union movement under Profintern auspices.[17] And although relations with the Socialists were publicly even more friendly after 1934, during the period of the Popular Front, in fact the Communists covertly carried on their undermining tactics, and delegations continued to be used to this end. Criticism of the Social Democratic leadership by the worker delegations after 1934 was greatly toned down, but as late as May, 1936, disparaging remarks were still being made.[18]

As we have seen, the ultimate objective in encouraging foreign visitors was to obtain for the USSR material gains—credits, foreign currency, trade, and technical assistance. The USSR's decision in the fall of 1928 to pursue a course of rapid industrialization affected its relationship with the capitalist world, since execution of the plans required outside help. The Sixth World Congress of the Comintern in September, 1928, outlined the path Russia had already adopted and would continue to pursue.

The simultaneous existence of two economic systems: the Socialist system in the USSR and the capitalist system in other countries, imposes on the Proletarian State the task of warding off the blows showered upon it by the capitalist world (boycott, blockade, etc.) and also compels it to resort to economic maneuvering with and utilizing economic contact with capitalist countries (with the aid of the monopoly of foreign trade—which is one of the fundamental conditions for the successful building up of Socialism, and also with the aid of credits, loans, concessions, etc.). The principal and fundamental line to be followed in this connection must be the line of establishing the widest possible contact with foreign countries— within limits determined by their usefulness to the U.S.S.R., i.e., primarily for strengthening industry in the U.S.S.R., for laying the

base for her own heavy industry and electrification and finally, for
the development of her own Socialist engineering industry. Only to
the extent that the economic independence of the U.S.S.R. in the
capitalist environment is secured, can solid guarantees be obtained
against the danger that socialist construction in the U.S.S.R. may
be destroyed and that the U.S.S.R. may be transformed into an
appendage of the world capitalist system.[19]

Thus, it was recognized that the continued independence of the
Soviet Union ultimately depended not on the pledges of the world
proletariat to defend her but on the attainment of the status of a
highly industrialized power.

Soviet leaders hoped that invitations to foreign businessmen
to visit the country would facilitate the granting of loans and
long-term commercial credits. But an acute need for foreign
currency forced the adoption of other measures which involved
foreigners. First, it forced the Bolsheviks to realize that they
could profit financially from people who thought a few days in
the USSR a proper way to end a European tour. These people
knew little about the Soviet Union or her problems and wanted
only to see where the Tsar had lived, and perhaps to buy a
souvenir of their visit. So the Soviet government ignored the
complaints that tables at the Grand Hotel lacked clean napkins
—and invested its travelers' checks in tractors and paving machines.

The regime also obtained foreign currency as an incident of
other longer-term arrangements when it granted permission
to foreign businessmen and newspaper correspondents to rent
apartments in houses constructed for Soviet citizens, or to students to live with Russian families.[20] The foreign currency so
acquired by Russian citizens eventually reached the government
through purchases made at Torgsin, a store which until its dis-
solution in 1936 offered superior merchandise for foreign exchange only.

In addition to credits and trade, the Soviet regime needed
technical assistance. The Communists realized by the time
they began the first Five-Year Plan in 1928 that foreign tech-

nological aid would be necessary to meet desired goals. The older Russian engineers not only lacked a knowledge of modern technology, but were politically untrustworthy in the eyes of the regime; there had not been time to produce a new type of Soviet engineer on which the country could depend, technically and politically. In 1926, the Soviet government invited Henry Ford to send a delegation to find out what was being done to service tractors in the Soviet Union and to begin the training of Russians to service tractors using Ford principles. The regime also hoped to encourage Ford to build a tractor factory in the country.[21] The Bolsheviks also encouraged such business groups as the American-Russian Chamber of Commerce to promote business-men's tours of the Soviet Union, promising the visitors the opportunity to talk to top Soviet industrialists.[22]

Foreign engineers and skilled workers were recruited to fill technological gaps as well as to help train future generations of Soviet engineers. Some came to the Soviet Union for a short time to install equipment; others for a longer period when their companies decided to play a role in Soviet economic construction. Some engineers and specialists, although not affiliated with companies doing business in the USSR, received personal invitations because their skills and abilities were known to the regime. The majority were gifted, hard-working specialists; they were apolitical, experts paid to do a job, their Russian interests limited to the technological challenge. Some were also interested in the Soviet experiment as a way to enrich human life. A small minority devoted more time to "social work" than to engineering and served the Soviet government as showpieces of success in winning over bourgeois engineers to the Soviet cause. Engineers and skilled workers were supplemented by semi-skilled laborers, lured by promises of work, better conditions, and instruction in any technical line. Many, perhaps even a majority of these workers had originally come from Russia and Eastern Europe and bore a sentimental attachment to that part of the world.

Since the achievement of many Soviet objectives depended

on the way the Soviet Union appeared to people outside its borders, the regime attempted to promote an image which appealed to many different groups, including the labor delegations. To the visiting worker, it promoted the image of a thriving society owned and managed by the working classes, the revolutionary fortress of the world proletariat. While this image may have appealed to visiting workers, Anne O'Hare McCormick viewed Soviet efforts more skeptically. "They all see the same factories; the same schools, the same clubs, the same sample fruits on the top of the proletarian apple cart," she said. "It is propaganda, a parlor exhibition, if you like—propaganda against ownership which is popular because it gives an illusion of ownership!" [23]

The Soviet regime hoped that a view of a truly dynamic proletarian society would revitalize the revolutionary fervor of the working classes. It believed that the proletariat lacked faith in its own possibilities, and thus was unable to serve the cause of world Communism. The Bolsheviks alleged that the leadership of the labor movement had come almost entirely under the influence of the capitalist class, an alliance which worked to undermine the vitality of the proletariat. Thus, to reinvigorate the foreign worker, the Bolsheviks planned to utilize radical elements within the rank and file.

Stalin, at the Fourteenth Congress of the Communist party in December, 1925, retorted to a complaint on the cost of entertaining the delegations that this was a shameful way of viewing the matter. Stalin remarked that in order for the proletariat in the West to succeed, they need to recognize that they can manage without the bourgeoisie. They must have faith in their own strength. By witnessing socialist construction, they will recognize that the working class can construct something new. The pilgrimage of workers to this country serves this end.[24] A *Pravda* editorial supported this statement by remarking that, "We must in every way possible help the workers of other countries who [are] coming to us [to] fortify their faith in their own strength, help them see with their own eyes what gigantic re-

serves of energy and activity lie latent in the proletariat. . . ." [25]
This theme of lack of belief by the workers in their own
strength was further developed in an article written in *Communist International* in 1928:

> No Communist holds the childish view that the proletariat of the
> capitalist world will arise and take up the struggle for power, just
> because they see the difference between their own conditions and
> those of their class comrades in the Soviet Union, and desire the
> former. Apart from the objective preliminary conditions of a suc-
> cessful revolution, there are the subjective, ideological prerequisites
> of the social revolution of the proletariat: the recognition of the
> danger of their ruin as a class, recognition of the impossibility of
> finding the road to safety within a capitalist order of society and
> by the methods of bourgeois democracy—the policy of the social
> democrats—and finally the faith in their own strength and capacity
> to exercise political power and to control industry. But just as the
> very existence of the Soviet Union, as a great State system with a
> socialist economy, sharpens the crisis of capitalism, and so hastens
> the coming to maturity of the objective conditions for the proletar-
> ian revolution in the rest of the world, so the object lessons of
> socialist construction in the Soviet Union help to form the subjec-
> tive conditions for the revolution.[26]

Visits to the Soviet Union would demonstrate, it said, that the
time had come for the possible building of a socialist economy by
the working classes. "The dissemination of this knowledge among
the social democratic and non-party working masses will prepare
the ground for the recruiting activities of the Communist Parties,
for in the long run such knowledge must lead to the realisation
that only the Bolshevik method of the proletarian class struggle
can have the desired result." [27]

Thus, the labor delegations must be studied as a technique
designed to further the attainment of certain ends. A Profintern
publication reminded its readers that it "must not be forgotten
that a delegate who has visited the USSR is for a long time
considered by the workers as 'authoritative' on questions of the
Soviet Union and that his social role and influence on the masses
are very great." [28] The Bolshevik method which the labor delegations observed was expected to become for them the only cor-

rect method of achieving a worker's society. Similarly, foreign
seamen, practically the only other group of laborers outside of
the delegations to visit the Soviet Union, were also to serve the
ends of "demonstrating to the proletariat abroad the achievements
of socialist construction and of showing its enormous importance
for the cause of an international proletarian revolution." [29]

The revolutionary image of the Soviet Union as a society run
by the proletariat was somewhat blurred for the benefit of the
few labor leaders whom the regime was able to attract and for
certain groups of intellectuals interested in the cause of labor.
Instead of stressing the Soviet role as the fortress of world revolution, which would have antagonized the moderate labor
leaders, the regime emphasized the portrayal of the Soviet Union
as a society where laborers were well off. This emphasis, the
Soviet leaders hoped, would convey the message that only under
such conditions as existed within the Soviet Union could labor's
position be improved. To implement this approach the American Communist party was instructed to organize a trade union
delegation whose report of its visit to Russia might be used "as
the findings of fair-minded impartial investigators, who, though
they were not Communists, had to admit that workers received
advantages that they did not enjoy in the capitalist countries." [30]
In the immediate future favorable opinions held by these individuals would aid such short-term objectives of the Soviet
Union as recognition; and in regard to such long-term objectives
as Communist expansion, any decrease in distrust by the labor
leadership would facilitate the breaking down of barriers to
Communist penetration.

In order to create an image of a society where laborers were
well off, the Bolsheviks found it necessary to suppress rumors
of famine which followed the massive collectivization campaigns
of 1931. A society which could not produce enough food to feed
its population could not be a society where laborers were better
off than elsewhere. Through various techniques, the regime
used the presence of visitors in the Soviet Union to combat such
rumors.[31]

Another facet of the image was the Soviet Union as a land of opportunity for foreign workers who came to link their destiny with their brothers. Wide publicity was given to the activities of foreign workers within Soviet borders in order to create the impression that they regarded the Soviet Union as their only home. Because of the persecution of workers and radicals in countries governed by reactionary governments, including those of the Fascist type, the Bolsheviks found themselves able to depict their nation as an asylum for groups fleeing dictators. The Soviet authorities offered a home and arranged transportation for many political émigrés, for example the Schutzbunder (Austrian Defense League), a group of radical Social Democrats whose 1934 revolt against the Dollfuss government failed.[32]

But the activities going on within Soviet Russia were of interest not only to the working classes. The despondency of foreign intellectuals, caused by the failure of modern Western society to provide ideals to which they could dedicate their lives, made them especially vulnerable to a different sort of appeal. To these people the Soviet Union portrayed itself as a humanitarian society, the chief world center of progress, spiritual cultivation, and enlightenment, which enabled all, regardless of class, to enjoy a better life. The intellectuals came to Russia looking for inspiration, and the Bolsheviks provided them with something to worship.

An article in *Communist International* stated some of the Soviet objectives in wooing the intellectuals.

The most fundamental reason for the sympathy of intellectuals lies less in the recognition and more [in] the unconscious feeling of what to us is a self-evident truth, that the crisis of capitalism and bourgeois society is also the crisis and the disintegration of its science and its culture. The nearer that the intellectuals stand to the masses and the more that they see in culture, not the privilege of a handful of "learned souls" but a vital part of the life of the masses, the more definite that feeling becomes. What prevents the development and operation of the sympathy of the intellectuals for the Soviet Union is the doubt that a dictatorship of the proletariat, based on a materialist conception of the world, is capable of developing science and culture, and the idea that the proletariat is only capable of controlling industry and technique. From this point of view, the delegations of "intellectuals" to the Soviet Union, merely by observing the facts, will be of advantage to the dictatorship of the proletariat.[33]

To acquaint foreign intellectuals with Soviet society, official invitations to witness the accomplishments of Soviet culture were offered to selected individuals. A letter by John Dewey expressing appreciation for an opportunity to see and learn about the activity of the USSR in "raising the cultural level" and "the creation of cultural values" serves as a testimony to the image that the Soviet regime hoped to promote.[34] Soviet literary critics regarded such letters, and literary works favorable to the Soviet Union, as weapons in the struggle then going on in the literary world, in which the Communists believed their enemies were trying to defame the Soviet state.

A group of intellectuals whom the Soviet regime tried in particular to attract were foreign scientists. Aware that large segments of the scientific community were dismayed at the gap between scientific theory and applied science, an attitude which gave rise in Great Britain about 1932 to the social relations of science movement, the Soviet Union attempted to appear to scientists as a society devoted to scientific advancement which would be used to benefit mankind.[35]

At the Second International Congress of the History of Science and Technology, held in London in 1931, the Soviet delegation, led by Bukharin, emphasized the new prospects opening up for scientists in the Soviet Union. The foreword to *Science at the Cross Roads*, the unabridged contributions of the Soviet delegation, states:

> The planned economy of socialism, the enormous extent of the constructive activity—in town and village, in the chief centres and in the remotest parts—demand that science should advance at an exceptional pace. The whole world is divided into two economic systems, two systems of social relationship, two types of culture. In the capitalist world the profound economic decline is reflected

in the paralysing crisis of scientific thought and philosophy generally. In the Socialist section of the world we observe an entirely new phenomenon: a new conjunction of theory and practice, the collective organization of scientific research planned on the scale of an enormous country, the ever-increasing penetration of a single method—the method of Dialectical Materialism—into all scientific disciplines. Thus the new type of intellectual culture, which dominates the mental activity of millions of workers, is becoming the greatest force of the present day.[36]

The Soviet delegation at the Congress impressed the foreign scientists, not so much with the theory of dialectical materialism, which was underplayed, as with the idea that the Soviet government recognized that science should be utilized directly to benefit society.

As visible evidence of its interest in the promotion of science, the Soviet regime played host to numerous international scientific congresses. The authorities also invited foreign scientists to study at Soviet academies, on the premise that those who became acquainted with the scientific life of the country would become convinced of the prestige accorded and attention paid to science in the Soviet Union.

The Soviet Union stressed to the intellectual not only the cultural and professional benefits but also the humanitarian aspects of the society. To present a humanitarian image to intellectuals and to businessmen as well, the Bolsheviks attempted to combat rumors of forced labor. To accomplish this they engaged foreign visitors and residents to testify to the groundlessness of such rumors; although evidence of forced labor did exist, the regime felt that certain foreigners would be willing to deny its existence because it knew that organizations, such as the American-Russian Chamber of Commerce, and individuals who were interested in a continuation of business relations with the Soviet Union would not talk about certain features of Soviet society. According to Eugene Lyons, an American correspondent stationed in the country, "an American 'commission' was dispatched to the lumber area, and in due time it attested truthfully that it had not *seen* forced labor." Lyons identified the three "commissioners" as men dependent on the official good will of the Soviet government: one was the resident secretary of the American-Russian Chamber of Commerce, Spencer Williams, hired by an "organization whose usefulness depended on maintaining cordial relations with Soviet authorities." Lyons noted:

> I knew all three men intimately, and it is betraying no secret to record that each of them was as thoroughly convinced of the widespread employment of forced labor in the lumber industry as Hamilton Fish or Mr. Deterding. They went to the North for the ride, or because it was difficult to refuse, and they placated their conscience by merely asserting ambiguously that they personally had seen no signs of forced labor; they did not indicate that they made no genuine effort to find it and that their official guides steered the "investigation." [37]

While the president of Freyn Engineering, an American company in charge of operations at Magnitogorsk, replied to an American-Russian Chamber of Commerce questionnaire that he observed no signs of forced labor there, John Scott, a foreign worker in Magnitogorsk, described in *Behind the Urals* the forced labor *kulaks*.[38] When interviewed, he stated, "There was no attempt to hide them. There were too many there to do so." [39] For business reasons it appears many individuals deliberately closed their eyes.

Finally, the Soviet Union attempted to appear to the business community as an economically thriving society with potential as a market for the products of capitalist industry and as a field for application of Western industrial techniques. But the regime's need for trade, credits, and technical aid could only be gratified if it could convince Western capitalism that economic intercourse between powers, irrespective of their socio-political systems, could be conducted on a mutually beneficial basis.

G. L. Piatakov, chairman of the State Bank, in a greeting to the British Trade Delegation which visited Russia in 1929, stated that he wished to emphasize the importance of the visit because "the exchange of visits between representatives of business circles of both countries cannot but assist the growth of mutual understanding, and consequently, the improvement and strengthening of our economic relations. . . . " [40] Saul Bron, who became head of Amtorg in 1927, remarked that "industrial leaders in the Soviet Union are fully awake to the value of utilizing American technical and industrial skill to assist in developing the rich natural resources of the country and promoting its industrialization." [41]

Foreign visitors and residents, then, had a functional value for the Soviet Union. The authorities hoped that they would serve as channels of communication to the outer world. It was also hoped that they would facilitate Soviet acquisition of economic materials needed for industrialization. Finally, the Soviet Communist party utilized foreigners to serve the objectives of international Communism as well as the objectives of the Soviet Union. To satisfy all these objectives, the Soviet regime opened up its doors and permitted limited foreign contacts within its society.

We may, therefore, conclude that the Soviet policy toward foreign visitors balanced the advantages which could be obtained by contact with the outside world against the disadvantages which such contact might bring to the maintenance of a closed society. Clearly, during the 1920's and 1930's, contact, however limited, was favored. It remains to be seen how and to what extent these contacts could be manipulated to maximize their advantages and minimize their disadvantages.

3

The Campaign to Woo Foreigners

In the Soviet strategy for manipulating foreign visits, it is scarcely surprising to learn that the organizational aspects occupied a major place. According to Alfred Meyer, one of the most penetrating students of Lenin's ideology, Lenin was "a revolutionary of a rare type, a revolutionary with a bureaucratic mind."[1] Basic to his philosophy was "a faith in organization and centralization as rational methods of decision-making." Lenin believed that the party's superior wisdom fitted it for the task of manipulating the rank and file of its followers as well as all others who came under its authority.

Beyond the party, Lenin envisaged a society completely converted into a network of front organizations, with its entire organizational and associational life guided by the leadership through control of party machinery.[2] The concept of "front organization" stemmed from the basic nature of the party as a small select group of totally dedicated people, a core which needed to attract a larger circle of sympathizers. This concept required that the fronts be "undogmatic, elastic in the way they were organized and in the activities they pursued, sensitive to the shifting requirements of local and temporary conditions, but firmly guided in whatever they were doing by the Party's leaders."[3] Such organization would thus enable the leaders to manipulate the masses.

32

Philip Selznick, in his study of Bolshevik strategy and tactics, asserts that organizations function as weapons "when a power-seeking elite uses them to maximize its own influence in a manner unrestrained by the constitutional order of the arena within which the struggle for power takes place."[4] Throughout the 'twenties and 'thirties, the Soviet elite attempted to enhance its prestige and authority throughout the world by employing the services of the people who visited the Soviet Union. In order to accomplish this task it utilized the resources of Soviet organizations which served other purposes as well, besides creating new organizations of access and control which would help transform any diffuse population into a mobilizable source of power.

Since organization played such an important part in the entire pilgrimage to Russia, it is necessary to examine the nature of the Communist organizational apparatus, and to study the specific features which enabled it to serve as a weapon in the struggle for power. How did the organizations involved in this effort compare with the models found in Communist theory? How did the mechanisms function during the initial stages of the recruitment and attraction of foreigners? To what extent did people decide on their own initiative to visit or work in the Soviet Union, and to what extent did Soviet and Communist authorities control or attempt to influence such decisions?

In attempting to answer these questions, the first thing that becomes apparent is the variety of organizations involved with the entire pilgrimage to Russia. The Soviet Communist party served as the hub, but a vast network of specialized agencies, some organs of Soviet government, others operating under Comintern supervision, played important roles. State organizations like Intourist catered to the ordinary tourist and minor intellectual. VOKS (the All-Union Society for Cultural Relations with Foreign Countries), the Union of Soviet Writers, and the All-Union Central Council of Trade Unions, governmental bodies which were made to resemble similar private organizations elsewhere, issued invitations to foreign guests and arranged itineraries for them upon their arrival. Other groups such as the

Dzerzhinsky Club (named for Felix Dzerzhinsky, founder of the Cheka—the Soviet secret police; later GPU, OGPU, NKVD), newspapers like the *Moscow Daily News,* and foreign departments in the various organs of the state economic structure attended to the needs of foreign technicians working within the Soviet Union.

Through the vehicle of the Soviet Communist party, the Comintern co-ordinated the work of the Soviet government with tasks performed by foreign Communists in their respective areas. Working under the Comintern were such parallel organizations as the Profintern, the international network of Friends of the Soviet Union, and the Societies for Cultural Relations, with national and local chapters under the supervision of national Communist parties. Such front organizations as the last two, as well as the multiplicity of ad hoc committees which appeared sporadically, were designed to attract people other than party members.

The complexity of the organizational setup served several purposes. First, many of the connecting links were almost invisible to the casual observer, and in the event of an attack the component parts were quick to deny the existence of interrelationships. Thus, the Soviet Union could simultaneously pursue varied aims without having publicly to assume responsibility for failures. Secondly, the existence of organizations which specialized in dealing with a particular clientele enabled the Soviet authorities to emphasize at a given time that part of the image intended for a particular group, thus following the advice of successful propagandists always to keep in mind the characteristics and inclinations of the target. Hence, revolutionary appeals could be directed toward foreign supporters of Communist expansion, while middle-class elements would hear only of the regime's interest in domestic development.

The Organizational Apparatus
and the Labor Delegations

The lines of control over labor delegations originated within the

Soviet Communist party and central trade union structure. Running through the channels of international Communism, local parties, and front groups, they ultimately reached their target— the radical elements with the labor movement. Both the method of organization and the composition of the rank-and-file delegations followed closely from the purposes they were to serve: to extend Soviet and international Communist influence among the masses of workers. Soviet authorities hoped that workers with many different political views would attend the meetings which chose the delegates, and would be represented on the delegations. However, Communist control was assured at all points in the selection process, and success depended on how subtly Communist control was exercised.

Documents seized by the Home Office during a raid on the headquarters of the British Communist party in 1925 illustrate the above statement.[5] Among the papers was "A Plan of Work of the Agitprop Department of the Executive Committee of the Communist International for the Next Half Year." Part of it described the project of visits to the USSR by worker delegations from different countries, and noted that priority in organization was to be given Germany, France, Czechoslovakia, and the United States. The margin of the statement contained an annotation in handwriting believed to be that of Tom Bell, general secretary of the British Communist party, which read: "We are doing this continually." [6] Another item in the collection was a letter addressed to the secretary of the Agitprop Department of the British Communist party, which read in part: "With regard to planning visits to the U.S.S.R. by workers' delegations we agree that this is valuable. . . ." [7]

Even the major American delegation which visited the Soviet Union in 1927 shared with other delegations such characteristics as a non-Communist façade and a subtle Communist control, though it served a somewhat different purpose. The members of the delegation were James H. Maurer, John Brophy, Frank Palmer, and James William Fitzpatrick. Unlike the rank-and-file delegations from Communist-infiltrated unions, whose major task after returning home was to help extend Communist influence within the labor movement, the 1927 delegation was invited, with its advisory staff, to help spread a favorable image of the Soviet Union. It was felt that such a report by non-Communist labor leaders would serve the Soviet policy of improving its image in the world. The Leninist conception of organization usually resulted in similar structural requirements despite the existence of different aims.

The organization in the Soviet Union which issued all instructions concerning the labor delegations was the Commission on Foreign Relations, which was attached to the All-Union Central Council of Trade Unions. The magazine *Mezhdunarodnoe Rabochee Dvizhenie* (*The International Working-Class Movement*), joint organ of the All-Union Central Council of Trade Unions and the Profintern, recorded that "the international work of the Soviet labor movement proceeds along a number of lines, one being to serve the numerous foreign worker delegations coming to the USSR from capitalist countries." [8] Invitations to the May and November celebrations were usually issued by the Commission, although occasionally invitations came from individual labor unions.

The Commission sent the instructions for selection of the delegates to the front organization, Friends of the Soviet Union, which generally handled this process. At the same time, instructions were handed down to national Communist parties and their "fractions" within the labor movement through Comintern and Profintern channels. Under the auspices of the Commission, a conference was held yearly or biennially, attended by the general secretary of the International Association of Friends of the Soviet Union, the secretaries of the national sections—who were usually Communists—and representatives of the Comintern and Profintern. [9] Participants criticized the previous work of these organizations, and a responsible member of the Comintern usually handed down new directions. Several people who worked for the Commission testified that it served secretly as the real center of the International Association of Friends of the Soviet

Union even though after 1927 the Association had its own structure and secretariat.[10]

The Association of Friends of the Soviet Union was officially begun in November, 1927, although the organization did bear some resemblance to an earlier group called the Friends of Soviet Russia; and the British section of the Friends of the Soviet Union actually called itself at times the Friends of Soviet Russia. The delegation functions undertaken after 1927 by the Friends of the Soviet Union had been performed since 1925 by different ad hoc committees: in Germany these were called "unity committees"; in Italy, "agitation committees"; in Great Britain, "committees to send a trade-union delegation to Russia." [11] A committee to send a delegation from France consisted of representatives from the French sections of International Workers' Relief and International Red Relief as well as from several peasant groups.[12] In the United States as early as 1925, in connection with the dispatch of an American labor delegation, a vast network of temporary regional committees was set up.[13]

Late in 1926 the All-Union Central Council of Trade Unions proposed the formation of an "International Workmen's Information Bureau for the purpose of disseminating among the workers of foreign countries information concerning the Soviet Union, which is to be based upon the observation of workers who have personally visited the S.S.S.R." A diplomatic report concerning the proposal stated that during the visit of an Italian workers' delegation the Council had raised the question "of coordinating the results of visits to the S.S.S.R. by foreign labor delegations with a view to bringing about closer contact between the working masses of the Soviet Union and those of Europe." [14] S. A. Lozovskii, a Soviet labor leader and head of Profintern, told the delegation that "the best way would be to found an International Association of Workmen who have visited the S.S.S.R. and form a wide information bureau, which would furnish extensive information about the S.S.S.R., information moreover which would be trustworthy as having been obtained personally by observation." [15] The Bureau would publish material on the USSR, based on the personal observations of visitors, and would compile all the materials obtained by the various delegations. The All-Union Central Council of Trade Unions proposed to send abroad a special delegation to discuss the opening of the Bureau and requested all labor delegates who had visited the Soviet Union to assist. The report concluded by saying that "the initiative in organizing a bureau of this sort is to be taken by foreign workmen, but the necessary subsidies would come secretly from the All-Union Central Soviet [i.e., Council] of Trade Unions." [16] Here is the theme that one meets over and over again in Soviet propaganda—a theme already noted in the preceding chapter—the emphasis on perception of the truth through personal observation.

One can guess that during the next year preparations were made to implement this proposal. In 1927 on the alleged initiative of a British labor delegation, an International Congress of Friends of the Soviet Union took place, taking advantage of the presence of the various delegations in Moscow for the November festivities.[17] At the request of the British delegation, a committee attached to the All-Union Central Council of Trade Unions undertook the arrangements. On this Committee for the Reception of Foreign Visitors sat representatives of the Communist League of Youth (Komsomol), the Soviet organization of co-operatives (Centrosoiuz), the Russian branches of International Red Relief (MOPR) and International Workers' Relief (MEZHRABPROM), and the Union of the Godless.[18] The Committee was later broadened to include representatives of the foreign delegations. The group selected G. N. Melnichanskii as its chairman and Ia. Iaglom as its secretary. It established an international press bureau composed of Karl Gei, Alfred Kurella, Robert Sievert, Paul Vaillant-Couturier, Scott Nearing, and Diego de Rivera.[19] The bureau distributed literature to the delegates and issued a bulletin edited by C. Umanskii in three different languages. The enlarged Committee later constituted itself as a Presidium for the Congress.

The agenda set up by the Presidium of the Congress set forth two tasks: a summation of progress attained through socialist construction and a discussion of the threat of war against the Soviet Union. The Congress began meeting on November 9, 1927, in the Hall of Columns of the Moscow Palace of Labor. Approximately a thousand delegates attended, representing 43 countries; Germany led in number with 173, followed by France with 146.[20] The Soviet press proclaimed the non-Communist nature of the Congress, but the inconsistency of stating the number of Communists present seems to indicate otherwise: while one source listed the proportion as 15 per cent, another gave a figure of 300.[21]

Pravda greeted the meeting as the symbol of "the presence of powerful spontaneous ties with the USSR before which stand revealed the weakness not only of world imperialism but of its sinister lackeys—international social democracy." [22] *Vestnik Truda* (*Herald of Labor*) said that the Congress of Friends of the Soviet Union, "representing itself as a clear illustration of the revolutionary tendencies of the non-Party and Social Democratic mass . . . served as a symptom of the growing might of Communist influence in all the world. It was evidence also that the united working front against capitalist thought shall be created despite all obstacles and it shall be created at once." [23]

Yet beneath the façade of a spontaneous, non-Communist movement, Soviet authorities continually emphasized the role and tactics of the party. During a discussion of the different tactical methods of class struggle, Comintern representatives stated that they regarded the question of the nature of these methods as critical at a Congress where the majority of members belonged to non-Communist and largely Social Democratic parties. Both Clara Zetkin and Nikolai Bukharin, speaking for the Communist International, discussed the problem openly:

For although neither the Comintern nor the C.P.S.U. convened the Congress, and although they refrained from directly influencing it, it would be foolish not to say that the methods of the class struggle which led to these results approved of by the delegates, are the methods of the C.P.S.U., and that the Communist International has placed before itself the task of employing these meth-

ods in other countries, in order to lead the working classes in those
countries by these, the only possible methods, to victory and to the
building up of socialism. It was not for this Congress to determine
how far the non-Communist delegates were clear on this point.
But the delegates at the Congress who formulated and spoke to
the two resolutions on the "Results of the Dictatorship of the Proletariat" and "the necessity to defend them against all attacks of
the bourgeoisie," will be compelled, in estimating the results of
their journey, to draw the logical consequences and to put and
answer, the question of method.[24]

The speech then continued to maintain that the very fact that
the delegates would have to consider the question of these
methods over and over again would have an effect on the entire
labor movement, and would help "prepare the ground among
the masses for a correct answer to this question; particularly
if the Communists set about their work of agitation and propaganda in the right place and in the right way." [25] Evidence
that the lesson was not lost on the labor delegates is found in
a resolution by an American rank-and-file delegation present
at the Congress. The delegation announced that the visit "opened
their eyes to the necessary role of a Communist Party, and had
convinced the delegates of the need of closer cooperation with
the American Communists than in the past." [26] Showing less
enthusiasm, Joseph Reeves, the leader of a visiting delegation
of co-operators from Great Britain, testified that it was a
"managed" congress. "The Cooperative group submitted resolutions," he said, "but they were so changed by the Presidium as
to be hardly recognizable." [27]

The Congress laid the work for the building, consolidation,
and resuscitation of various groups, committees, and leagues of
the Friends of the Soviet Union. It also elected a permanent
presidium for the international movement consisting of Clara
Zetkin, Henri Barbusse, Arthur Ewert, and Arthur Holitscher.[28]
In an article written the following May, Barbusse noted that
such groups "keep themselves apart from the actual political
struggle and concentrate their work upon proving documentarily
the warlike attitude of the capitalist powers toward the Soviet

Union and upon working against these tendencies openly." [29]
The major motive behind the consolidation of the Friends
of the Soviet Union was to create a mass organization which
would unite people of different persuasions in activities connected
with the defense of the Soviet Union and the popularization
of its achievements—particularly people who were pro-Soviet
but not yet ready to join a Communist party. The Communist
leader of the French section of FSU, A. Herclet, advised the
militant members of the party and the CGTU who participated in the formation of the section not to urge the intellectuals
and Socialists to adhere to Communist tactics of action, "the
transference of the imperialist war into a civil war." "All we ask
is willingness to defend the USSR in case of aggression." [30] In
1926 at the Twelfth Session of the Enlarged Executive of the
Comintern, Mikhail Pavlovich Tomskii had reminded his audience that in mobilizing the non-party masses extreme slogans
should not be used. He remarked that many of the comrades
did not realize that winning over the non-party masses was "not
merely a question of agitation and propaganda but a question
of detail work in the trade unions and in the other non-party
Labour organizations." [31]
The Sixth Congress of the Comintern continued to call for
mass work in non-party organizations. In its resolution on "the
struggle against imperialist war and the tasks of the Communists," it urged that the tactics of the "united front from below"
and work in the "hands off Russia" committees be conducted
more effectively than hitherto.[32] The plenums of the national
Communist parties that met following the Congress confirmed
such resolutions. The American Communist party at its Thirteenth
Plenum resolved to assist the building of the FSU into a mass
organization and to assist in the organization of worker delegations as important steps to advance the struggle for the defense
of the Soviet Union.[33]
Although the Friends of the Soviet Union did not concern
itself exclusively with the organization of worker delegations,
it did, in the words of *Soviet Russia Today*, the official magazine

of the American branch of FSU, regard this activity as "one of our most important tasks." [34] Writing in *Imprecorr*, Albert Inkpin, general secretary of the international organization, remarked:

> The delegation campaigns bring the F.O.S.R. into close contact with ever widening circles of workers, provide opportunities for the creation of groups and committees in the workshops and factories and for building up the "Friends of Soviet Russia" as a *real mass organization*, based upon the widest possible united front from below, and it is that which constitutes the principal task of the F.O.S.R. and is the end to which the organization of delegations is one of the various means.[35]

Following the Congress of 1927, labor delegations from Western Europe and the United States went about the tasks of setting up national chapters in areas lacking them and of consolidating and reorganizing existing groups. A French section which stated that it would work independently of political parties made its appearance on December 29.[36] A report of the Tenth Congress of the Communist party of Great Britain noted, following the return of the British labor delegation from the Soviet Union, the formation of a Friends of Soviet Russia chapter similar to those founded elsewhere after the Moscow Congress.[37] The organizational structure of the chapters in both countries included a national executive committee headed by a secretary, with district and local committees composed of delegates who had visited the Soviet Union, supplemented by active trade unionists. The British section had no general membership since the various committees worked within existing organizations, unions, cooperatives, and political parties.[38]

While the local sections of the organization attempted to consolidate, a conference of leaders of the International Association of Friends of the Soviet Union opened in Cologne in order to organize the defense task "more methodically and in a more centralised fashion than before." [39] Soviet delegates were absent from the meeting because of their inability to enter Germany, but representatives of MEZHRABPROM and the League against

Imperialism attended the meeting. It was announced that the assembly was called through the initiative of the English section of Friends of the Soviet Union with the assistance of the All-Union Central Council of Trade Unions.[40]

Questions on the agenda included election of an International Committee of Friends of the Soviet Union, "the fight against the war danger," "international trade union unity," and "the struggle against Fascism and the White Terror." An International Committee consisting of two members each for Great Britain, France, and Germany was set up; its tasks were to publish an information bulletin, to establish organizational contact with those national and international trade union organizations which embraced workers engaged in industries most vital to the conduct of war, and to complete immediately preliminary work for the organization of a second international congress of Friends of the Soviet Union.[41]

A new directorate appeared to be in charge at the Cologne meeting; the list included William Lawther, a member of the British Labour party, Pierre André Cannone, a French Socialist party member, and Robert Sievert, a German Communist. All three had participated in the work of organization for the 1927 Congress.[42]

After several cancellations, the second international congress was finally held in Essen, Germany, in March, 1930. The cancellations were attributed by the leadership to the fact that intensified anti-Soviet campaigns everywhere made it inadvisable for the leaders of the national chapters to leave their countries.[43] A third congress was held in Paris in 1933, but little information is available on it.[44]

Until 1933, a central secretariat for the International Association of FSU existed in Berlin. Later it moved to Amsterdam to escape Nazi persecution.[45] Although the Secretariat was nominally headed by a former secretary of the British Communist party, Albert Inkpin, a former employee of the Commission on Foreign Relations of the Central Council of Trade Unions noted that it was actually subordinate both to the Commission and to the Comintern, from which it received money.[46]

THE RECRUITMENT CAMPAIGN

The campaigns to recruit delegations to the Soviet Union attempted to involve as many people as possible, both in selecting delegates and in financing the delegations. The All-Union Central Council of Trade Unions sent out its invitations long before the May and November festivities to enable the Communist parties and front organizations to plan and organize the agitation campaign. Local members of these groups and subdivisions of ad hoc "unity" or "united front" committees then began to visit sympathetic workers' organizations, labor unions, co-operative groups, and factory units to urge them to nominate candidates for the delegations and to elect delegates to future selection conferences.[47]

In the United States a national convention of Friends of the Soviet Union opened the drive for delegations. A call was issued by the National Committee to trade unions, factory groups, fraternal organizations, political party locals, anti-war groups, and Negro associations to send delegates to the convention.[48] For weeks before this date *Soviet Russia Today* urged its readers to exert pressure on their organizations to send delegations. The magazine later reported that the highlight of the convention was the report of the national secretary on the importance of sending delegations to the USSR. The presiding officials asked each convention delegate to submit in writing to the National Committee suggestions and proposals for recruiting delegates to the Soviet Union from his area.[49]

In Great Britain, the National Committee to Send a Workers Delegation to the USSR in 1927 announced that final selection of candidates for the London area would be held at a conference called for that purpose after nominations by individual labor organizations were made. However, the decisions of the conference were to be subject to final ratification by the National Committee.[50]

Selection of delegates to the Soviet Union from the United States and Great Britain evidently took place at regional or district conferences. In Germany and Belgium, on the other hand, delegates appear to have been selected at the factory level without intervening conferences, partly by "unity" groups and partly by the trade unions.[51] After the initial steps, committees (aided in propaganda activity by the various national divisions of the directing organizations, the "unity" committees, or national FSU chapters) were set up within factories to conduct the campaign. Some called themselves "factory committees"; others, "agitation committees" or "committees for proletarian unity."[52] A report on activities published by the Communist Youth International noted that during the campaigns to recruit delegations to Soviet Russia such questions as life in the Soviet Union and the conditions of Russian youth compared to those of youth in the capitalist countries were discussed. Measures for the joint struggles of young workers on a national and international scale were also discussed. The report stated that "in most countries, therefore, the young workers' delegations became the starting point for United Front action, in defense of the economic and political interests of the young workers."[53] *Workers Life,* describing the factory meeting held to elect representatives to a Friends of the Soviet Union campaign committee, commented: "in this way, too, will be laid the foundations of the all-embracing Factory Committees that are the pressing need for successful working-class struggle today."[54] The achievements of socialist construction were continually praised, and agitation was conducted at all meetings around the slogan "Defense of the Soviet Union."

Communist publications continually emphasized the mass character of these campaigns, and especially the involvement in them of those who were not Communist party members. Instructions issued by the All-Russian Council of Trade Unions and the Secretariat of the International Association of FSU ordered that elections were to be conducted in all shops with a minimum of 500 workers and must involve the participation of as many organized and unorganized workers as possible.[55] All the publicity on the selection meetings stressed the number of workers in attendance.

The personal account of a selection meeting by Margaret McCarthy, a weaver in Lancashire, who in 1926 was secretary of a branch of the Guild of Youth (the youth organization of the Independent Labour party), deserves summarizing here, for it provides a graphic illustration of Communist tactics in arranging a delegation and suggests the climate of opinion in Britain which made these tactics effective.[56] Miss McCarthy received a letter from a "Mr. H. Lee" of the Manchester Labour League of Youth, inviting the interest as well as the moral and financial support of her branch in the delegation campaign. Her first reaction was to be impressed that someone outside her organization had noticed its existence. She liked the general idea of the project because she "believed that young workers from different countries should meet and make friends." Mr. Lee appeared pleased with her interest, and by letter invited the branch to attend the selection conference in Manchester which would choose the youth delegates to represent the Lancashire section of the delegation.

She found the conference very exciting. For the first time she heard about Russia and met Communists. She was enthusiastic about the important role played by Soviet youth and agreed with the description of the terrible conditions of young workers in Great Britain: "In these speeches I heard the echo of my own hopelessness, hatred of factory life, the poverty of my parents. . . ."[57] She felt "a sudden sense of belonging"; and when the leader of her delegation counseled her about voting for the Communist resolutions, she was shocked that anyone should tell her how to vote. She states that she was so much in sympathy with the Communist platform that she voted against her colleagues. Information about the Communist direction of the meeting did not change her mind because the Communist delegates still appeared to be the only ones really concerned about the conditions of the working class. Their youth delegates seemed "more purposeful, more confident, more self-sacrificing, and better organizers" than the rest of the delegates present. Despite opposition among representatives of the Guild of Youth to Communist direction of the election meeting, the leader of the group consented to go along with the delegation.[58] More important, the selection meeting extended Communist influence among new groups of young people, previously unfamiliar with the activities of the party.

In addition to securing broad representation at selection meetings, the organizers of the delegation campaigns were attempting to get many people involved in the raising of money for the trip, even when the cost was handled by the Comintern. The instructions of the All-Russian Council were that the fellow workers of delegates who had been selected should help finance the campaign by voluntary contributions.[59] In England an incentive was introduced by providing that if an enterprise or combination of enterprises could raise over £25, the average cost of sending a delegate, its nominee would be guaranteed a place on the delegation.[60] Another method of raising money for this purpose was through the sale of stamps. In Germany, a group called the "Committee of Unity," similar in character to the Friends of the Soviet Union, issued a list of signatures headed by a greeting to the Soviet proletariat on the occasion of the Tenth Anniversary of the October Revolution. Each person who signed the list paid ten pfennigs for a stamp with printed slogans such as "Fight the enemy," or "Stretch out a brotherly hand to the workers of the USSR." [61] The money collected was supposed to finance the trip of the German delegates.

While the major 1927 American delegation to the Soviet Union differed from the other delegations in its composition and the fact that the visit was independent of the May and November festivities, to some extent it was similar in basic organizational principles, such as the involvement of many individuals in the process of selection and the masking of Communist influence. Recruitment of the delegation was carried on behind a façade of independent committees employing the services of several prestigious persons. In view of the abundance of unusually reliable information as to the organization of this delegation, the affair deserves special attention.

According to Benjamin Gitlow, the Comintern entrusted the American Communist party with the organization of a delegation of labor leaders.[62] The party also organized a nineteen-man technical, advisory, research, and secretarial staff, which included several unacknowledged party members as well as such prominent persons as Professors George S. Counts and Rexford G. Tugwell. A knowledgeable oral source confirmed Gitlow's statement, declaring that the undertaking was handled in the Secretariat of the Communist party by Benjamin Gitlow, William Z. Foster, and Jay Lovestone, with the latter put in charge because of his position on the Executive Committee of the Comintern (he was then secretary of the American Communist party).[63] The papers of Frank P. Walsh, a liberal labor lawyer and close personal friend of Lovestone, also give us insight into the situation.

Lovestone hoped to get Walsh interested in the delegation, for his name would lend it considerable prestige. In a letter to Walsh of January 30, 1926, Lovestone advocated organizing a national committee to spark the delegation, and urged the decision to enter the field be made immediately.[64] In a subsequent letter of February 6, Lovestone told Walsh of the free hand he had in the matter [65] and he expressed the hope that Walsh had received the report of the British Trades Union Delegation to the Soviet Union.

Subsequently, Lovestone evidently asked Walsh to write letters to prominent labor men to interest them in the delegation, but Walsh felt that this was a matter for personal contact: "It would seem to me that in the Labor Movement there are many outstanding, fine men, who could be trusted to make a study of industrial conditions in Russia, and make a report which would stand up forever. . . ." [66] In addition to enlisting the efforts of Frank Walsh and his friends, the American Communist party inspired the erection of a complex network of regional committees throughout the United States, all designed to agitate for and to help select and finance a delegation to go to the Soviet Union.[67]

Instituted under a non-Communist façade, the delegation was able to attract several labor leaders and quite a few young intellectuals. Paul Douglas, a member of the advisory group, expressed to me in an interview his genuine surprise when Jay Lovestone told him in 1949 about Communist manipulation of the strings. He later commented in a letter that the information that Lovestone got Walsh to help sponsor the trip to Russia, if true, was completely unknown to him, and that he had never heard of it; since he did not read the *Daily Worker*, he did not know of the Communists' activity.[68]

The leaders of the American Federation of Labor, particularly William Green, seem to have had doubts about the nature of the delegation. In 1926 a number of minor labor leaders had requested the American trade unions to send a delegation to the USSR. Albert Coyle, editor of the *Locomotive Engineers Journal*, had persuaded Timothy Healy, president of the International Brotherhood of Stationary Firemen, to work to promote the delegation.[69] Green was asked by Coyle to serve on the national committee which had been formed, or to send a substitute. Green did not approve of the undertaking and was especially suspicious of its financial sources.[70] After considering the question, the Executive Council of the AFL decided that "no good purpose could be served through such action. In fact we seriously doubt," said the Council, "the good faith of such a self-constituted Commission." [71] A similar proposal had been turned down by the Convention of the AFL meeting in Atlantic City in 1925. In 1926 the Committee on Resolutions again asked the Convention to turn down the proposal, which it did indirectly by accepting the recommendations of the Committee.[72]

The group organizing the delegation continued to stress that although the AFL had decided not to pay expenses of an official mission to Russia, "the present delegation in no way conflicts with this decision since its members are going in their private capacity and not as an official body." [73] The seventh vice presi-

dent, James Wilson, called this statement a "deception," noting
that the Convention at Atlantic City in 1925 had said "that no
delegation should go to Russia, and we made no reference to any
delegation going if they saw fit to pay their own expenses." [74]
The fact that the AFL refused to support the group probably
helped to delay the trip for over a year. Matthew Woll, fifth
vice president of the AFL, later called the delegation "a self-
appointed group hostile to the position of American labor." [75]

Paul Douglas has reported that when Coyle approached him
in the spring of 1927 and asked him to join the trade union
delegation, he told Coyle that he wanted to satisfy himself in two
respects. The first was that the trip was not being financed by the
Communist party but was being independently financed; he
pressed Coyle on this point and Coyle assured him that the
Communists were *not* financing it. Coyle had previously told him
that he was trying to raise money for the trip from American
liberals and unions. As Coyle then had a good reputation, and as
Douglas had himself been in Clarence Darrow's apartment on
the Midway in Chicago when Coyle had called on Darrow and
asked for a contribution, and so knew at first hand he was making
such an effort, he did not question his statement. Douglas' second
condition for joining the delegation was that no Communist be a
member of the delegation or staff. Coyle seemed to agree, but
asked whom Douglas was suspicious about. When Douglas replied "Robert W. Dunn," Coyle said that Dunn was not a member
of the Communist party but was an independent writer. Douglas
has written: "I had no evidence to disprove this. Later Benjamin
Gitlow wrote that Dunn was a secret member of the Communist
party. I certainly did not know this and Coyle specifically denied
it." [76]

Gitlow, however, asserts that the Comintern informed the
American Communist party that the costs of sending the delegation, as well as of preparing the subsequent report, would be paid
by Moscow.[77] This statement has been confirmed by a knowledgeable oral source.[78] Gitlow also remarked that to mask the
financial source, the report implied "that the money came from

contributions of workers and liberal friends, who supplemented a nucleus from the Purcell fund. But," said Gitlow, "we had no Purcell Fund. Purcell's tour did not pay for itself." [79] Further, he noted that contributions from workers and liberals were negligible.

Other sources reveal that fund-raising activities with reference to a delegation to the Soviet Union were going on during 1925, 1926, and 1927. The *Daily Worker* during 1925 and 1926 described the activities of the local committees set up all over the country to raise funds for the delegation.[80] Letters in the Walsh Collection mention an attempt to raise money among affluent individuals. Coyle wrote Walsh that he was lining up some mutual friends for a meeting, to be held at a private residence, of possible contributors in the $500 to $1000 range.[81] He asked Walsh to suggest persons who might make contributions.

Many non-Communist delegates were unaware of the financial manipulations, however; they believed that (as the published report of the delegation also states) "various members of the delegation paid part or all of their own expenses." [82] Paul Douglas informed me that he believed that other members of the delegation as well as he himself were paying their way to the Soviet Union; in order to be sure that he would not be under financial obligations to anyone, he paid his own fare over and later contributed enough to pay his way back.[83] A letter of December 17, 1927, in the Walsh Files indicates that Douglas paid Coyle before the delegation left and supplemented it after his return when he learned Coyle was in debt because of some money that had disappeared.[84] Walsh himself, believing that the delegation had difficulty in raising funds, signed a note for the delegation; Coyle later made payments on the note through the use of royalties from the labor delegation's report.[85] John Brophy, a member of the labor delegation, states in his autobiography that the money came largely from the Garland Fund (American Fund for Public Service), although some delegates were able to pay part or all of their expenses.[86] According to a highly informed oral source, the money raised to finance the delegation's trip went into the party's coffers.[87] So, although individual and group contributions were made to finance the trip, thus supporting the statement in the report of the labor delegation, the fact that these funds went into the party's general funds and did not directly pay for the trip suggests the basis for Gitlow's statement that the money came from Moscow.

One of the most important aspects of the rank-and-file delegations was their composition in regard to such characteristics as age, sex, race, occupation, and political affiliation. The composition of the delegation was deliberately arranged to suggest that workers of all types and affiliations expressed interest in the Soviet Union. The Central Council of Trade Unions dispatched instructions concerning this aspect of the delegation to national and local FSU chapters shortly after it had issued invitations to visit the Soviet Union.

In regard to the American delegations, the Central Council and the Communist International proposed that delegates be "bona fide" workers, employed in basic industries which could be quickly converted into war use. Instructions also stressed that each delegation should include farmers, Negroes, youth, women, Socialists, unemployed workers, and trade union members. "In choosing the delegates," the directions continued, "we should secure such workers, honest and sincere, who, as yet, are not entirely convinced of the victories of socialist construction in the U.S.S.R., but who can be relied upon to give an unbiased report on their return." [88] "Conditions in the American labour movement are such," said *Imprecorr*, "that this delegation [referring to an American rank-and-file delegation] if it is to be effective in advancing the organisation of American workers' sentiment for the recognition and defence of the Soviet Union should bear a pronounced non-Communist character. This means that while notorious non-Communists would be welcome, no trade unionist who by his militancy had come to be known as a member of the Communist Party would be considered altogether a most desirable member of the delegation." [89] The International Committee of Friends of the Soviet Union recommended that "measures be taken to ensure that the preponderant majority of the delegates chosen are workers who do not realise clearly the significance of the work of socialist reconstruction, or the real situation of workers in the U.S.S.R. . . . those workers who feel instinctive sympathy for the proletarian state, but are still greatly in doubt." [90]

Communist instructions specified that the major American labor delegation of 1927 should be composed of "fair-minded, impartial investigators, who, though they were not Communists, had to admit that conditions were excellent. . . ." [91] In a letter of February 8, 1926, Frank Walsh agreed with Jay Lovestone that "a strictly Trade Union delegation composed of conservative members, yet with open minds, progressive ideas, and bravery of purpose could do a monumental work. Their conclusions," wrote Walsh, "would have vastly more effect, one way or the other than any other body of investigators which I could vision." [92] He suggested that W. Jett Lauck be invited to accompany the group. "His established reputation as an impartial economist, as well as his vast experience in organizing investigations covering large territory, would insure not only the economical prosecution of the idea, but a truthful report which would stand up against adverse attack." [93] In a subsequent letter, Walsh stressed again that "the investigation should be an impartial one, and a fair, open-minded man should be able to arrive at conclusions which would be valuable, regardless of any predilections he might have with reference to the Soviet Republic or the Communist Party." [94]

The enthusiastic response of individuals like Walsh to the idea of an impartial delegation confirmed Soviet beliefs that a neutral façade would direct suspicion away from the motivating source of the delegation. In addition, when a favorable report emerged, as Communist authorities intended, it would have a better reception because the investigators were not thought to be biased by Communist or other radical affiliations. Through the manipulation of such a delegation, the Soviet propagandists hoped to penetrate circles hostile to Soviet Russia and its activities.

The Communists also paid special attention to delegation

composition in other countries. The British National Committee to Send a Workers Delegation to the USSR mentioned in its publicity certain occupational characteristics a nominee must have, stressing that all "must be trade unionists of good standing and active in the working-class movement for at least five years." [95] *Cahiers du bolchevisme*, the journal of the French Communist party, in a story describing the selection campaign conducted by one locality, praised the fact that non-party members were included on the organization committee and comprised the vast majority of delegates finally selected. [96]

While the Soviet Union welcomed the rank and file of different political parties as delegation members, the leaders of the parties were not acceptable. This tactic fitted into the general policy known within Communist circles as "the united front from below," which sought to separate the masses from their non-Bolshevik leaders. Youth organizations were particularly susceptible because they often proved to be more radical than the parent organization. [97]

For example, in 1925, the Communist Youth International proposed that the Socialist Youth International join them in sending a young workers' delegation to the Soviet Union. [98] Understanding Communist tactics, the SYI accepted with the proviso that the composition of the delegations should be arranged with "the full agreement of the Central Committees of the Socialist Youth Organizations in the various countries." It further declared its readiness to send its own delegation if it could select the members and have its own interpreters, and was assured "full rights to get in personal contact with imprisoned members of Menshevist Youth organizations in the Soviet Union." [99]

The CYI replied that while the Socialists were discussing details, many delegations which included young Social Democrats had already gone to Russia, despite warnings from their own leaders about participation. The CYI thus pointed out what it said was the difference between the words and deeds of the

Social Democrats, and declared itself ready "to set up a committee with equal representation from the Social Democratic Youth
organizations for the organization of delegations, stressing, however, the absolute necessity that the delegates should be young
workers elected by youth working in the respective factories."
The CYI refused to consider sending a delegation of Social
Democratic leaders, since they "could not expect an unbiased
judgment of the position in the Soviet Union from avowed
political enemies." [100]

The CYI then accused SYI of misinforming its members by
asserting that the Communists refused a joint delegation. However, a German Socialist paper did admit, said the CYI, that
"we only rejected a delegation from the Central Committees, and
not a delegation of young workers from the factories." [101] What
is very curious in the use by the CYI of this article to support its
case is that it contains a passage which exposes the Communist
bias: "they [the Communists] do not want, therefore, a delegation
which has sufficient knowledge necessary for this purpose, but
they only want young workers, who go on their journeys totally
unprepared in order that they should report as facts that which
they have heard, without any criticism." [102] The Communists
attempted to refute the statement by saying that it "was an insult
to the 'simple' young workers, members of the Socialist Youth
International, but it proved again that the Socialist Youth International was not at all keen on sending an unprejudiced young
workers' delegation, but wanted to send a delegation of counterrevolutionary social democratic leaders consciously opposed to
the Soviet Union." [103]

Communist suspicion of staunch Socialist leaders can also be
illustrated by their reluctance to grant a visa to Norman Thomas
in 1937. The Soviet authorities, caught between granting a visa
and thus opening up the country to a critic, and declining to
issue a visa during a period marked by surface co-operation with
Socialists, finally decided to follow the first path. After some
delay the visa was granted Thomas by the Soviet consul with the

words (referring to Thomas' association with the Committee for Justice to Trotsky), "I hope you will form a committee for justice to Russia." [104]

While Communist literature on the delegations continually stressed the number of Socialists, reformists, Catholics, and non-party members who visited the Soviet Union, it practically ignored the existence of a Communist "fraction" within each delegation. The Communist party selected the "fraction" members of the delegations from Communist-controlled labor unions such as the old Ford local of the United Auto Workers or party affiliates like the Slovak Workers' Society of the International Workers Order, to which the party had sent election directions. [105] In one 1929 delegation from the United States, the Communist "fraction" comprised eight out of forty-eight members. The majority of the others were sympathizers of one degree or another, with the nominal leadership of the delegation in the hands of a non-Communist, Louis Hyman. [106] In another delegation of twenty-six members, ten were part of the Communist fraction. Several delegates had just been contacted by the Communists, who hoped to use their association with the delegation to draw them closer to the party. [107]

A baker from Hamburg, Germany, who went to the Soviet Union with a German delegation in 1926, wrote in an article published in *Der Socialistische Bote* that when the delegation was being formed, members were told "that it would be exclusively composed of Social Democrats and Non-Party men," but upon leaving for Russia, they discovered that the delegation included eight Communists. [108]

ORGANIZATIONAL CONTROL WITHIN THE SOVIET UNION

Within the Soviet Union, officials and interpreters attached to the Commission on Foreign Relations cared for the delegations. [109] While interpreters had to show some evidence of loyalty to the regime, it is debatable whether they were always party members. During the early years the Commission recruited them from the ranks of the former intelligentsia. The range of knowledge among interpreters varied. As one said, "I had no knowledge of the trade-union life of the West, but in the USSR a shoemaker is amazed not a bit if they prescribe his fate. Specialization of function—about this one does not ask." [110] In addition to the interpreters, there were various trade union officials who acted as political organizers and accompanied the delegations. One person mentioned several times as traveling with delegations was a secretary of the Central Council of Trade Unions, M. Slutsky, who had served from 1921 as general secretary of the International Committee of Propaganda and Action of the Revolutionary Coal Miners. John Ballam, American representative to the Profintern, was another person who accompanied delegations. [111]

While the Friends of the Soviet Union was the primary organization involved with delegations, organizations such as International Workers' Relief and World Tourist also participated, although to a much lesser degree. World Tourist, ostensibly organized as an independent travel agency, constituted one of the many organs of international Communism. Headed by Robert W. Weiner, financial secretary of the American Communist party, Alexander Trachtenburg, and Jacob Golos, World Tourist was designed to be a profit-making enterprise for the American Communist party and the Comintern. It was designed also to encourage tourists, primarily of working-class background, to visit the Soviet Union, where they were promised preferential treatment. [112] According to one source, however, the main purpose of the organization was to function as a front for Soviet espionage and intelligence activity, receiving directions directly from Moscow. [113]

The international Communist organization International Red Relief, which proclaimed as its aim "to accord assistance to all victims of the revolutionary struggle," concentrated on propaganda work among sailors, operating, together with the trade unions, the international clubs at Soviet ports. [114] Other activities of the organization included participation in the work surround-

ing the 1927 Congress of Friends of the Soviet Union and
providing transportation for Schutzbunder to come to the Soviet
Union.[115]

The Organizational Apparatus and the Intellectuals

The channels designed for attracting and manipulating intellectuals differed from those operating primarily within labor circles.
Except for the Bureau of Revolutionary Literature, organizations designed to handle intellectuals rarely expressed revolutionary sentiments. There were apparently some differences in
regard to clientele among the various organizations catering to
intellectuals: VOKS (the All-Union Society for Cultural Relations
with Foreign Countries) was concerned with the more prominent
bourgeoisie; Intourist, with the lesser-known people in this
category and the ordinary tourist; and the Bureau of Revolutionary Literature, with foreign writers already identified as
possessing revolutionary sympathies.

While the dividing line between Intourist and VOKS was
blurred in many instances, the division of labor between VOKS
and the Bureau of Revolutionary Literature appeared much
sharper. Liam O'Flaherty, the Irish writer, was told by an English-speaking Soviet employee working in the Bureau that this
organization was "the center of a world organization to coordinate
the activities of proletarian writers." The Bureau specialized in
the entertainment of proletarian writers, avowing to unite "the
principal writers of the world under its control, for the purpose
of demoralizing capitalism and encouraging the working class of
the world to make war on their oppressors." The Soviet employee
explained that all foreign writers who visited Russia came there
for information and guidance, "except such as are entirely
bourgeois, which go to the society for cultural relations. Such
people, which we cannot very well forbid to come, are nevertheless brought around by that other society, so that they may see
what is best and be unable to tell too many lies." [116] O'Flaherty
expressed astonishment, after a visit to VOKS, at the difference
in psychology between its officials and the individuals at the

Bureau of Revolutionary Literature. "Not a word did he [the gentleman at VOKS] speak about the revolution, or about the liberation of the world proletariat. He was concerned solely with the aggrandisement of his country, Russia." [117] VOKS was the major Soviet organization which dealt with foreign intellectuals. Established by decree of the Council of People's Commissars in August, 1925, it replaced an earlier information bureau located in Moscow.[118] The organization consisted of representatives from all the union republics, members of people's commissariats interested in developing relations with foreign countries, and delegates from the large scientific and cultural institutions of the Soviet Union. It was first headed by Madame Kameneva, the sister of Trotsky and wife of Leo Kamenev.[119] Professor Feodor Nikolaevich Petrov, a former head of the Chief Scientific Section of the Commissariat of Education of the Russian Soviet Republic, occupied this position from 1929 to 1933, followed by A. Y. Arosiev.[120] Although the Soviet regime tried to make it appear that VOKS was only a semi-official group, in order to facilitate its work with non-Communists, the organization was, in fact, supported by the Soviet government. Party control over VOKS was exercised through a Communist fraction within the organization and through members of the GPU (State Political Administration) who served as section heads and interpreters.[121]

VOKS had diverse goals and activities, but its major aims were to popularize Soviet culture abroad and to mobilize foreign intellectuals against alleged plans for military attack on the Soviet Union. An article in *VOKS Weekly News Bulletin* remarked that the new generation of intellectuals "must lay the foundations of cultural cooperation between the nations and must always remember that this can only be achieved by preserving peace, that their struggle for peace is facilitated by cultural relations which draw the nations nearer together." [122]

The society hoped through various means of communication to spread more adequate information about the cultural and scientific life of the Soviet Union, and "to assist in the establish-

ment and development of cultural connections between the
various institutions, public organizations and individuals active
in the scientific and cultural field in the Soviet Union and those
similarly engaged in other countries." [123] To aid this purpose it
published a weekly news bulletin in French, German, English,
and Russian.

The society was divided into a number of different sections
which performed such activities as sending Soviet exhibitions
abroad, exchanging books with other countries, and compiling
bibliographies. One of the most important sections was the
Bureau for the Reception of Foreign Visitors. VOKS provided
visiting intellectuals with access to materials, institutions, interpreters, and Soviet officials with whom they wished to speak;
it sponsored lectures by visiting intellectuals during evenings of
cultural rapprochement; it generally assisted these visitors in
getting acquainted with Soviet life.[124]

VOKS also sponsored or co-sponsored many special activities.
To help crystalize the interest in Soviet science that existed
among the world scientific community, it sponsored a Franco-
Soviet Week of Scientific Rapprochement in May, 1934.[125] During
this week it played host to a large number of French scientists
and academicians who had come to acquaint themselves with
the activities and achievements of Moscow scientific institutions.
Other VOKS activities directed toward the interests of scientists
included sponsoring a series of courses for foreign physicians in
Moscow to acquaint them with public health work in the Soviet
Union and making the arrangements for several international
scientific congresses.[126] It also served as a sponsor on the Soviet
side of the Anglo-American Summer School held at Moscow University in 1933 and 1934.[127]

One of the functions of VOKS was to assist the various friendship societies and national societies for cultural relations which
had blossomed out in many countries. It is not clear whether
they arose spontaneously or through the efforts of the Comintern,
but whatever their beginnings, evidence suggests that these

societies served as fronts for Communist activities. A plan of work for the Agitprop Department of the Comintern Executive Committee, found among Communist papers seized during the raid of the headquarters of the Communist party in London, had, next to a point reading "elaboration of the question of artistic forms of agitation," a note believed to be in the handwriting of Tom Bell, stating, "The Society for Cultural Relations between G.B. and USSR doing this." [128]

A statement in the *Soviet Culture Review* of October 25, 1931, further clarified the relation of these organizations to Soviet policy.

> Our foreign societies would, however, be entirely wrong in limiting their work to disseminating neutral information which often hides a desire to efface our victories. These societies must organize their work so as to attract such representatives of the working intelligenzia who, in times of great trial, could stand in defense of the USSR. These societies must create a ring of trust, sympathy and friendship around the USSR, through which all plans of intervention will be unable to penetrate.[129]

The article remarked that the societies for cultural relations with the USSR then embraced only the more advanced intellectuals who had not yet formed clear-cut programs of activity, but that the day was not distant when the wide scope of the work outlined would attract all intellectuals.

On November 14 and 15, 1927, delegates from the various societies met in Moscow for the Tenth Anniversary of the October Revolution.[130] VOKS was entrusted with the task of organizing an international federation of these groups. The assembly called on existing societies to get in touch with other organizations interested in the cultural and economic life of the USSR. Subdivisions and branches were held to be desirable in larger countries, and the assembly decreed that each national society should, like VOKS, consist of a number of specialized sections. Close co-operation between VOKS and the independent units was pledged: the national societies agreed to send regular reports of their activities to the Soviet organization; VOKS, in return, offered to help them organize their programs and to provide them with material.[131]

The activities of the societies in their own countries included sponsoring programs about the Soviet Union, serving as information centers, and arranging special excursions designed to attract particular groups of professionals such as doctors and educators. The societies resembled such groups as the Friends of the Soviet Union in that they sent delegations to Russia; but since it was less difficult to attract delegations of intellectuals than delegations of laborers, this constituted a less important part of the societies' work.

The American Society for Cultural Relations listed as its object "to bring together those Americans who are interested in Russian life and contemporary culture, and to collect and diffuse in the United States and the U.S.S.R. developments in science, education, philosophy, art, music and drama in both countries." [132] The British Society vowed "to take any action deemed desirable to forward the intellectual and technical progress of both peoples." [133] Both societies boasted a distinguished list of directors, led by Dr. John Dewey, Professor E. A. Ross, and Lillian Wald in the United States, and H. T. Hobhouse, John Maynard Keynes, E. M. Forster, H. G. Wells, and Julian Huxley in Great Britain.[134] These liberal, non-Communist intellectuals had visited the Soviet Union, and after liking what they saw, had agreed to "tell the truth about Russia."

Liam O'Flaherty was asked by the director of the Anglo-American Section of VOKS to set up a branch of the Friends of Soviet Russia in Ireland, with the suggestion that O'Flaherty contact either George Russell or William Butler Yeats. When O'Flaherty seemed puzzled why these men, who were far from being Socialists or Communists, should be contacted, the director answered: ". . . but they might help to propagate the ideas of the new Russian culture. It is not necessary for people to be Communist or even Socialist in order to be of assistance." [135] In fact, it was to the Soviet advantage that prominent non-Communist intellectuals join these organizations: they would be star attractions and proof that the organizations were independent groups of well-wishers of the Soviet Union.

The visitor to Russia, was, for the most part, quite different from tourists to other parts of the world. While a few came for adventure and excitement, and for the opportunity to tell others that "they had been to Russia," a greater number came to visit relatives or out of intellectual curiosity. It is difficult to divide visitors into categories such as intellectuals, tourists, etc. Besides the select group of writers, educators, sociologists, and others who were taken care of through the auspices of VOKS, much larger groups of people in these categories and others were individually or collectively supervised by Intourist.

Organized in the spring of 1929 after its predecessor, the Travel Bureau of the Soviet Merchant Fleet, had failed to handle the increasing number of visitors, Intourist did not attain a high standard of efficiency until several years later.[136] During the 1930's it expanded its operations, opening up offices in the major cities of the world and carrying on business with private travel agencies. Its president, Wilhelm A. Kurtz, on his arrival in the United States late in 1933, described it as "an independent organization, but at the same time under the supervision of the Central Executive Committee [of the All-Union Congress of Soviets]." [137]

Popular magazines like *Scribner's* and the *Review of Reviews,* as well as those which appealed to special interest audiences, such as the *Nation* and *Survey Graphic,* contained Intourist advertisements offering many different types of tours and accommodations. Intourist employed a staff of several hundred Soviet interpreters and guides, usually university students with training in foreign languages, well acquainted with Soviet history and government as well as with the major tourist attractions.[138] In the earlier years, because of a shortage of trained people, the organization utilized the services of the "children of the former ruling classes," but they were replaced with more reliable assistance as soon as possible. In addition to providing interpreters, in each of the major Soviet cities Intourist operated one or two hotels which catered exclusively to foreign tourists and accepted only foreign currency. Intourist also assisted VOKS with many of its special scientific activities as well as with the Anglo-American Summer School at Moscow University.[139]

THE ORGANIZATIONAL APPARATUS
AND THE BUSINESS DELEGATIONS

In entertaining business delegations not only Intourist but such other Soviet economic organizations as the USSR Chamber of Commerce for the West and the State Bank played a part. While many of the invitations came directly from Moscow, the central organizations were assisted by the Soviet trade delegations in foreign countries.

The USSR Chamber of Commerce for the West, composed of sections devoted to different Western countries, helped plan the itineraries of foreign business delegations and carried on relations with foreign business organizations in the Soviet Union and abroad. Working with Intourist, it organized the visit of the delegation of American businessmen in 1929 which was sponsored by the American-Russian Chamber of Commerce, and arranged access to Soviet officials for business talks.[140] However, despite the position of power the USSR Chamber of Commerce for the West had in the hierarchy of Soviet organizations, Spencer Williams stated that the American-Russian Chamber of Commerce maintained better relations with Mostorg (Moscow Trade Organization) because of its better contacts with men in the Commissariat for Foreign Trade.[141] Amtorg also played an important role both in the Soviet Union and the United States. In the Soviet Union it apparently acted as intermediary between foreign businessmen and Soviet commercial organizations. Businessmen found that they could not negotiate with any Soviet commercial organization except those selected by the Moscow office of Amtorg.[142] In the United States, Amtorg publicized Soviet trade possibilities and invited firms to send representatives to Moscow. In addition, it took a part, which will be mentioned later, in the recruitment of foreign engineers and specialists.

Before American recognition of the USSR in 1933, an organization called the Soviet Union Information Bureau existed in the United States. Testifying before the Congressional hearing on subversive activities conducted by the Fish Committee, its director, Boris Skvirsky, remarked: "I attempted through the bureau to make available a modicum of reliable information about the Soviet Union for American business organizations, government departments, and general inquirers." [143] To perform this task, the organization turned out the monthly periodical *Soviet Union Review*, which provided information on the economy, culture, and general nature of the Soviet Union. The magazine was sent to government departments, business firms, and banks.[144] The Bureau also assisted a number of government officials and businessmen who wished to visit the Soviet Union.

THE ORGANIZATIONAL APPARATUS
AND FOREIGN SPECIALISTS AND WORKERS

Before considering the nature of the organizations concerned both with specialists and ordinary workers, one must stress the difficulty of attempting to differentiate between the two groups. One difficulty is caused by the failure of Soviet sources to define sharply the two categories in order to serve propaganda ends.[145] Thus, while I have divided foreign workers into two groups— specialists and ordinary workers—based on such criteria as nationality, methods of recruitment, salaries, and housing accommodations (a differentiation I believe supported by evidence appearing in Soviet sources), the careless use by the Soviet authorities of the terms "worker" and "specialist" makes it impossible to arrive at a definitive judgment on the meaning of the words in specific contexts. This difficulty should be kept in mind during the following discussion.

It appears that many of the Soviet organizations involved with the recruitment and utilization of engineers and other specialists also attended to the needs of ordinary workers. However, some differentiation of organization between specialists and workers seems to have existed, reflecting, perhaps, a difference of Soviet objectives. The Soviet regime, realizing that the interest of most foreign specialists in Soviet Russia was motivated by the technological challenge, concerned itself primarily with making use of the specialists' technical skills, making few attempts to integrate them into Soviet society. Hence state organizations dealt more with the specialists than did party organizations. On the other hand, although the workers did contribute technical skills to Soviet industrialization, they were equally important in their role in Soviet propaganda work. So the state organizations' interest in foreign workers was supplemented by special attention from party organizations, both during the recruitment stage and during the workers' residence in the Soviet Union.

Plans for the recruitment and utilization of foreign specialists were formulated by the Supreme Economic Council, which then gave permission to individual economic organizations and trusts (i.e., state monopolies) to negotiate independently with foreign specialists through technical bureaus located abroad, trade representatives, Soviet export-import organizations, foreign business contacts, or through representatives sent abroad for the specific purpose of hiring foreign engineers. Instructions published in the *British-Russian Gazette and Trade Outlook* in 1929 suggested that Soviet economic organizations might utilize the recommendations of foreign concerns, use foreign employment agencies, engineering associations, and the techniques of direct advertising in the foreign press. The article noted, however, that final contracts had to be signed in the Soviet Union.[146]

In addition, according to a 1934 resolution of the Council of Labor and Defense on the "Procedure in Concluding Contracts with Foreign Specialists," the contracts of "foreign specialists, invited to work in the U.S.S.R., must be ratified by the competent people's commissars and chiefs of the central administrations, after the People's Commissar for Finances of the U.S.S.R. has agreed to the amount and conditions of remuneration stipulated by these contracts." [147] Earlier, contracts had had to be registered with the People's Commissariat for Labor as well.[148] Party supervision of the process was carried on by the Assignment Division of the Central Committee Secretariat and the Cadre Department of the Supreme Economic Council, which the Central Committee charged with inspecting the personnel employed by the economic combines to handle foreign contacts and with submitting to the Orgburo of the Central Committee a report concerning future recruitment and utilization plans.[149]

While the documents cited above concerning the recruitment of foreign engineers do not refer to ordinary workers, the resolution on party supervision adds the words "and workers" next to the word "specialists," and associates the words "specialists and workers," with the phrase, "the line of policy of the Supreme Economic Council," implying that the Supreme Economic Council co-ordinated the recruitment of both groups to some extent.[150] Possibly there was a division of labor between the Assignment Division of the Central Committee Secretariat and the Cadre Department of the Supreme Economic Council in regard to workers and specialists, although there is no evidence of this in the resolution.

Most of the men coming to the Soviet Union as specialists or workers on personal contracts had been contacted through Amtorg, Arcos, its British equivalent, or other trade delegations, or had applied at these agencies after seeing their advertisements about work in Russia. Representatives of different Soviet trusts also searched abroad for specialists who would be interested in Soviet employment opportunities. John Littlepage, an American mining engineer working in the Soviet coal mines, received such an invitation from Alexander P. Serebrovsky, head of the Gold Trust, whom he had met when Serebrovsky visited Alaska.[151] A Soviet agricultural delegation visited Midwest universities during the late winter of 1929 and the spring of 1930.[152] Workers were recruited through similar devices. Although Amtorg was located in New York, it often sent representatives to the major industrial areas to recruit men on the spot. In several other cases, although the Soviet trade delegation made final arrangements, Soviet organizations directly maintained representatives at key locations. The Soviet Automobile and Tractor Trust maintained an office within the Ford Plant in Detroit which recruited men for work in Russia.[153]

However, in addition to recruiting methods cited above, Soviet agencies used several less official contacts, including individuals born on the territory of the former Russian Empire. Nathan Glazer comments that "the most striking characteristic of Communist Party membership throughout the twenties was that it was overwhelmingly composed of relatively recent immigrants."[154] The Finnish, Jewish, South Slavic, and Russian sections of the party had the largest memberships in 1925.[155] Although the foreign language federations disappeared after 1925 with "Bolshevization," i.e., the enforced adoption by all foreign Communist parties of the official views of the Russian leadership as ordered by Stalin in 1924, former immigrants continued to play an important part within the party, as is apparent from the following incidents.

One worker reported that during one of his calls on his old company seeking re-employment he was approached by an employee who told him that work might be obtained in Soviet Russia. This man escorted him with several others to a toolmaker, a naturalized American citizen of Russian descent employed at the White Motor Company, who he said had full authority to hire laborers and arrange their transportation to Russia. Although the toolmaker described working conditions and salary, the contract was completed in the New York office of Amtorg with a representative of Instrumenttrest of Leningrad.[156]

A Karelian Technical Bureau had an office in New York which tried to recruit among the Finnish population in the United States. Large-scale propaganda was carried on among former Finnish nationals in favor of emigration to Karelia, but often no definite mention of place of work or wages was made, nor were those interested required to sign a contract.[157] Several Finns named a Finnish Communist, Matti Tehunin, as carrying on the propaganda through a paper called *Työmies* (*The Workman*) which he published in Superior, Wisconsin.[158]

Amtorg appears to have been covertly connected with a tractor and auto school in Brooklyn, New York, designed to recruit and train American workers for employment and payment in rubles in Soviet Russia.[159] One man decided to apply after seeing an advertisement of the school in the Sunday edition of the *New York American*, stating that some 15,000 miners and many thousands of automobile and tractor mechanics were wanted in Russia, where they would be paid good wages and furnished with comfortable living quarters. After calling at the school, he was advised to enroll for a general mechanics course and told that he would be given the job of garage superintendent in Russia. After he had paid $100 for an eight-week course (which was not actually given), the school sent him to a farm maintained for practical training, a short distance from New York, where he was taught to operate and service tractors. There he had to pay $800 in extra fees to cover living costs and special instruction.[160] He ultimately reached the Soviet Union and was given the position of garage manager on a grain farm near Kherson at the salary of 250 rubles a month.

A major organization involved in recruiting foreign labor was the Society for Technical Aid to Soviet Russia, located in New York. It arranged the passage of thousands of American residents, mainly aliens and naturalized citizens, to the Soviet Union. Although the Society kept its real identity well masked, Benjamin Gitlow alleged that "this was a Russian organization which was run by the members of the Russian Federation of the American Communist Party." [161] Its director, Arnold Finkelberg, a one-time associate of Gitlow, stated in an interview with a State Department agent that the object of his office was "to purchase machinery and raw materials for Russian industry and to facilitate the emigration to Russia of suitable expert labor—which in most cases was constituted by persons actually of Russian origin, who had become American citizens, learned their trades here, and were now returning to permanently settle in the Homeland." [162] A circular letter of the People's Commissariat for Internal Affairs for the RSFSR dated July 28, 1925, recognized the role of the organization.[163]

The Society interested the State Department because most persons traveling under its auspices did not have American passports; they had Soviet travel documents in the guise of letters of introduction. After the Russian border was crossed, these letters carried the weight of Soviet passports.[164] In the opinion of the State Department agent who investigated the organization, "the system was a very neat camouflage of actual consular status." [165] This opinion was confirmed by a statement by Gitlow that the Society issued visas for the Soviet government before the United States recognized Soviet Russia.[166]

Representatives of major foreign companies were invited by the Soviet Union to investigate the possibilities of assisting with Soviet construction. Reports following the excursions were not always favorable; Ford officials wrote a negative report after their 1926 journey.[167] In 1928, however, the Soviet regime sent two delegations to see Ford in Detroit. The first was unsuccessful, but the second, headed by Valery Mezhlauk, then vice-chairman of the Supreme Economic Council, reached an agreement.[168]

In recruiting foreign specialists and workers, Soviet policy favored invitations to two or more firms, sometimes in regard to the same project. While Ford was responsible for setting up the tractor factory at Gorki, the actual construction of the factory building was done by the Austin Company of Cleveland.[169] Both German and American firms operated at Dnieprostroi. The chief Russian engineer on the project said that by consulting with two firms and combining methods, the possibility was increased that the work would be terminated on the date set by the government, while with the use of only the methods proposed by Hugh Cooper, the American director, the date of termination would have been prolonged almost a year.[170] American engineers appear to have been favored during the first few years of the plan, because as V. Mezhlauk declared, construction of this nature, i.e., of assembly-line factories, had been developed only in the United States. "This does not mean," said Mezhlauk, "that we shall close the door for technical assistance from other countries, but a leading role must belong to American engineers and technicians."[171] However, in a report given before the meeting of the German section of the All-Union Chamber of Commerce for the West, Soviet officials toned down this expression of policy. The head of the Foreign Section of the Supreme Economic Council said that they had neither an American nor German orientation but a Soviet one, being prepared to learn from each country the area in which that country was superior.[172] By the beginning of 1932, individuals leaving the Soviet Union reported a decline in the number of American engineers there, partly because German engineers were satisfied with lower salaries in general, and in particular with salaries paid almost entirely in rubles.[173]

Although the Soviet government attempted to carry on recruiting in an organized fashion so that jobs and housing would await those employed, Intourist, and to some extent Amtorg, made recommendations that contradicted the policy of the central authorities. Intourist sold one-way tourist tickets good for from five days to one month to workers, assuring them that they would be able to find positions once they reached Russia. On arriving in the USSR, however, these workers found it difficult to locate jobs, and on the expiration of their tourist visas, they found themselves without jobs or money to return home.[174] After having some groups checked for political reliability by the Profintern, the Commissariat for Labor and the trade unions managed to find positions which the emigrants were forced to take regardless of working conditions and salary.[175] To remedy this situation, authorities issued in early 1931 a series of orders which restricted immigration but left enough loopholes to enable someone possessing a badly needed skill to come to Moscow on a tourist's visa and still obtain work.[176]

Since one of the objectives of the Soviet regime was to integrate foreign workers into Soviet life as well as to utilize their skills, party and trade union organizations played more important roles among workers than among specialists and engineers. *Partiinoe Stroitel'stvo*, which covered all types of party activity, printed numerous resolutions passed by the Central Committee of the party which criticized the effectiveness of party and trade union work among foreign workers while giving new directives to lower party and union apparatus and to responsible instructors of the Central Committee charged with duties in these areas.[177] The party charged the foreign bureaus which existed at the different levels of the trade union hierarchy with the duty of involving foreign workers in cultural and social activities through the operation of workers' clubs and special sections of local houses of cultures.[178] In November, 1932, the Soviet regime implemented one of these recommendations by organizing a foreign bureau attached to the All-Union Central Council of Trade Unions to establish more intimate contact between foreign workers and Soviet life. VOKS also carried on cultural activities among foreign workers and trained instructors for work in the provinces where the greatest number of foreign workers resided.[179]

Unlike the engineers or workers, who had many organizations supervising their activities, journalists came under the control only of the Soviet Press Office attached to the Commissariat for Foreign Affairs, but the Politburo of the party had ultimate decision-making powers.[180] The Press Office exercised the duties of censorship. Until 1930 Theodore Rothstein, member of the executive staff of the Commissariat for Foreign Affairs, occupied the position of Soviet censor. He was replaced by Jean Arens, an important member of the GPU.[181]

The last of the Soviet organizations which needs mention is the GPU, which affected the lives of all foreign visitors and residents. It is interesting to discover that to foreigners the GPU presented both a favorable and a negative image. Its favorable image was related to its role as an administrative public service agency directing foreigners to places where they could spend the night, operating information centers in railroad stations, and getting foreigners space on overcrowded trains.[182] It also aided foreign engineers when they were hindered or abused by trust officials.[183]

But the darker side of the GPU was also visible. Its role was evident in the sabotage trials which involved foreign engineers during the late 'twenties and early 'thirties. Although varying in degree, some surveillance of foreigners by the State security organs was always present. GPU members were believed to staff Intourist hotels and to function as interpreters for foreign visitors. They checked foreign residences in the absence of the tenants and watched activities involving both foreigners and Russian nationals.[184]

NON-SOVIET ORGANIZATIONS

During the period of this study a number of foreign organizations independent of Communist control played a role in the pilgrimage to Russia; some were able to operate within the Soviet Union. Among these agencies were independent travel bureaus such as the Amalgamated Bank Travel Service and Pocono Study Tours, which co-operated with Intourist and made arrangements for tourists who wanted to visit the country.

One of the more important organizations was the Open Road, which described itself as a "membership organization maintained in the interest of international friendship and education." A brochure it put out stated that "it is the function of The Open Road to serve those who wish to widen their horizons by observation of peoples, manners, and traditions in other countries." [185]

The involvement of the Open Road in the Soviet tourist trade began when Dr. Stephen P. Duggan, Director of the Institute of International Education, went to the Soviet Union in 1926 on an educational mission.[186] He returned to the United States with the strong feeling that students and professional people should be able to visit the USSR. Since there was no machinery for such visits at that time, he urged John Rothschild, director of the Open Road, to go to the Soviet Union, set something up, and then interest other Americans in going. Rothschild did not believe the plan to be feasible without State Department approval, so Duggan, through Allen Dulles (who was then a practicing lawyer, but had close State Department connections), arranged a meeting for Rothschild with the head of the Slavic Desk, Robert Kelly. After getting Kelly's approval, Rothschild went to Moscow, where he talked with Mme. Kameneva, head of VOKS, about this project and a reciprocal project which would permit Soviet students to come to the United States. Talks were also held with Sovtorgflot, the state shipping company and predecessor of Intourist, and with the central trade union organization, both of which wanted to participate with VOKS.

Late in 1927, a proposal came from Sovtorgflot. Since it was near the end of the travel season, only a very small group of students went to the Soviet Union that year, but the Open Road had decided to enter the Russian tourist trade. As the work grew, the organization hired a Mrs. Rosa Laddon Hanna, a bilingual American citizen of Russian background. The New York office depended on her for information on conditions and for overseeing the arrangements in the Soviet Union. Although the Open Road had to use Intourist interpreters, she knew who the best guides were and was able to get the best treatment possible for patrons of the Open Road.

While the Open Road worked with Intourist and was obliged to buy services from it, American experts on the Soviet Union, such as Maurice Hindus, Louis Fischer, Julian Bryan, Maxwell Stewart, Henry Shapiro, and Philip E. Mosely, led the various excursions. Featuring special interest tours, the Open Road, in the words of another representative of the organization, Herman Habicht, had room to operate alongside VOKS and Intourist because "we personalize our services." [187] In most cases, however, the standard Intourist itinerary was followed with "extras" provided by the leader.[188]

Intourist gave the Open Road considerable latitude in designating itineraries, but Intourist wanted to do a mass production job, one which was administratively easy to supervise, while the Open Road was interested in special attractions.[189] Itineraries in many cases were made by the tour leader in consultation with Intourist. "But sometimes," said an Open Road employee, "we had to fight to get what we wanted." [190] By 1936 it became more difficult to maintain an Open Road representative in Moscow. Intourist appeared to resent the presence of the organization, arguing that it was duplicating services. Although the Open Road was made aware of such feelings before 1936, not until 1936–37 did Soviet authorities begin to create difficulties over visa renewal for the Open Road representative within the country. [191]

Another American organization which was able to maintain a representative within the Soviet Union was the American-Russian Chamber of Commerce. This organization was founded by a number of American businessmen and engineers who wished assistance in dealing with the governments of both the Soviet Union and the United States on American-Soviet business matters. Reeve Schley, president of Chase-Manhattan Bank, served as president of the Chamber for most of the 1924–1937 period; Hugh Cooper, consulting engineer for Dnieprostroi, took over for several years during the middle years of the period under study.

Activities of the Chamber included sponsoring business delegations to the USSR and maintenance of a permanent office in Moscow; this was headed until 1930 by Charles H. Smith, vice-president of the Chamber, followed by Spencer Williams, a former newspaper man. [192] The Moscow office kept a file of interpreters, Russian and English clerks and stenographers, lawyers, engineers, and other specialists desiring to represent American firms in the Soviet Union; it furnished information on visas and other travel essentials. The Chamber's representative attempted to get information about Soviet trade opportunities for members of the organization.

A Russian-British Chamber of Commerce operated in Great Britain with the aim of developing trade relations with the Soviet Union. Although composed of and governed by representatives of each country, its membership was mostly British, because of the nature of the Soviet trade monopoly. [193] According to Spencer Williams, it was far less independent than its American counterpart, for it needed subsidies from Arcos to survive. Its Executive Council was composed half of Arcos men and half of British

industrialists, but since some of the British representatives did
not show up at all meetings, Arcos played a leading role. Arcos'
equivalent in the United States, Amtorg, possessed no similar
veto, since Russian subsidies were not needed to finance the
American-Russian Chamber of Commerce.[194]

During the summers of 1933 and 1934, Moscow University
played host to a special summer-school program for American
students, who enrolled in courses taught by Soviet faculty. An
American sponsor, the Anglo-American Institute, was organized in
late 1932 with encouragement from Intourist and the Open Road;
the interest of the latter was apparently attributable largely to
its desire to promote the tourist traffic to Russia.[195] In late 1932,
a representative of Intourist suggested to the Institute of International Education that it join the other sponsor. The IIE
promised to give favorable consideration to the request, but the
program began without IIE participation.[196] In early 1934, IIE
agreed to become an academic sponsor of the project; its decision
was based on the belief that the student and citizen in a democracy had a duty to acquire knowledge and understanding
about political forces abroad, whether hostile or friendly. The two
main purposes of the project as described at the time were "to
provide facilities and services for serious study and research on
the Soviet Union" and "to make possible the publication of material on Soviet education, society and cultural movements for the
information of students from all English-speaking nations." [197]

During the summer of 1934, the second session of the Anglo-
American Summer School was held at Moscow University, the
Soviet sponsors being the All-Russian Commissariat for Education, VOKS, and Intourist. Despite certain misgivings and
disappointments at the end of the summer, IIE decided to continue sponsorship of the program for the summer of 1935,
when two hundred students left for Moscow, only to find upon
arrival that the session had been summarily cancelled. The Soviet
government explained that it needed to use the faculty for other
purposes and that other English-speaking professors were unavailable. The IIE remarked that although it believed the Soviet

government did the best it could in arranging other activities for these students, the Institute "doesn't feel justified in sponsoring an activity characterized by inefficient administration." [198]

In conclusion, what can we say about Soviet organizational devices? We find a proliferation of organizations, characterized by specialization in regard to function and clientele. We find a constant use of the front organization, operating to deliver the party's message. Like a dynamo which supplies central power via transmission belts and gears to all the machinery of a factory, the front organizations received their driving force from Soviet Russia. Thus, through the maintenance of tight discipline at all levels, Soviet and Communist mechanisms were geared to serve as weapons. Equipped with a distinctive code of strategy and tactics, as well as an acute perception (in most cases) of the nature of the terrain in which they were to work, front organizations were able to penetrate, at least during the initial stages, the defenses set up against them.

The organizational framework utilized in the pilgrimage to Russia paralleled those used in other contexts. Despite a constant effort by the regime to depict Soviet and Communist economic and cultural organizations as resembling their non-Communist counterparts, Lenin's faith in centralization and party control remained dominant.

Communist control over the attraction of foreigners varied according to the groups involved. During the initial stages of attracting and recruiting labor delegations, the Communist apparatus played a major role. Except for a few scattered visits by small groups of laborers independent of the November and May festivities, the impetus behind and the direction of the movement to Russia had a Soviet source. Unlike more affluent groups, workers could not afford to travel to the USSR unless special arrangements had been made.

While less manipulation was involved in attracting intellectuals than workers, the Soviet regime did issue personal invitations to important writers and educators, who were given special attention after they crossed the border. In addition, such front organizations as the societies for cultural relations arranged trips for professional people and other members of the middle class. On the whole, more opportunity existed for independent investigation by intellectuals, even though they traveled under Intourist, than existed for workers. And probably more individuals from the middle class and professional category than from the working class decided to go to the Soviet Union on their own initiative.

The desire to work for the Soviet government was not so much created in the minds of foreign specialists and workers by Soviet advertising and recruitment techniques as stimulated by them. There existed among many groups a tremendous interest in the Soviet Union, which was intensified by Soviet public relations techniques.

While the Soviet Communist party, was, in all cases, the hub of the organizational network, organizations designed to carry out such short-term objectives as recognition and economic aid were more often state than party organizations. A business delegation was convinced that the propaganda activities of the Comintern were only "a sort of smoke screen behind which the men who are really running the country are quietly building up a vast productive organization whether directly State-controlled or by means of the innumerable cooperatives." [199] In regard to longer-range aims, such as the battle for a united trade union movement, party organizations became more prominent. Party organizations also played an important part in the integration of foreign workers into Soviet life. Once foreigners made the decision, or had the decision made for them, to remain permanently in the Soviet Union, the same organizational forces which affected Soviet citizens applied.

An interesting feature of this period was Soviet permission for certain organizations such as the Open Road and the American-Russian Chamber of Commerce to operate within the Soviet Union. These were exceptions, because at the same time the Soviet regime combated all attempts by foreigners to establish clubs independent of Soviet control. By 1937 the functioning of even these agencies became impossible.

Finally, we find that much of the apparatus became more efficient, from the Soviet standpoint, during the years 1924–37. VOKS and Intourist were definitely more efficient during the 'thirties than during the 'twenties. Foreign sections and bureaus proliferated in attempts to control foreign workers. But what became more efficient from the Soviet point of view became more obnoxious for the foreigners who came into contact with these organizations. Their increased effectiveness was qualified by attitudes of hostility toward them.

Despite the trend toward efficiency, one notes a certain continuity among organizations. Even when some part of the apparatus did not function as designed, the Soviet regime found itself unable to correct the defects because of its inability to decentralize. The concept of front organizations, as noted early in this chapter, required that fronts be "undogmatic, elastic . . ., and sensitive to the shifting requirements of local and temporary conditions," although firmly guided by the party leadership.[200] In practice, especially in that part of the apparatus concerned with labor delegations, centralized control by the party voided any possibility that such groups as the Friends of the Soviet Union could be elastic and sensitive to the local scene and temporary conditions. FSU identified itself so closely with the Communist party that only the completely naive and those who had little previous contact with Communist tactics were attracted by its activities. Among workers FSU did achieve some success by appearing more purposeful than their own organizations and readier to act immediately against inadequate labor conditions.

Front organizations more successful in broadening the number of Soviet sympathizers were the societies for cultural relations. These were allowed more flexibility than FSU, and it was more difficult to see behind their façade. Thus they were able to attract many non-Communist intellectuals, although these individuals too appeared quite ignorant of the nature of Soviet Communism. Similarly, ad hoc committees organized to send delegations to the Soviet Union and headed by influential non-Communists were also more successful than many of the permanent organizations because it was difficult to see behind their façades.

Communists also used the device of the "fraction" to advantage. Although the "fraction" often intimidated other members of the delegation, it performed the very important role of steering the delegation, as will be seen in Chapter 5.

Another effective device used by the Soviet regime was stressing the alleged voluntary nature of what were in fact state-controlled organizations, such as the Soviet Chamber of Commerce, the Union of Soviet Writers, and VOKS. Judging from the comments of many of the visitors, the Soviet regime was successful in persuading foreigners that these organizations were not unlike those existing in the West. The organizations suffered, however, from inefficiency, a condition not characteristic of those existing in the West.

Finally, Soviet recruitment of foreign engineers and workers was generally successful, but this was in large part because of unemployment in the West; many semiskilled workers hoped to improve their situation in the Soviet Union. Misrepresentations of conditions by Soviet trade delegations and other Soviet agents, as well as lack of co-ordination between these agents and the central authorities, often ruffled relations between the regime and such foreigners.

Despite its defects, the Soviet organizational apparatus did serve the purpose of manipulating the pilgrimage to Russia and of decreasing the amount of spontaneity permitted foreigners within the Soviet Union. Lenin's prescription for organization reached its fullest development during the Stalin era.

4

Indulgence and Integration: Soviet Treatment of Foreigners

I have described the Soviet and non-Soviet Communist organizations involved outside the USSR in the pilgrimage to Russia and how they operated to attract and recruit foreign visitors; here the subject is the functioning of the apparatus within the Soviet Union. Unlike free societies, closed societies must restrict genuine investigation by foreign visitors in order to limit contacts between societies. But when a closed society finds it advantageous to allow foreigners within its borders, official hospitality employs the centralized resources of the state, and pampers its foreign guests with banquets, receptions, gifts, publicity, and other kinds of special treatment which tend to dull the critical senses of the visitors and to divert their attention from the lack of opportunity to penetrate beneath the surface.

Apparently even those who temporarily settle within the society for some specific purpose are given special privileges as incentives for remaining and to prevent their painting too dismal a picture after their departure. If this is true, then for those who attempt permanent residence, little or no expenditure of official resources would occur. In fact, concessions under these circumstances would be distinctly disadvantageous to the regime, making native citizens aware of differences in treatment between themselves and residents from abroad.

In order to prove these statements, we must examine the techniques used toward both these categories of the foreign visitors to the Soviet Union to determine whether different objectives dictated different treatment. To what extent did the Soviet desire to use foreign visitors as potential opinion leaders result in privileged treatment? And to what extent did deliberate plans by the Soviet authorities permanently to integrate certain categories of foreign workers into Soviet life result in treatment which scarcely differed from that accorded natives?

Many who visited the Soviet Union came to believe that in this new society their contributions were regarded as important. Those people who esteemed honor and recognition more than wealth as life's objective were especially vulnerable to Soviet attempts to praise their accomplishments. André Gide, discussing his voyage to the Soviet Union, where he had been a guest of the Union of Soviet Writers, commented on the favors and indulgences awarded to writers, remarking that he could hardly make a dent in his ruble balance since everything was given him:

> The immense privileges that I was offered amazed and terrified me and I was afraid of being seduced and corrupted. . . . And every time I took out my note-case to settle a hotel or restaurant bill, to pay an account, to buy stamps or a newspaper, the delightful smile and authoritative gesture of our guide stopped me. "You're joking! [he said]. You are our guest, and your five companions too." [1]

Fear of being corrupted motivated some men, like Norman Thomas, to refuse official invitations. In the early 'twenties, Thomas was invited to visit the Soviet Union at the government's expense. He refused, feeling it was against his principles to have such a trip paid for by the host country.[2] A similar invitation to Dr. Judah Magnes, first president of the Hebrew University in Jerusalem, was also refused at about the same time.

Others were less sensitive. Soviet officials invited prominent persons to attend anniversary festivities in the hope that their acceptance would help publicize the events. Theodore Dreiser was one of the many intellectuals invited to attend the celebration of the Tenth Anniversary of the Revolution. The invitation was offered through the secretary of the front organization, International Workers' Relief, which had been designated by Soviet authorities to serve as intermediary.[3] Fred Biedenkapp, the secretary of the organization, visited Dreiser in his studio one day and invited him "to witness for yourself what has been accomplished for Russia by the Soviet Union in the ten years of its existence."[4] Biedenkapp remarked that Dreiser was being invited because of his status in America as a potential opinion leader in intellectual circles. When Dreiser expressed reluctance to visit Russia during the period of the November festivities, Biedenkapp stressed the importance of the timing for the Soviet Union because, he said, it "would like to be able to announce that you are coming to that."[5] Soviet authorities wanted so strongly to be able to advertise Dreiser's visit that several days after he had insisted on a direct official invitation, notes were received from Maxim Litvinov, then Assistant Commissar for Foreign Affairs, and Mme. Kameneva, head of VOKS.[6] In addition to providing Dreiser the benefits that other guests were given while they traveled within the country, the Soviet authorities agreed to pay for his passage to the Soviet Union.

Among the writers invited to visit Soviet Russia was Panait Istrati, a Rumanian author sympathetic to the regime. Directors of Soviet propaganda felt that in Istrati the regime had found "a man who would contradict 'the lies of the capitalist press.'"[7] Unfortunately for the Soviet government, the previously favorable tone of Istrati's writing and speeches changed after his visit to the USSR.

While official invitations to intellectuals were issued with the hope that they would paint a rosy picture of the country after their departure, businessmen were formally invited to visit the country as guests of the government to assess the potentialities for foreign participation in economic construction. Besides the invitations to the Ford Company referred to earlier, representatives of companies like the engineering firm of Stuart, James and

Cook were encouraged by such individual Soviet economic units as the Donugol Coal Trust to inspect their facilities and to offer suggestions for modernization.[8]

Finally, official invitations were issued by the Soviet trade unions to labor groups throughout the world, inviting them to witness the May and November festivities as the guests of the Soviet government. Other invitations to enjoy Soviet hospitality throughout the year went to foreign sailors docking at Soviet ports.[9]

In addition to having all their expenses paid within the Soviet Union, important visitors were the recipients of various gifts. When the 1929 Ford delegation left Moscow for Leningrad, all with whom they had been associated came to say goodby with presents of luxury food items—caviar, cigarettes, and wine. This farewell reception was repeated when they left Leningrad.[10] The British Miners' delegation which arrived in 1926 to collect funds for the striking British coal miners was also the recipient of gifts on departing: a samovar for the delegation as a whole, and an album filled with pictures of the trip for each delegate.[11] A Communist member of another workers' delegation reported that all items lost by its members were fully replaced.[12]

But more important than the expense-free visit or the gifts was the acclaim that greeted foreign guests. Liam O'Flaherty described a reception in his honor given by the Bureau of Revolutionary Literature as "worthy of a worthier person than myself." [13] Banquets, receptions, and lavish entertainment accompanied the visits of all kinds of delegations. Ford representatives were entertained by Soviet officials on a yacht which journeyed up the Volga, and then given a huge reception in the Nizhni-Novgorod city hall.[14]

One foreign engineer described the banquets given in honor of visiting foreigners as "a sumptuous affair," with "silver plate, cut glass dishes, flowers, fine linen, many courses of excellent food, and a table covered with wines and liquors." [15] No wonder one of the delegates to the 1933 celebration could write in *Soviet Russia Today* that rumors about severe famine were false.[16] To please the American business delegation of 1929, Soviet authorities adjusted meal hours to American habits. A meal for them at Tiflis included hors d'oeuvres, soup, fish, meat and fowl, as well as dessert, wine, coffee, and fruit.[17]

To demonstrate the significance attached to delegations, top Soviet officials were present to greet the guests and attend to their needs. Stalin, commenting on the visits of labor delegations remarked:

> You have heard how leaders of the Soviet state met a British workers' delegation and a German workers' delegation. Have you noticed that our comrades, directors of various spheres of administration, not only provided the representatives of the workers' delegations with information but actually rendered account to them? . . . I have read that the directors of our oil industry— Kosior in Grozny and Serebrovsky in Baku—not merely gave the workers' delegates information as is done to tourists, but rendered account to these workers' delegations as if to a higher supervising authority.[18]

Labor delegations attended receptions presided over by some of the great figures of Soviet and foreign communism, such as A. I. Rykov, S. A. Lozovskii, M. P. Tomskii, Krupskaia (Lenin's widow), Clara Zetkin, M. N. Roy, and Mme. Sun Yat Sen. On one occasion Krupskaia and Lozovskii urged the delegates to further the revolutionary cause in their own country and to join the Communist party if they were not already members.[19] It would take a tremendous amount of discipline for an individual who was already disposed to radical sentiments to remain objective in an atmosphere such as this.

The use of prestigious figures was a very effective mechanism of persuasion even for those who were not already inclined to sympathize with the Soviet Union and Communism. To communicate the seriousness of Soviet intentions in regard to business relations with foreign countries, top Soviet leaders consented to conversations with business delegations and individual businessmen. The vice-president in charge of foreign sales of an American locomotive company, after a trip in the private car of the general manager of the Western Division of Russian Railways, was met

at the Moscow station by a delegation from the Foreign Commissariat, Amtorg, and the Russian Railways.[20] To communicate
the Soviet's deep interest in science and medicine, the Commissar
for Health for the Ukraine welcomed the first American medical
tour to the Soviet Union at the railroad station at Kiev.[21] Prominent
individuals who desired to visit the country unofficially often
found it difficult. In 1934, Sir Walter Citrine, head of the British
labor movement, attempted a private visit, but was met at
Leningrad harbor by Moscow and Leningrad trade union
officials.[22]

To charm foreign intellectuals, the Soviet regime enlisted the
aid of its own intelligentsia. Prince Dmitri Svyátopolk-Mirsky,
the Russian aristocrat who was converted to Marxism in London
and allowed to return to Russia through Gorky's intercession,
made an appearance whenever someone who spoke fluent English was needed to address meetings held to edify English-
speaking visitors.[23]

Some visitors found, to their surprise, that everyone who
crossed their path in the Soviet Union was acquainted with their
names and their work. It is possible that this knowledge was
gained primarily from the publicity given visiting celebrities and
delegations in Soviet papers, but a study of various incidents
leads one to believe that briefing campaigns preceded each visit.

Everyone on John Dewey's itinerary knew his name, which
seemed to be a "password" for entrance into schools, homes,
factories, and government bureaus.[24] Writers, whether they had
published many noteworthy books or few of mediocre quality,
found popular recognition. People whom they met all seemed to
know their work by heart, and the literary officials frequently
expressed the wish to publish a story by the writer.[25] The 1929
Ford delegation found itself greeted everywhere by workers who
had previously worked in the Ford plants.[26]

Many of the intellectuals fêted in the Soviet Union, however,
had less of a reputation than Gide and Dewey. Eugene Lyons
termed the Soviet capital "a paradise" for misfits from abroad.[27]
Adulation was given to painters and sculptors whose art had

never been shown outside of independent shows and cafés. The qualifications of some engineers and workers were overvalued by the Soviet government. John Scott told of a draftsman from Amsterdam who passed as a famous Dutch architect and a lineman from Germany who pretended to be an electrical engineer.[28] When several Ford officials visited the Moscow Motor Truck Factory in 1929, they found foreign workers there who had previously worked in Detroit. The Russians recruited them as "experts," although none had been more than bench workers in Detroit.[29]

Tolerance of such a state of affairs by Soviet authorities had unforeseen results. When Soviet industrial managers finally fired individuals because of their incompetence, the foreign friends of the Soviet Union were more ready that the Soviet authorities to recognize the justice of these dismissals; the authorities realized that admission of such failures would open up their hiring policy to criticism.

The regime invited prominent personalities to address Soviet audiences. The British political philosopher Harold Laski lectured at Moscow University; I. V. Sollins, an American director of the Anglo-American Summer School at Moscow University, presented a radio talk on education. Foreign engineers and specialists were asked by the All-Union Chamber of Commerce for the West to address meetings held under its auspices on their special subjects. If a potential audience was lacking, VOKS could speedily produce one. William C. White tells how a "self-styled" leading American drama critic read several papers on "The Need for a Proletarian Note in American Drama" to an audience composed partly of Moscow producers virtually compelled to attend by VOKS.[30]

The Soviet authorities reserved special treatment for writers, lecturers, and producers of film travelogues. Burton Holmes, the noted producer of travel films, was offered a 25 per cent discount on his trip by American representatives of Intourist, who explained: "we are happy to have writers and lecturers visit the Soviet Union and report about conditions." [31]

But more important were the offers of publication and the subsequent royalties which came from Soviet authorities. Before Gide left for the Soviet Union, he learned from Moscow newspapers that in a few months Soviet distributors had sold more than 400,000 copies of his books.[32] Immediately after Liam O'Flaherty signed a pro-Soviet statement, the cashier of the Bureau of Revolutionary Literature paid him for a story printed in its magazine five years previously, and told him that on the following day the State Publishing House would pay him a thousand rubles in royalties.[33] Eugene Lyons found on his arrival in the Soviet Union that a great many of his articles on American themes were being published by Soviet magazines; shortly afterwards, his biography of Sacco and Vanzetti was published twice in Russia under different auspices. The Soviet press highly commended the work, and the first edition was quickly exhausted.[34]

Publication of work by foreign visitors included technical volumes. A professor of chemistry at Stanford University discovered that one of his books which had sold less than a thousand copies in three years in the United States was a big success in the Soviet Union. ". . . I was surprised to hear it casually mentioned that it had been translated and was being issued this year in an edition of 10,000 copies, with the request that I should write a new edition for next year." [35]

Finally, Arthur Koestler tells of being invited to the Soviet Union to write a book entitled "The Soviet Land through Bourgeois Eyes." Although at the time of the visit he was affiliated with the German Communist party, his experiences can serve as an example of general Soviet policy.

> When I arrived in a provincial capital, say in Tiflis, I went to the local Writers' Federation, where I produced my Comintern letter. The Secretary of the Federation thereupon arranged the usual banquets and meetings with the political leaders and members of the intelligensia of the town, appointed somebody to look after me, and put me in touch with the editor of the local literary magazine and the director of the State Publishing Trust—in this case the Trust of the Georgian Soviet Republic. The editor of the magazine declared that it had been for many years his dearest

wish to publish a story by me. I handed him a copy of a story published some time ago in Germany; and the same day a check for three or four thousand roubles was sent to my hotel. The director of the State Publishing Trust asked for the privilege of publishing a Georgian translation of the book I was going to write; I signed a printed agreement form and was sent another check for three or four thousand roubles. (The salary of the average wage-earner was at that time 130 roubles per month.) I thus sold the same short story to eight or ten different literary magazines from Leningrad to Tashkent, and sold the Russian, German, Ukrainian, Georgian and Armenian rights of my unwritten book against advance payments which amounted to a small fortune. And as I did all this with official encouragement, and as other writers did the same, I could wholeheartedly confirm that Soviet Russia was the writer's paradise and that nowhere else in the world was the creative artist better paid or held in higher esteem. Human nature being what it is, it never occurred to me that my contracts and cash advances had been granted not on the strength of my literary reputation, but for reasons of a different nature.[36]

Koestler remarks that at the time of the incident he had not yet published a single book and his name was completely unknown in the literary world. But, says Koestler, the average visiting author knows little about publishing in a country where this activity is under state control. "And the little which his intuition makes him guess, his vanity will quickly make him forget."[37] Payment in rubles which could not be removed from the country served other purposes as well, such as stimulating recurrent visits by authors or their friends to expend unused balances.

Thus, we have a picture of lavish entertainment of visiting foreigners, including many who (in their own opinion) had been underrated and ignored at home. Every individual was made to feel important. How could one criticize a host who contributed to one's sense of dignity and expended the valuable time of important top officials in this endeavor?

Beyond the official hospitality and financial rewards offered foreigners, the central authorities made available to foreign professional groups certain facilities and conveniences. A number of special conferences and courses devoted to science have been noted before.[38] Several international scientific congresses, including those concerned with physiology, soil science, and geology met in the Soviet Union. Besides plenary meetings, visits to Soviet scientific institutions and receptions were included in the program. Before the opening of the Second International Soil Congress in Leningrad in July, 1930, plans specified that delegates make a seven-day visit to Murmansk and to the White Russian Agricultural Exhibition at Minsk as well as a number of excursions around Moscow and Leningrad. On adjournment of the Congress, the delegation spent twenty-four days studying soils, inspecting new factories, state and collective farms, and agricultural institutions. For the benefit of the delegates, several works on the soils and agriculture of the USSR were to be translated into English and German, accompanied by a comprehensive guidebook containing descriptions of climate, geology, vegetation, and agricultural experimentation within European Russia.[39]

The Soviet government granted full co-operation to a British astronomical expedition which journeyed to Omsk in 1936 to watch a solar eclipse. Special orders were issued by central authorities expediting customs formalities and ensuring the direct transit of equipment in special vans to Omsk.[40] As late as 1937, visitors who attended the Seventeenth International Geological Congress in Moscow participated in a Urals excursion, made in a special train with seven sleepers, two diners, and coaches for servants and baggage. A member of the excursion related that everything was prepared in advance, from the excellent guidebooks describing the geology and mineral deposits to the packing boxes for specimens.[41]

The Anglo-American Summer School held sessions during the summers of 1933 and 1934.[42] The first year, the school offered courses entitled "Experimental Education Programs in the Soviet Union" and "Institutional Changes in the Soviet Union." [43] During the second summer a wider range of courses in education, art and literature, sociology, psychology, and political economy were offered. Field work and inspection trips supplemented class work.[44] The Institute of International Education, however, described the student body as "miscellaneous, a large, if not preponderant number having been attracted by the new opportunity to travel in the Soviet Union at the special rates for students." [45] The absence of examinations and the fact that lectures were in English also attracted a less serious type of student.

Several more serious students obtained permission to work in the Russian historical archives or study in Soviet schools. George Bolsover (later director of the School of Slavonic Studies of London University) after some preliminary difficulty obtained access to the reports of the Tsarist Foreign Ministry for 1830–31.[46] Philip E. Mosely (Director of the Russian Institute, Columbia University, 1951–1955, and head of the European Institute since 1963) received permission to use the archives of the Imperial Ministry of Foreign Affairs for the years 1838–1842 inclusive. He published *Russian Diplomacy and the Opening of the Eastern Question in 1838 and 1839* (1934), as well as a number of articles.[47] Geroid T. Robinson used the archives for research on what later became the book *Rural Russia under the old Régime.*[48] John Curtiss was also permitted to do the research for *Church and State in Russia, 1900–1917* within the Soviet Union.[49] Soviet authorities allowed John Hazard (later Professor of Public Law at Columbia University) to study law at the Moscow Juridicial Institute.[50] By allowing certain scholars and students to use its archives, the Soviet regime apparently hoped to demonstrate that a Bolshevik regime was not hostile to intellectual scholarship per se, and also to improve their image in the United States at the time of receiving diplomatic recognition from the United States.

Because general living standards were low, the regime had to grant foreigners certain privileges and conveniences not available to the native population in order to persuade them to stay longer than a few months. Among the more important privileges were higher salaries. Amtorg, discussing this question, reminded the economic organs (i.e., the trusts and department ministries) that salaries of 400 rubles were inadequate for prominent engineers because even the beginning engineer received more in America.

"We need not rank and file," said Amtorg, "but highly qualified specialists." [51] The Soviet trade delegation argued that even though recruitment would be costly, several highly competent American specialists would bring the Soviet Union more returns than dozens of less well qualified engineers.

As early as 1926 a meeting of the Foreign Section of the Supreme Economic Council emphasized that high salaries were essential for attracting eminent foreign specialists. It suggested that economic trusts be granted the right to guarantee foreign specialists wages exceeding existing norms and to produce corresponding amounts to acquire living quarters for them. [52] But not all Soviet officials agreed with this policy. Criticizing excessive wages, A. Kilinskii in a 1931 issue of *Voprosy Truda* declared that the proper authorities "must sum up experience from last year and pick out the most typical mass pay rates which to some extent may serve as [a] criterion for a scale of orientation." [53]

The type of currency in which wages were paid was as important as the amount of wages received. The more highly qualified specialists were paid a large percentage of their wages in foreign currency, deposited directly in foreign banks. However, beginning in 1932, new contracts and those that were renewed generally provided for a much smaller part, if any, to be paid in foreign currency; as a result, many top engineers departed. [54] Exceptions to this trend occurred, however, in fields such as gold mining where new people continued to be hired on a valuta (foreign exchange) basis. [55] The salaries of ordinary foreign workers, although higher than those of Soviet citizens, were closer to the latter than to the wages of specialists from their own countries, and were paid in rubles. [56]

Foreign engineers, and in particular American engineers, were provided with relatively comfortable living quarters. At Magnitogorsk, an American sector was created for top specialists, with well-made houses equipped with central heat and running water. [57] Apartments for foreigners with bath, kitchen, and other modern conveniences were constructed in Moscow under the auspices of the Supreme Economic Council, employing the services of a noted foreign architect, Zara Witkin. The living quarters of the ordinary foreign worker, on the other hand, although better than the facilities of the Russian worker, did not reach the standard of housing for foreign specialists. At Magnitogorsk the workers lived apart from the specialists in what was called "Socialist City," in houses inferior in construction and conveniences to the specialists'.[58] The less fortunate lived in barracks with the Russian workers. Many of the privileges which nominally existed for foreign workers were actually unavailable in some of the smaller industrial, mining, and agricultural districts to which they were assigned.

However, the sharpest difference in treatment among foreign residents was said to be less that between specialists and workers than that between those who came to the Soviet Union under contract and those who came seeking political asylum.[59] The latter category included Austrian Schutzbunder (after the initial propaganda goals of the Soviet regime had been served), Italians who fled Mussolini's Italy, as well as political refugees from various Slavic countries. They were forced to work where the Soviet government sent them, and were subject to arrest without explanation. Often their economic condition approximated that of the Soviet worker.

German specialists seem to have been less favored than Americans. Observers noted German specialists working for salaries paid in rubles long before 1932.[60] Those Germans who did have valuta contracts received much less foreign currency than their American counterparts. While American specialists had entire houses to themselves, their German counterparts were often quartered in one room and compelled to eat with Russians.[61] In most cases, Germans lived quite separately from other foreign specialists.[62] Apparently all this was true because so many of the Germans were political refugees, who had no alternative but to work in the Soviet Union. German engineers were more likely than Americans to be Communist sympathizers or even party members, who, because they needed few inducements to stay in Russia, do not appear to have received better treatment than capitalists except in special cases. Also, a higher percentage of German engineers had personal contracts directly with the Soviet government rather than with foreign companies which had been given assignments in the Soviet Union, another explanation for their fewer privileges and less security.[63]

To supplement the distinctive living quarters provided for some foreign specialists, special shops and stores, better stocked and administered than the average, were opened to provide for the needs of foreign visitors and residents.[64] Unlike the retail distribution mechanism which served the native population, these shops paid attention to consumer demand as far as possible. In July, 1930, new customs regulations went into effect that enabled foreign technicians to import at lower rates such items as tobacco and coffee.[65] Antique shops and Torgsin offered tourists numerous art items for foreign currency. In addition, an art object bought at a state or co-operative store did not require a special permit to be shipped out of the country.[66]

One outstanding privilege given to foreign visitors must be stressed: private transportation sharply differing in quality from that of Soviet citizens. Most descriptions of Russia during the late 'twenties and 'thirties paint a picture of overcrowded, outdated, uncomfortable trolleys and trains. But unless foreigners went off the tourist track or resided in the country for an extended period, they enjoyed quite a different type of accommodation. Private sleeping and dining cars were provided for all delegations on trips through the Soviet Union, which were so superior even to Intourist Hotels that the coaches served both living and traveling purposes.

The difference between these facilities and those used by Soviet citizens can be best expressed through the comments and observations of foreign residents. A German musician employed by the Soviet regime, who was recuperating from an illness in the Caucasus, was amazed to see luxury trains standing at the railway station one day instead of the usual hard-class coaches. He later learned that they had been provided for a German labor delegation.[67] The American engineer John Littlepage comments that Soviet travel for the non-tourist was primitive and unpleasant. When the eastbound express with tourists aboard came through, Soviet officials found it advisable to get out of sight the people thronging the railway station waiting for tickets.[68] The American journalist William Chamberlin, commenting on the Trans-Siberian Railroad excursion for resident newspapermen and important guests, was surprised at how smoothly everything went, after past experiences of roughing it.[69] On one regular trip of a Volga steamer, the entire first- and second-class cabin space was occupied by an "unofficial" delegation of foreign businessmen, leaving no decent quarters for other passengers.[70] Soviet trusts put new Rolls Royces and expensive American cars at delegates' disposal. For labor delegations, wrote Anne O'Hare McCormick, "automobiles wait outside the doors of hotels all day long while the rest of us take the cobbles or a tram. . . . They never stand in queues for tickets or enjoy the reek or the racy talk of the hard trains." [71]

George Chicherin, Commissar for Foreign Affairs, once assented to a statement made by Louis Fischer that foreigners, especially Americans, enjoyed extraterritorial privileges in Soviet Russia.[72] Privileges ranged from being allowed to board streetcars at the wrong end to having ignored infractions of police regulations which might have meant fines or arrests for a Soviet citizen.[73] The GPU even opened up gasoline stations on holidays or after closing hours for foreigners traveling by automobile.

Thus, some foreign visitors or temporary residents lived a privileged existence. Realizing that the average member of the bourgeoisie liked his creature comforts, the Soviet regime catered to his whims. The radical labor delegation was given luxury facilities to suggest that only in the Soviet Union could the workers enjoy such benefits. But for those who possessed no satisfactory alternative to settling permanently in the USSR, these accommodations were not available.

The Soviet regime attempted to set apart as sharply as possible the privileged groups of foreigners from the native population, considering the visitors bourgeois capitalists whose ideology could not be changed. But they tried to integrate foreign workers completely into Soviet society. "The foreign workmen employed in the USSR," said P. P. Postyshev, "should be turned into class-conscious and staunch Bolsheviks." [74] There were two targets of the plan to integrate workers into the Soviet population. First, there were the political émigrés who sought asylum from reactionary governments in their native countries; second, there were the naturalized citizens and alien residents of countries other than the Soviet Union who had been born in the territory included in the former Russian Empire. A large majority of the foreign workers classified as American by the Soviets turn out on further examination to have been members of this latter group. The Soviet Union, according to several foreign residents, classified as American any laborer who had worked in the United States and who used American methods and tools.[75] The *New York Times* mentioned that most of the "American" miners and steel workers were Europeans who had emigrated to the United States five to twenty years earlier.[76] Out of thirty-seven people who came to Russia on one particular ship, only eight could not speak Russian, and these were the American-born children of Russian immigrants.[77]

Evidence is available that a very tiny percentage of Americans at plants such as Stalingrad Tractor were native-born. One worker at Stalingrad, born in a Volga-German colony in Russia and educated in the United States, said that the Americans at Stalingrad were not really Americans but former alien residents of the United States of Russian extraction. Few had American passports.[78] Maxwell Stewart commented that "to the native Americans in Russia, they were Russians, but Russians considered them Americans." [79] Soviet hiring agents had, in fact, focused their efforts in the United States on large areas where immigrants had congregated and had deliberately used the facilities of the foreign language press and ethnically oriented organizations.

Many workers, at least on arrival in the USSR, were sympathetic to Communism, although party membership was often the consequence of economic conditions rather than ideological affinities. A large number of German workers at Stalingrad appeared to one observer to be Communists, openly sympathetic to and supporting the Soviet regime. Similar observations were made at Chelyabinsk, and Krasny Uralsk.[80] It is difficult to discover the exact number of Communist sympathizers and party members because the Soviet regime masked party affiliations for propaganda purposes. The authorities wished to give the impression that Socialists, liberals, and other non-party members, as well as Communists, were coming to the Soviet Union to offer their assistance to Soviet workers. Yet, despite the actual political affiliations of these individuals, several foreign residents stated that the Soviet authorities viewed them contemptuously. The attitude appeared to be, "You're just one of us; why do you deserve better treatment?"[81]

Attempts to incorporate some categories of foreign workers into Soviet society began on their trips to the USSR. Americans traveling under the auspices of the Society for Technical Aid carried a letter which had the weight of a Soviet passport.[82] Several of the Americans who later returned from Russia said they had "signed unwittingly a statement to the effect that not only will they not at any time entertain a claim against Soviet Russia or any of its institutions, and a second statement that they 'agree to travel on a Russian travel document.'"[83] It was reported that any passenger who still had an American passport after the boat reached Le Havre had it confiscated by Soviet agents in accordance with what they called "the established policy of the Soviet Union in cases of naturalized Americans who were born in what is now Russia."[84]

The treatment of these individuals on the passage to Russia foreshadowed their treatment once they reached the Soviet Union. While Amtorg furnished engineers and specialists with first- and cabin-class sea and rail transportation, the workers occupied third-class accommodations. In making arrangements for such people with the shipping lines, Amtorg called them "Soviet state employees." That a distinction was made among categories of foreign workers was testified to by the agent of North German Lloyd, who told an employee of the American Legation in Riga that " 'Soviet state employees' are distinguished from engineers and specialists on either individual or technical aid contracts. They are not paid on the same scale or are entitled [sic] to the same privileges and accommodations." [85]

Material conditions for these "Soviet state employees," once they were in the Soviet Union were inferior. Workers who came without contracts, and those who were paid only in rubles lived in poverty. One Finnish-American who managed to leave Russia told the American Legation in Helsingfors that the food and living conditions of the thousand Finnish-Americans in Petrozavodsk were only a little better than those of the natives.[86] A native-born American mechanic employed on a ruble salary found it impossible to find living quarters in Leningrad which approached the standards of an American skilled mechanic. On arrival at a factory which made precision instruments, thirty kilometers from Leningrad, he was given for himself and his family one small room without toilet facilities in a dirty little hotel. An apartment funished him later was also dirty and had a leaky roof.[87] Fred Beal, an American Communist agitator at Kharkov, remarked that, although the several hundred foreign workers at the tractor plant were a privileged upper class, their standard of living was low. The poor food, long working hours, and irregular pay inspired repeated rebellion, especially among the wives of foreign workers.[88]

The Soviet regime attempted to incorporate foreign workers into Soviet society through the numerous organizational activities required of Soviet citizens (whether these efforts progressed far beyond the paper stage is a question which will be examined later). A reader of the *Moscow Daily News* (a Soviet paper for English-speaking foreigners) or of the publications of the All-Union Cooperative Publishing House of Foreign Workers (a branch of the State Publishing House) gets the impression that a majority of the foreign workers were actively and voluntarily participating in numerous activities—trade unions, MOPR, International Labor Defense, socialist competition, shock brigades, study circles on current politics, and Soviet elections. They were also apparently involved in cultural and sports programs, language instruction, and excursions organized by the trade unions, VOKS, and local houses of culture. An English-speaking troupe of actors was created, which dramatized important historical events and performed proletarian plays. A Foreign Language Experimental Theater, staffed by Soviet actors and actresses, opened in Moscow, to provide entertainment for foreign workers.

Foreign engineers were invited to join the foreign section of the Dzerzhinsky Club, which George Burrell described as "a somber place" where he heard "tedious controversy through translators about complaints the foreign specialists presented concerning lack of co-operation and inadequacy of housing." [89] Foreign workers were assigned to clubs operated by the trade unions, which possessed fewer comforts and were more concerned with political indoctrination.

The Soviet authorities took special pains to keep the foreign specialists and workers apart in these activities. When the wives of some of the more radical American engineers and workers wanted to adopt a collective farm on the outskirts of Moscow under the auspices of the Dzerzhinsky Club, Soviet officials protested that the wives of workmen could not serve on a committee under the auspices of the club for specialists.[90] A joint meeting of American and Russian specialists was called to consider what kind of club Americans should form. When an American bricklayer began to talk about the difficulties in organization, he was told "that this club was not for bricklayers but specialists." Anna Louise Strong, in a letter to the *Moscow Industrial Gazette,* commented that the bricklayer then nearly broke up the meeting by speaking indignantly on class distinctions in the Soviet state.[91]

The struggle over control of the English-language paper, the *Moscow News,* while primarily a struggle between party orthodoxy and effective journalism, also reflected differences in approaches to specialists and ordinary workers. The *Moscow*

News originally was designed to serve as liaison between the American specialists and Soviet society, as well as to be of interest to tourists and English-speaking people abroad.[92] The paper was also designed to parallel for English-speaking people the efforts of a German-language paper *Moskauer Rundschau* which serviced Germans working within the Soviet Union.

The *Moscow News* was headed by Anna Louise Strong, an American girl who, after obtaining a doctorate from the University of Chicago at a very early age, became a Communist sympathizer and went to the Soviet Union to work for the coming Utopia. Although highly favorable to the Soviet Union, she conflicted with party leaders because of her unwillingness to toe the line of party orthodoxy. She conceived the idea of running a newspaper for foreign specialists herself when Michael Borodin, director of the Paper Trust, told her that the comrades who were handling complaints of Americans thought they needed a news organ to help them.[93] Miss Strong went to Valery Mezhlauk, vice-chairman of the Supreme Economic Council, told him about the plan, and asked if she, a foreigner and not a party member, would be allowed to do the job. He responded that it would be to the paper's advantage if such a person were to take charge.[94] So the *Moscow News* was born on October 5, 1930, with Miss Strong as managing editor and G. Vasutin, a Russian Communist, as editor-in-chief. The paper, which appeared five days a week, was financed by Ogoniok Publishing Company of Moscow with backing from institutions and firms employing English-speaking specialists and from Soviet schools teaching English.[95]

The birth of the paper also marked the beginning of a struggle by Miss Strong with the Communist editors. She accused them of "toning down vivid, flashing statements in favor of 'the exact line.'"[96] Disturbed by the fact that the circulation of *Workers News*, another English-language periodical, was growing faster than that of her paper, she decided to resign, but the other editors refused to remove her name from the masthead.[97] At a hearing before Stalin, Kaganovich, and Voroshilov, she then asked for the merger of the *Moscow News* and the *Workers News*.

S. I. Gusev, head of the Press Department of the Central Committee, explained that the two papers had different purposes. It was the idea that "for engineers and circulation abroad," said Gusev, "we need more or less a liberal paper. . . . But for the increasing number of American workers coming into our industries, we needed something more serious—more of a party organ." [98] Stalin disagreed with Gusev, remarking that if the workers stayed long enough they would get their theory from the Russian papers. The meeting resulted in the requested merger, the new paper taking the name of the *Moscow Daily News*.[99]

The merger did not end the major conflict over the nature of the newspaper—the struggle between party orthodoxy and effective journalism. Revolutionary theory and propaganda dominated the journal. While Miss Strong wanted the paper to show some journalistic polish, the new Communist editor, Michael Borodin, subordinated this goal to long columns of statistics. Another conflict arose during the famine. Miss Strong was convinced that the journalist must paint the whole picture of collectivization while Borodin, the party official, told her: "I think we give a clear picture to anyone who has intelligence to read. Our readers know of the food shortage from their own food cards and from Stalin's report." [100]

The propaganda nature of the paper was very evident. An assistant to Walter Duranty remarked that although the American residents in Moscow welcomed the birth of the *Moscow News*, they soon became annoyed at its propaganda. When they made their annoyance known, members of the staff admitted that the tone was determined by T. L. Axelrod, one of the Communist editors. Axelrod was not in the least receptive to suggestions from his American subordinates regarding policy.[101] George Burrell termed the paper a Bolshevik publication which was inspired by the Soviet government, printing only the things that the government permitted in print.[102] An oral informant described it as "helpful, because it told you what was going on. However," he added, "most of the description was exaggeration." [103]

The *Moscow News, Moscow Daily News,* and *Moskauer Rundschau* fitted into the role prescribed by Communist theory for party and state news organs. Along with its primary task of political indoctrination, the Soviet press has always performed the more activist role of mobilizing individuals to complete the tasks prescribed by the regime. Along these lines, the foreign-language papers took an active role in efforts to conciliate foreign engineers and workers by calling meetings to listen to their grievances.[104] They also assumed the task of criticizing the conduct of activities among foreign workers, and sponsored conferences at which they welcomed suggestions to remedy errors.[105] On the other hand, they served as "hack men" of the regime, casting abuse on any departing foreigner who criticized the Soviet Union.[106]

As part of the effort to recruit political propagandists among the foreign workers an evening college, with separate English and German sections, began operating at the Vyborg House of Culture under the supervision of the Leningrad Council of Trade Unions; it offered courses in economics, Leninism, Russian language, and politics. "The aim of the University," said the *Moscow News,* "is to prepare foreign worker and specialist propagandists for work among the ever-increasing number of foreigners coming to work in the Soviet Union." [107] An American worker at Magnitogorsk, John Scott, was accepted into "Komvuz," to study Russian language, political economy, Leninism, Communist party history, and dialectical materialism. He intimated that Communist authorities probably admitted him with the hope that like other graduates he would become a professional agitator.[108]

Party organizations played a very important part among foreign workers. Once foreign workers entered the Soviet Union with the intention of permanent residence, the Soviet Communist party sought to exert its control over them, even when groups were composed of foreign radicals and Communists.

Fred Beal, an American Communist, was in charge of propaganda and cultural activities at Kharkov Tractor Plant, where he served as the main contact man between Soviet authorities and foreigners. Beal, who worked under Isador Erenburg, a Los Angeles Communist and native of the Ukraine, was instructed to supervise living conditions for foreigners, as well as to organize political excursions and cultural entertainment.[109] Before leaving Moscow for Kharkov, Clarence Hathaway, an American Communist party representative at Comintern headquarters, had explained Beal's duties as follows: "Do *not* yield to the materialistic desires of the foreigners, but cajole them and try to make them happy with as little as possible in the way of food and other requirements." [110] To quiet the continual protests about poor material conditions, Beal described the even gloomier life under capitalism and got them to endorse resolutions which "proclaimed to the world the wonders of Socialist construction, the solving of unemployment and the fight against the kulaks and the wreckers, agents of imperialist powers trying to sabotage the Workers' Revolution!" [111] Another foreign Communist, A. Rudolf, taught a course in politics to wives of German workers at Elektrozavod which was designed "to raise the political level of the foreigners, to explain to them the politics of the Communist party, and to appease them if they were too discontented because of the daily difficulties." [112]

The presence of foreign Communists was reported at other factories such as the Stalingrad Tractor Factory, where an observer declared they told him that they were ordered to have nothing to do with Communists in the United States when they returned home.[113] The Soviet Communist party probably required this to mask the fact that foreign Communists were carrying on agitation among foreign workers in the United States.

Soviet displeasure with the activities of foreign Communists was expressed in the September, 1932, issue of *Partiinoe Stroitel'stvo*, which criticized local party units for following what it called the path of least resistance:

> In practice it often occurs that instead of selecting comrades able to conduct work among foreign workmen, the Party organizations follow the line of least resistance and entrust all the work to active Communists from among the foreigners themselves (for ex-

ample at the Kuibyshev plant at Irkutsk, at certain mines of the Donets Basin, etc.). Meanwhile, foreign Communists do not, for the most part, know the Russian language, have not immersed themselves in the Soviet cauldron, and are not familiar with our conditions. Is it any wonder that these comrades are not in a condition to introduce Soviet reality to foreign workers. Instead of linking Party-mass work with concrete tasks of socialist construction, only reports on international questions are given. . . . As a result of such an organization of work among foreigners, their isolation takes place, the creation of special organizations for foreigners only.[114]

An engineer at Kharkov confirmed the existence of the problem by remarking that most of the propaganda being carried on among American workers was concerned with furthering international Communism. Foreign workers did not seem, he said, to be encouraged to take any interest in favoring Communism in Russia.[115]

The February, 1931, issue of *Partiinoe Stroitel'stvo*, had suggested that a proposal be submitted to the Communist International for its national sections in Moscow to assume "patronage" (i.e., tutelage) of workmen of their nationalities. The article had proposed that "the Communist International periodically commission comrades to the various localities with a series of reports, talks and lectures," and "supply them with new literary publications of a political nature, etc.," as well as have the foreign Communists among the workers "organized into a faction entrusted with the leadership of various voluntary organizations among foreign workers." [116] The discrepancy between measures proposed by the two articles might be explained by the fact that a proposal earlier thought to promise dividends had proven ineffective on application because of different emphases between Soviet and international Communism.

Soviet distrust of foreign Communists continued to exist. When Fred Beal attempted to call a meeting of the most pro-Soviet among the foreign workers at Kharkov to help increase the efficiency of the entire group, Soviet officials were angered by its being done without their knowledge and without the presence of a Soviet Communist party member.[117] Other radical groups that did not follow the discipline of the Soviet Communist party were also criticized. An article in *Partiinoe Stroitel'stvo* singled out a group of men at Stalingrad affiliated with the Society for Technical Aid to the Soviet Union, and although describing them as "a left group" criticized them for the vagueness and sectarian nature of their policy. The party organization at Stalingrad "failed from the very beginning to place the Society upon the proper basis; while several American Communists are among its members, no faction has been organized and their transfer to the All-Union Communist Party (b) [Bolshevik] is being delayed through obstructions in the legalization of their membership at Moscow." [118] The article suggested that the group be taken under the direct supervision of the plant committee of the All-Union Communist party.

Stalin's efforts to erase all signs of internal deviation extended to intense surveillance of all foreign Communists and radicals. Although by 1931, the date of the article discussing the Society for Technical Aid, the actual fight against Trotsky and the "left opposition" (Zinoviev and Kamenev) had long been over, Stalin continued to be suspicious of any deviation in that direction.

To remedy the errors committed by foreign Communists, Soviet party organizations were instructed to conduct more efficient work among foreigners. In a resolution dated November 21, 1930, the Central Committee ordered republic, *krai* (territorial), and *oblast* (regional) organizations to ensure without delay the execution of decisions taken the preceding August. The Central Committee proposed that these bodies

> take measures to get rid of the isolated situation of foreign workers —aiding them to master the Russian language, attracting them into udarnik [superior worker] brigades, social competition, the working out of industrial-financial counterplans, attracting them into active participation in the trade-union work, drawing the best of them into the zavkom [trade union committee] structure and so forth. Special attention must be given to the acclimation of these workers to the Soviet press, establishing for them [oral] readings of the papers in translation.[119]

The resolution also forbade the creation of separate clubs for foreign workers, and ordered party and Komsomol members to establish comradely relations with foreign workers, helping them, and leading individual and group work among them while fighting scornful and unfriendly attitudes toward them on the part of isolated native workers. Women party-members were to be assigned to wives of foreign workers to draw them into the work of the children's crèche, co-operatives, dining-room committees, and delegate meetings. The party organization was ordered "to carry on among foreign workers broad educational work attracting them to open Party meetings and attracting the best of them into the Party." [120]

An article in the February, 1931, *Partiinoe Stroitel'stvo* proposed, after criticizing previous work, that political education among arrivals be improved and that adequate agitation and propaganda forces of the party be mobilized for the work.[121] This article was followed shortly by a new resolution of the Central Committee, dated March 23, 1931, again criticizing the quality of mass political and cultural work among foreigners. The Central Publishing House of Nationalities of the USSR (Centrizdat) and the All-Union Central Council of Labor Unions, together with the Department of Cultural Propaganda and the Department of Agitation and Mass Campaigns of the Central Committee, were asked to draw up, within ten days, a plan of literature to be published for foreign workers and specialists, and to ensure its early publication.[122]

Still another resolution of the Central Committee, dated August 16, 1931, decreed that a member of the bureau of a party committee or of a party cell at enterprises employing foreign workers and specialists be assigned to work among them. Committees at the *krai* and *oblast* levels of the party as well as the Central Committees at the national republic level were ordered to allot responsible instructors for party work in the areas where foreign workers and specialists were employed. The resolution also recommended that responsible instructors of the Central Committee be attached to those krais, oblasts, and national republics, and be charged with the task of systematic observance and control in the execution of enactments of the Central Committee. Finally, the Central Committee ordered the All-Union Central Council of Trade Unions to create a foreign bureau attached to its secretariat which would specialize in work among foreigners and would assure the assignment of special workers in the Central Committee of the union structure, and in trade unions and machine-tractor stations in areas where foreign workmen and specialists were located.[123]

The last article on this subject, in September, 1932, noted that there had been little improvement in integrating foreign workers. Plant organizations were criticized for undervaluing the political significance of party and mass work among foreigners, especially when a particular plant had few foreign workers. The article suggested that in those cases work should be carried out on an individual basis. It cited what it called an "absolutely erroneous opinion that foreign workmen cannot understand our difficulties because they are 'petty-bourgeois,'" and cited this as "a defeatist attitude." It called on all local organizations to help the Russian workers rid themselves of this tradition and to develop mass political work. And again readers were reminded that the aim of political work among foreigners was not to create special organizations to carry on such work, but to create activists among the foreign workmen who might assist local party organization.[124]

These articles and resolutions criticized severely the attitude held by many party officials that work among foreigners was unimportant. The Central Committee urged local party organizations to expend a greater percentage of their resources on integrating foreign workers into Soviet society. To further the integration process, Soviet citizenship policy was geared to deprive foreigners of the protection of their country of permanent residence. The RSFSR and other union republics granted the political rights of Soviet citizens to foreigners of the laboring and peasant classes who had settled within the territory of the republics to earn their living.[125] Soviet authorities launched campaigns to involve foreigners in Soviet elections and to serve

as candidates to local soviets. *Izvestia, Trud,* and the *Moscow
News* published appeals to foreigners to participate. Slogans
stressed the proletarian duty of foreign laborers to take an active
part in building up socialism, in discussing the activities of soviets
and executive committees, and in preparing new election instructions to be given the soviets by their constituents.[126]

One of the major problems facing the Consular Division of the
American Embassy when it opened in 1934 was the status of
many Americans who alleged that they had been forced to
renounce their American citizenship.[127] The large majority of
these cases were naturalized citizens who, though born in the
Russian Empire, had left before the Revolution. Until 1933 the
Soviet Union regarded these people as "potential" Soviet citizens,
unless they had been divested of Soviet citizenship or allowed to
renounce it by decree of the Presidium of the Central Executive
Committee of the USSR or of a constituent republic.[128] This procedure was changed by a decree of May 27, 1933, which deprived
of Soviet citizenship all former Russian subjects who went abroad
prior to October 25, 1917, and acquired or applied for foreign
citizenship.[129]

Despite these regulations, the Consulate General found it almost impossible to obtain from the authorities definite answers
to specific questions about the cases of Americans who had
acquired Soviet citizenship.[130] An analysis of all cases of Soviet
naturalization which had come to the attention of the Consulate
General tended to show that the Soviet authorities had attempted
to cause as many foreign citizens as possible to acquire Soviet
citizenship. This was especially true, said the report, of skilled
workers born within the Russian Empire, who were needed for
special work; they were subjected to considerable pressure by
the authorities.[131] However, American citizens who flatly refused
to give up their citizenship were not forced to do so; therefore it
could not be inferred that the definite policy of the government
was to force all foreigners to become Soviet citizens.[132]

Officials in the various foreign departments were apparently
instructed to induce all the foreigners they could to acquire Soviet

citizenship, and the most ardent of these officials tried to carry out the policy to the extreme. The report quoted a member of the consular staff who had been connected for two years with the Foreign Bureau at the Gorki Automobile Plant. He reported that one person in the department used every means at her disposal to induce or force foreigners to become Soviet citizens, until higher authorities were forced by the complaints registered to warn her against carrying this policy too far.[133]

Other bits of information, some probably available to those who wrote the report, although not included in it, provide further confirmation of Soviet citizenship policies. One worker at Gorki was asked on arrival to surrender his passport. "Word got around," he said, "that it would be wise to ask for its return quickly, for those without passports generally found it difficult to leave the country." [134] The fifteen or twenty Gorki workers who did take out Soviet citizenship were mainly naturalized citizens or alien residents of the United States; they were told that their status would improve if they became Soviet citizens and that a good future in Soviet industry would open up to them. Lacking resources outside of Russia and tiring of the continual pressure, they yielded to Soviet demands.[135]

This point about lack of finances leads one to believe that financial pressures as well as direct political pressures induced foreigners to become Soviet citizens. Since most were paid in rubles, which could not be taken out of Russia, many lacked the money to return home. A Finnish-American mechanic said that the large fees for residence permits, which had to be renewed with increasing frequency, encouraged people to become Soviet citizens. If a foreigner's passport had expired when he applied for extension of his permit, he was offered Soviet citizenship papers to sign, and most accepted for lack of money.[136] An American consular official remarked in an interview that he heard many stories of this type. "Later," he said, "these people would try to contact the American Embassy to try to get a passport to return to the United States. The State Department took a lenient view of such situations and tried to help." [137]

For political émigrés, the pressure was of a third sort. They became Soviet citizens because the only other alternative was to return to the prisons of Hitler and Mussolini or other governments.[138]

The Soviet regime did not directly prevent the departure of those workers who had financial resources and still retained foreign passports. However, by paying their salaries in rubles, and by attempting to confiscate their passports and pressuring them to become Soviet citizens, it made departure very difficult. Why it pursued this policy is a matter for conjecture. A survey of the conditions for foreign workers within Soviet Russia suggests that they would scarcely have disseminated a favorable image of Soviet society abroad after leaving the country. As long as they remained within the country and subject to Communist control, the Soviets could use them to support the boast that only in the Soviet Union could foreign workers find a real home, and to "prove" to Soviet citizens that the blessings of Communist society were sufficient inducement to remain. It is true that the departure of foreign workers could be justified by referring to the tasks that still must be performed by the proletariat throughout the world, but it could also be seen by Soviet workers as evidence that conditions, no matter how bad outside, were still worse within their country.

Thus, we find differences in the treatment of foreign guests by Soviet authorities: privileged treatment for short-term guests and members of the bourgeoisie, who, after leaving Russia, would serve the regime as disseminators of a favorable image of Soviet society; harsher treatment and few concessions for those whose major propaganda value to the regime existed only as long as they remained within the Soviet Union. To integrate foreign workers into Soviet life meant to subject them to the same type of treatment accorded Soviet citizens in terms of living facilities and indoctrination. When foreigners refused to co-operate voluntarily with Soviet plans for their integration, the regime supplemented persuasion by using citizenship decrees and payment of salaries in non-exportable rubles to make it extremely difficult for foreigners to leave the country.

Finally, we note that foreigners ideologically close to the Soviet position received fewer concessions than those further away. On the one hand, the Soviet authorities saw less need to provide incentives to convince those already faithful to the regime. On the other hand, they were suspicious of all those who came close but did not quite toe the party line, and treated them with little deference. The Soviet "passion for unanimity" in doctrinal matters dictated a close surveillance of all foreign radicals and an intense drive to subordinate them to party discipline. The Soviet regime could afford to cater to the whims of the bourgeois foreigner, but the whims of the foreign radical had to be suppressed. To their regret, the Soviet authorities found that many of the faithful became disillusioned when forced to endure Soviet reality.

5

Protecting the Soviet Image

As we have seen, the positive techniques of flattery and privileged treatment of foreigners operated to promote a favorable image of the Soviet Union; at the same time, control techniques functioned to prevent negative factors from interfering with that image. The fact that many of these controls produced a negative image apparently did not enter the minds of the Soviet authorities, or else was subordinated to other considerations.

While some of the controls were tangible, many were of a more subtle nature, their success or failure depending very much on the preconceptions, attitudes, and language skills of individuals and groups concerned. Controls, then, were based on a combination of specific techniques and an opinion of human nature.

DIRECT CONTROLS TO PREVENT THE DISSEMINATION OF A NEGATIVE IMAGE

The "Fraction" and Political Organizer

The Communist "fraction" was among the more explicit and overt controls utilized to manipulate foreign opinion.[1] It served the twofold purpose of ensuring the proper direction of the delegation during the visit to the Soviet Union and of seeing that favorable resolutions emerged during and after the journey.

A Hamburg baker who visited Russia in 1926 reported that after his delegation reached the Soviet Union it was divided into three groups, each headed by a Social Democrat. The real leader, however, was the deputy chairman, a Communist; and "the Socialist majority was simply led by the nose." [2] Another illustration of the functioning of the fraction is found in a description by a Communist member of an American rank-and-file delegation. When the nominal leader of the group (Louis Hyman, who, though not a Communist himself, headed the Communist-controlled Needles Trade Industrial Union) began to criticize Communist policy in American trade unions, the fraction quickly silenced him.[3] On the basis of available evidence, a Communist fraction appears to have operated within the major American trade union delegation of 1927, although its role was not clear.[4]

The fraction generally assisted the political organizer who supervised the activities of the labor delegation in the Soviet Union. In one delegation, when the political organizer required someone to address a Russian audience, the fraction members were likely to be chosen. The fraction in this delegation supervised the work of the Soviet interpreter, ensuring that translations of speeches by the delegates adhered precisely to the party line. One of the English Communists accompanying the delegation of coal miners in 1926, who was the editor of the *Sunday Worker*, served as publicity agent for the group, sending to English papers of leftist inclination photographs of their visit as well as hundreds of telegrams about the "triumphant journey." [5]

A Soviet interpreter commented on the service of the fraction as gadflies helping in the attempts by the political organizer of the British Miners' delegation to force delegation leaders to disown such moderate Labour party leaders as McDonald, Thomas, and Henderson. She described how silence filled the room after the political organizer asked the delegation members, "Do you think that your leaders, Thomas, Ramsay McDonald and others defend the interest of the working class?" Suddenly the silence was broken by the English Communists sitting on the couch. "Down with the traitors, Thomas, McDonald, down with

Baldwin and Hicks," they exclaimed. "Long live a Soviet England." [6]

The Communist fraction played an important role within labor delegations, but in some cases, especially when young people were involved, was not considered sufficient in itself to direct the delegation. Margaret McCarthy remarked that a young woman Communist from London party headquarters, fluent in Russian, traveled with her youth delegation throughout its entire Russian trip: "No doubt she was the actual Party director of our youth delegation, although the official Young Communist fraction leader was a miner from South Wales." [7]

The political organizer of a trip was often a Russian Communist leader attached to the Commission on Foreign Relations or a foreign Communist attached to the Comintern and Profintern Headquarters in Moscow. The organizers handled the arrangements within the Soviet Union, seeing that everything was in order at each stop, and supervised meetings between delegation members and Soviet citizens. One interpreter noticed small pieces of paper floating into the delegation's carriages. They carried messages written by Soviet workers drawing attention to the deceptive nature of the excursion. As she pondered whether and how to translate them, she observed the watchful eye of the political organizer upon her. [8]

In addition to supervising the visits of delegations, the political organizers tried to ensure that delegation members signed their names to the pro-Soviet resolutions drawn up within the secretariats of the Comintern and Profintern. In the delegation of the Great Britain Federation of Coal Miners, the organizers operated a system of mail censorship to guarantee that all outgoing mail dispatched by the delegation contained only sentiments favorable to the Soviet regime. In addition, they inspected all incoming mail lest such items interfere with Soviet plans for the delegation. When the Soviet authorities extended the trip of the delegation so that additional time could be spent in Grozny, Tiflis, and Baku, the Federation became concerned and began to bombard the delegation with telegrams. "I myself perceived," said the interpreter, "that the telegrams disappeared into the pockets of Gorbachev [Secretary of the Central Committee of the Union of Soviet Coal Miners], and [that] the English knew nothing about them until their departure." [9]

Equivalent, perhaps, to the work of the political organizers in the labor delegations were the activities of foreign Communists among the foreign workers, discussed in Chapter 4.[10] They supervised the contacts with Soviet society and directed the foreigners' political education, utilizing them for propaganda purposes.

Restrictions on Freedom of Movement of Foreign Visitors

Although the task of the Communist fraction and the professional organizers was to guide the delegations, the authorities worked constantly to keep delegates from knowing they were being guided. This illusion of freedom was most important for intellectuals, who prided themselves on their independent and critical minds.

To create this illusion, the regime tried to convince foreign visitors that they could go wherever they desired. A popular technique during the 'thirties was to send "favored guests on free tours of selected parts of Russia" or to allow them access to areas previously closed to foreigners, while exercising a subtle surveillance.[11] To combat the belief that visitors were shown only "models," the Soviet authorities permitted limited access to some of the squalid areas, which were passed off as part of the Tsarist heritage. Soviet officials held in such low esteem the critical abilities of their guests that, following collectivization, the regime allowed tourists to enter the famine-stricken areas long before they were opened up to foreign journalists.[12]

But could visitors really choose their own itineraries? For labor delegations coming to the November festivities, orders would go out to regional and other local committees alerting them to the delegations' arrival. In 1927, for example, local executive committees and councils of people's commissars of the autonomous republics were instructed by the All-Union Council of People's

Commissars to co-ordinate delegation schedules with the Moscow Soviet before the delegations left the republics for Moscow.[13] A list was made of factories and farms to be visited and the authorities notified. A German Social Democratic member of a labor delegation described this process: "When our delegation arrived in any centre the heads of the professional [labor] union came to meet us, and they submitted a list of various undertakings which were considered suitable for our inspection." [14] Silas Axtell, a member of the advisory staff of the major American labor delegation of 1927, declared that their being permitted to go "anywhere they wanted" was related to a state of mind. "While we did have the choice of whether we would go to a candy factory or a rubber factory or a steel plant, it cannot be said that we were given free privilege to browse about and see anything we wanted to." [15]

These descriptions of the choice of places to be visited have been confirmed independently by two former employees of the Commission on Foreign Relations of the central Soviet trade union apparatus, the organization most concerned with labor delegations. "The delegates don't suspect," declared A. Rudolf, "that all choices offered have been inscribed on a list previously confirmed by the Communist International." [16] Soviet interpreter Tamara Solonevich remarked that beneath the façade of allowing the delegations to go wherever they desired lay a plan confirmed by the Comintern, Profintern, and Soviet trade unions.[17]

The authorities denied that advance notice had been given the communities and institutions visited, and to prove this cited changes made by members of a delegation in its itinerary. A German Social Democrat commented: ". . . it is true that the Crimea and Ural group had changed their programme somewhat, but that was only done *with permission of the Russian trade unionists*: the alteration was decided on a *week* before the delegation left, and all the places visited *had been warned* of their visit." [18] An interpreter attached to the British Miners' delegation of 1926, Tamara Solonevich, asserted that although she did not see the actual directives and letters she was certain that telephone calls and telegrams went from Moscow to other points where the delegation was to stop. The reception of the delegation at each place reflected prior knowledge of the visit. The delegates were met by "spontaneous" demonstrations, invited to attend "improvised" meetings, and addressed by "figurehead activists" who pronounced similar memorized speeches.[19]

Walter Citrine, general secretary of the British Trades Union Congress, tells how a friend went with some members of a delegation to the home of a printer. Questions addressed to the host elicited the information that his monthly wage was 700 rubles, which seemed strange to Citrine's friend, since he knew that the average wage the previous year was about 189 rubles. The meal served the delegates "would have taxed the best efforts of a good-class restaurant." When these delegates compared notes with another group which had visited a home in a different part of the city, it was found "that they, too, had been to the home of a similar typical worker who was about to serve them on the spur of the moment with a sumptuous dinner such as my friend experienced." [20] When Citrine himself, traveling in Russia in 1934, tried to visit a worker's apartment, which he thought he had selected at random, he had an idea that people knew he was coming.[21]

In some cases, when, for example, a foreigner knew no Russian, allowing a small amount of freedom was no sacrifice. The freedom of a visitor without Russian to wander around Moscow alone, presented few problems for the regime and helped promote the view that one could go where one wanted. The experience of Julian Huxley, who visited the Soviet Union in 1931 with other scientific and medical men on a tour sponsored by the Society for Cultural Relations, illustrates this situation. Some medical men who did not wish to see the scientific institutions devoted to research to which visits had been arranged for them obtained from their interpreter the names of various hospitals and directions on how to reach them. They went off by themselves, "invaded this or that hospital, waited until some one was produced who could speak English, French, or German, and then asked to be taken round—a request which was invariably granted." Huxley stated that "their impressions were based on the everyday routine of ordinary institutions, not on prearranged visits to showplaces." [22] Apparently he discounted the fact that a Soviet interpreter furnished the original list of hospitals.

Some visitors who expressed a desire to probe further than their "guided tours" met only excuses and delays. The Karelian timber camps, Solotvetsky Island, and other places where political prisoners were kept at forced labor were permanently off limits, as most Soviet officials admitted. In other cases, places were "temporarily" closed to foreign inspection.

When one member of a delegation asked to see a small bakery after visiting several large enterprises, he was told it was not possible, and instead was taken to the largest establishment in town. A particular sausage department which interested him could be inspected only after three, the hour that dinner was scheduled.[23] A journalist who wanted to see a small textile factory near Moscow found it difficult to get permission; Soviet authorities kept insisting that he visit a large factory in Moscow.[24] The writer E. M. Delafield through her own initiative spent some time in the Seattle Commune; she was requested by her Intourist guide after she later joined a tour "not to encourage any other tourists to demand the same privilege, as it would certainly not be granted to them." [25] Although his Moscow travel bureau knew of Edmund Wilson's desire to see Ulianovsk, his Intourist guide tried everything possible to dissuade him from going, but was unsuccessful. Commenting many years later on this experience, he expressed the belief that the rundown condition of the city was "one of the real reasons" for opposing his going there.[26] Several individuals at different times during the 'thirties asked to visit the Gorki Tractor Plant. Though in Moscow they were not discouraged about the possibilities of such visits, they found on arrival that inspection was not possible: the Plant was being reorganized; there was not enough time to stop there; visitors disturbed the workers.[27]

At other times it appeared impossible to obtain transportation to various places. Silas Axtell remarked that he asked his interpreter fifteen times to secure a car and chauffeur to take him to the Amo [Automotive] Plant.[28] Professor Samuel Harper of the University of Chicago found in 1930 that factory authorities at Stalingrad created many obstacles to his visiting the American engineers working there, refusing, for example, to send a car to take him and his party out to the Plant.[29] Both eventually were successful in visiting the factory.

One might argue that a logical explanation can be found for each case of this kind. Several visitors believed that prohibitions were imposed by the local authorities, independent of orders from Moscow. But the accumulation of these and similar incidents suggests a pattern of excuses and delays whenever a visitor wished to exercise his independence of planned itineraries. With tourism centrally controlled in the Soviet Union, an explanation based on lack of co-operation by local authorities seems too simple. Furthermore, many of those who were denied permission to visit certain areas were known as friends of the regime; their complaints were not those of hostile individuals. So, it seems safe to conclude that the Soviet regime attempted to discourage visits to places off planned itineraries, or to sites of activities which they wanted hidden from public view, or to places where poverty was evident.

However, qualification is required. In certain cases, persistent efforts made by travelers netted results, perhaps because further obstructiveness might produce a worse impression than the hidden object.[30] Some visitors had more freedom than most: Edmund Wilson commented that he would have been controlled by Intourist if his friend Dos Passos had not arranged to have the latter's unexpended royalties transferred to him.[31]

And finally there is the time factor. Foreigners not traveling with delegations seem to have had more freedom during the late 'twenties and early 'thirties than during the later 'thirties. Intourist was not established until 1929, and as we have noted, did not achieve even a minimum of efficiency until several years later. A visitor to Russia in both 1931 and 1936 remarked that by 1936 there was less freedom of independent investigation;[32] Intourist looked after the well-being of the traveler and kept him within a prearranged and well-supervised itinerary.

Not until 1934 did individuals begin commenting that the only way to get long-distance train tickets was through Intourist.[33] Maurice Hindus stated that up to 1936 (excluding the famine period) every foreign journalist could travel freely, except in Central Asia and the Arctic, if he was willing to risk discomfort in the provinces; but from then on, one had to outline one's itinerary. Then the Commissariat for Foreign Affairs would get in touch with the chairman of the local soviet to warn him of the journalist's arrival. The local administration took and kept one's passport until one checked out and told the police where one would go next. "One couldn't just get off the train at some place on a whim."[34]

Yet even as early as 1929, one American couple, hoping to spend some time on their own, complained: "We were absolutely captives of the Russian setup for tourists and barely permitted to go any place or do anything without our guide. We could not stay one moment longer than arranged for in each place. We were always checked in and checked out."[35] Thus, while there was some tightening of controls on foreign tourists as time passed, independence was hard for some to achieve even during the early period.

But while there may have been more opportunity for independent travel during the earlier than during the later years of the period, a device operated throughout to limit such opportunity. The lack of rubles available at a fair rate of exchange forced the visitor to utilize prepaid group travel arrangements, and limited him to the special facilities which accepted foreign currency. After Intourist was established, commented Eileen Bigland, the organization "forced you to use them [i.e., Intourist's services] in the sense that unless you were a millionaire, prices would be too steep."[36] F. S. Miles wrote that, while a tourist could wander around by himself, Intourist restricted his movement by not allowing him to have any currency rubles.[37] Eugene Lyons commented that the Metropole Hotel, which catered to foreign tourists, offered a valuta as well as a ruble menu, with great differences in service and price: the ruble menu, intended primarily for Russian patrons, was more expensive; the service accompanying it was poorer.[38]

Lack of rubles restricted the pleasure of one American's visit: ". . . We were strangers here, more deeply so than anywhere we had been," he said. "Our money was no good except in this hotel. We couldn't go to a play or a picture without making arrangements in advance. . . ."[39] The great majority of the American students who attended the Anglo-American Summer School at Moscow University expressed a similar grievance. As one put it, he wished for some solution of the problem of money exchange "so one would be able to move around freely without being forever 'carried about' by Intourist."[40] Another regarded the problem of foreign currency as quite serious; the official rate of one ruble, thirteen kopeks, to the dollar was outrageous. Financial controls, he added, limited one to group sightseeing. Although he disagreed with the idea that in Russia one was allowed to see only what was chosen for him, he admitted that "currency difficulties do have the effect of usually limiting the visitor."[41]

The English writer Violet Conolly, when asked about this problem, said that during her visits in 1928 and 1936 one could always obtain rubles on the black market.[42] Although this was true, many foreign visitors must have hesitated to obtain rubles in this manner, for fear of the consequences if caught. A 1926 incident which bears on the situation is related by Tamara Solonevich. Some members of the British Miners' delegation, waiting outside a restaurant for the rest to finish, saw a store that sold cigars. They entered and exchanged an English pound, receiving 100 rubles in return. This exchange created some excitement among both the delegation members and party officials. They had been receiving only twenty rubles to a pound through the service of the officials. The officials, much perturbed, lectured the delegates: the man in the store was a malicious speculator, a remnant of the bourgeoisie; in the future they must be on guard against enemies of the proletariat.[43] As we have seen, foreign workers were also restricted by currency problems. All of this seems to suggest that the Soviet authorities had a dual interest in limiting the number of rubles available to the visitors: to limit their range of freedom, and to profit by the exchange ratios.

In 1936, Soviet authorities abolished the direct use of foreign currency, which had two curious and to some extent contradictory effects. Theoretically, the decree allowed the individual visitor more freedom to travel independently, since there was no longer a difference between services paid for in rubles and those paid for in valuta.[44] On the other hand, since all foreigners now had to use rubles in everyday transactions, and the ruble was stabilized at five to the dollar, foreign residence was prohibitively expensive.[45]

Currency controls which forced the less affluent to use the facilities of group tourism limited their freedom to explore the country because of certain characteristics of this method of travel. Frederick C. Barghoorn has remarked that the Soviet authorities have always favored group tourism since ". . . it is, on the whole, easier to keep members of groups, with full schedules of formal activities, away from sights and sounds and smells not intended for foreigners"; besides it is "more economical to assign top-flight interpreters and skilled guides to groups than to individuals."[46] Many arguments were used in travel literature to encourage group tours: a group carried more weight than an individual in Soviet Russia; conferences with top Soviet officials would be impossible to arrange for any but the most important individuals; visas were easier to obtain for members of a group.[47]

Group tourism facilitated a "guided" tourism, making it easier for the Soviet regime to stage large productions for guests. A French doctor visiting the Soviet Union expressed his exasperation at the Russian practice of showing off hospitals as they showed off museums. With some other doctors, he asked to see an operation performed at one of the Soviet hospitals, apart from ordinary tourists. Conducted by a Soviet guide, they proceeded to the Mechnikov Hospital. As they waited for the operation to begin, suddenly the doors of the operating room opened, admitting over a hundred tourists. The French doctors left immediately, not wanting to be any part of the propaganda show.[48] Even Burton Holmes, who commented at one point in his book that his guide seemed to know just what he wanted to see and that he did not feel that anyone was trying to steer him, complained of the constant scrutiny and interference by guards and the insistent urgings of guides to keep together in the Kremlin. Here, he said, "sightseeing . . . is limited to a cursory survey of such buildings as the tourist can see from where he passes as a marcher in a tourist troop. . . ."[49]

Substitution of group for private interviews with a single Soviet official began in the 'thirties. After 1932, one student of the Soviet economy reported, interviews became group affairs with a panel of experts headed by a chairman answering the questions of groups of foreign visitors, in his case economists.[50] In other cases, where one visitor was granted an interview, several Soviet officials were present in the same room.

Another aspect of group tourism which distressed foreigners was the pace of the activities. A Flemish worker who traveled with Intourist found his days so crowded with activities that everything seemed kaleidoscopic.[51] A French journalist complained that the Intourist guides propelled one through an endless maze of workers' clubs, maternity homes, crèches, farms, and museums, leaving not a moment to oneself.[52] A former Communist member of the Commission on Foreign Relations agreed that the itinerary of the labor delegations gave "no minute of respite, no occasion to reflect," since one thing followed another without pause.[53] Even an individual traveling alone with a guide would cry out at the pace. Liam O'Flaherty commented that the guide "carried me along in such a hurry that I was blind and deaf to my surroundings. I saw churches, theatres, newspaper offices, clubs, and crèches which merely bewildered me without teaching me anything." [54]

One's critical senses were dulled by the momentum of guided travel. People found it difficult to evaluate what they had seen, especially when they had never before seen such places as a prophylactorium (an institution for the rehabilitation of prostitutes). As one visitor remarked: "But I had never visited a factory nor a crèche before, and therefore had no standards of comparison by which to judge whether these Russian examples compared favorably or not with those of other countries. I strongly suspect that many 'Intourists' who have returned full of enthusiasm for such show-places had as little previous experience by which to judge them as myself." [55]

An analogy can be made between showing the foreign visitors the maximum number of things that could be squeezed into one day and filling the day or week of the resident foreign worker with as many activities as possible. A November calendar for foreign workers at the Kharkov Tractor Plant left only two evenings empty for private activity.[56] But this has been true of all Communist activity: Communist parties have been called "parties of total integration" because they demand in addition to dues-paying membership, extensive influence over all spheres of individual life.[57]

Contacts of Foreigners with Russian Citizens

Various techniques were tried to prevent most foreign visitors from genuine and close contact with the native population, for fear that the visitors might have a detrimental influence on Soviet citizens or get an unfavorable image of the country.

Russian citizens were instructed to remain quiet or were told what to say during the visits of foreign guests or delegations. A Soviet teacher who was a summer custodian for one of the lesser royal residences at Peterhof spoke timidly to Anne O'Hare McCormick until she found that the journalist was not a labor delegate. "She then," according to Mrs. McCormick, "confessed to a hopeless passion for china of the Russian Elizabethan period." [58] A former employee of the Commission on Foreign Relations of the Soviet trade unions declared that during the interviews which labor delegates had with Russian workers and soldiers, the latter were carefully instructed in what to say. "Besides, no one under the eyes of interpreters would dare to criticize or complain." [59] Only in unusual cases would an interpreter even hesitate in deciding how to translate an unfavorable answer or statement. Andrew Smith, the American Communist who worked at Elektrozavod, explained that during the visit of any delegation the workers were ordered to pay attention only to their machines and let the officials do the talking.[60]

A former Soviet citizen described to me the visit of an English delegation to a resort where he was staying, as a small boy, with his mother.[61] The Russians at the resort were ordered not to speak too much in the presence of the delegates, even in Russian, for it was not known how much Russian the delegates could understand. Wanting to practice his English, the boy approached the delegation. The NKVD officer in charge was puzzled about how to keep the delegation from seeing that contacts with Russian citizens were discouraged. He finally decided to invite the boy to share a special meal with the delegation apart from the rest of the Russian vacationers. Afterwards, other officials questioned the boy about what he and the delegates had asked or replied to each other. My informant commented at the end of the story, "How could I in this atmosphere tell them [the delegates] if anything was wrong?" This man remarked that the failure to impress Gide was costly to those who organized the trip. Although Gide was allowed some contact with Russians, people along his route were told in advance what to say and were later asked what they had said. After his return to France, Gide complained that most of the people whom he met were "vague" and "redundant" in answering his questions.[62] "Of course," my informant said, "Gide found Soviet youth monotonous. At the time of Shaw's visit, there still was genuine enthusiasm. . . . By 1936, there were no views at all either positive or negative. One just repeated *Pravda*." [63]

In some instances the Soviet authorities went further than briefing Russian citizens on what to say in the presence of foreigners: they ordered the replacement of the actual inhabitants of an area, factory, *kolkhoz,* or prison by Soviet propagandists and GPU men. To counteract reports of famine in the area inhabited by the Volga Germans, factories, party units, and trade unions throughout the USSR were ordered to select the best foreign workers to participate in an excursion up the Volga. Accompanied by Soviet officials, propagandists, and photographers, the excursionists finally arrived at what they were told was a Volga German colony. There they were photographed sharing a festive picnic with the supposed residents of the colony. Andrew Smith later discovered that the "Volga Germans" present were *udarniks* (superior workers) and propagandists shipped from Samara after the real colonists had been evacuated.[64]

A former Belgian consul who had remained in the Soviet Union after the Revolution witnessed the preparations made to receive the British Trades Union delegation at Rostov in 1924: several hundred workmen at one of the major plants who were considered politically unreliable were given a vacation while GPU men replaced them.[65] During visits in 1926 of a German workers' delegation and of an American delegation of intellectuals to Kharkov prisons, the political prisoners were replaced by agents of the GPU who told the delegates that life in prison was very comfortable.[66] The story of an Italian-American working on a farm visited by Intourist where the political committee dressed up in peasant attire to replace the regular workers when foreigners were visiting will be recounted in detail.[67] The GPU and other officials must have been very active in posing as workers, peasants, or prisoners, judging by the number of similar incidents reported.

While separate facilities for foreign guests were, perhaps, necessary in view of the poor housing and transporation available to Soviet citizens, such facilities also served to keep foreigners and Russians apart. While the German musician Unger was recuperating at a Russian health resort he took a walk one day in a park and noticed that certain paths were completely railed off; he observed that German workers were being shown around, unable to have any contact with Russian workers.[68] Theodore Seibert describes the evacuation of all Russians from a hotel where he had been staying when the German workers' delegation arrived.[69] Intourist also ran a separate network of hotels reserved for foreign visitors. Soviet citizens who attempted to use the facilities of such places or who visited people there were kept under surveillance.

The motivating factor in providing separate facilities for resident foreign engineers seems to have been less the desire to separate them from Soviet citizens than the need to provide these minimum standards of comfort. Nevertheless, providing separate living quarters also served Soviet purposes in keeping the foreign specialists apart from the Soviet community. To a lesser degree, foreign workers also had separate lodging. An American worker at Gorki believed that the foreign workers were purposely located near a little peasant village and away from the settlement of Russian workers.[70] In Magnitogorsk, many of the foreign workers (excluding political émigrés) lived in a place called "Socialist City."[71] Despite these examples, foreign workers did share the facilities of their Soviet comrades more than did the specialists.

Soviet guides accompanying foreign delegations or individual tourists showed annoyance at efforts made by persons under their care to talk with Russians, or even with foreign workers and specialists working in Soviet factories. Silas Axtell commented that whenever he tried to get out of his car and talk to some peasant, his interpreter tried to stop him.[72] A Frenchman who visited the Soviet Union with a group of co-operative members complained that whenever he tried to talk with passers-by his guide stayed nearby. He doubted whether, under these circumstances, people could talk freely.[73] A Flemish worker on an Intourist tour noted extreme displeasure on the face of his Dutch- and Flemish-speaking guide when he talked in French with a French engineer working at Elektrozavod.[74]

Foreign engineers and other foreign residents reported lack of contact with Russians outside of their jobs. Many foreign specialists, it is true, kept apart by preference, refused to learn Russian, and were interested only in getting their technical job done. This happened especially when companies sent to the Soviet Union large numbers of men who formed their own sep-

arate communities. On the other hand, many foreigners wanted
to get to know their Russian counterparts better but were stopped from doing so. A Russian railroad engineer, Andre Lebed,
who worked with foreigners on the railroad, said that there were
no written orders on the subject of contact with foreigners, but
plant managers recommended, through instructions handed down
by word of mouth, that there should be no contacts but official
ones.[75] Another Russian engineer stated that it was dangerous
to associate with foreign engineers.[76] An interpreter for an American engineer at Kramatorsk was taken to task by her labor union
for accepting some personal favors from him. She was warned
to keep her distance from Americans and associate with them
only in her work. When the friendship continued, articles began
appearing in the local papers condemning her too friendly relations with foreigners. Her union appointed an investigating commission. The American tried to defend her at an open meeting,
which cleared the atmosphere for a while, but the articles soon
began again and stopped only when she quit work.[77] A circum-
stance that poisoned relations between Russians and Americans
was that most of the journalists' secretaries were employed by
the GPU or were obliged to report on their employers. The journalist Paul Scheffer thought the Commissariat for Foreign Affairs
waged "an underground war" on Russians who worked for foreign
correspondents. Scheffer believed that the isolation of foreign
correspondents began as early as 1926, and intensified as time
went on.[78]

Invitations to Russian homes were extremely rare. An American specialist employed with the Archer-Wheeler Company
reported that "Americans come and go quietly when visiting Russian friends so neighbors would not be aware of their presence."[79]
The wife of a foreign engineer wrote:

> In our dealings with various Russian friends it was necessary to
> keep our conversations very carefully in compartments, so to speak.
> This entailed a constant watch on one's tongue. [Someone], of
> course, must have known all about our friendship with the [a
> Russian family] and that we were constant visitors at their flat, but

it seemed to me very unnecessary to mention the fact. Even to [a close friend] I also felt it to be unwise to speak much of our other friends. It was so impossible, in the majority of cases, to know who was who behind the scenes.[80]

George Burrell remarked that his many Russian friends were interested in learning about the outside world. "Hence they sometimes overcame fear of censure from the Party and visited us at our apartment, and we visited them. Not infrequently they would telephone us not to come to their houses until they notified us. Apparently something had happened so that they felt it wise to forego too much fraternization for a time." [81] Walter Rukeyser noted extreme reluctance on the part of Soviet engineers to meet their counterparts anywhere except in public places.[82] Although foreign workers generally had closer contacts with Soviet workers than did foreign specialists, one worker in Gorki commented it was difficult to meet Russians in their home: the only time he could talk freely with them was during a walk in the woods.[83]

The presence of GPU agents at social gatherings attended by both foreigners and Soviet citizens further inhibited contacts between foreign residents and Russians. Eugene Lyons, who had come to the Soviet Union well disposed toward the regime, quickly became disillusioned, partly because gatherings to which he invited both foreigners and Russians aroused the suspicions of the GPU, which sent people there to spy.[84] As time passed, Lyons wrote, "we learned to curb our social instincts and waited always for Russians to make the first gesture toward continued relations to spare everyone concerned possible embarrassment." [85] The American photographer James Abbe, who had a *dacha* (country house) at Cliasma, remarked that, "although the foreign colony and the Soviet bureaucrats' *datchas* . . . often adjoin, they remain two distinct 'sets' and do not mingle. Only around the town pumps, of necessity social centers, you can pass the time of day in neighborly fashion with the Bolsheviks." [86]

Other foreigners complained of isolation from Russian life. The American students who attended the Anglo-American Summer School at Moscow University recommended for future summers far more contact than they had enjoyed with Russian students. One student reflected the general consensus when he remarked: "I feel strongly that for certain *students* arrangements should be made so that they can *live* in a more typically Soviet environment than offered by the extremely artificial one existing in the Institute last summer." [87] Other students complained of the general lack of free contact between the students and the Soviet community. A visiting American editor, Ray Long, found that VOKS and the Union of Soviet Writers prevented him from contacting directly Soviet writers to solicit material which would appeal to the American and British publics.[88]

Journalists, too, were affected. Anne O'Hare McCormick remarked that "'the man in the street' so useful to the reporter elsewhere," represented the government viewpoint or feared to talk to foreigners if out of the "reliable" circle.[89] An English colleague commented: "Thus, by the end of the first week, I found myself acquainted with almost everyone whom the Law allows you to know in Russia, but cut off from all those I really wished to meet. It takes time and patience to dig under the surface of officialdom into those social strata which are groaning under the Bolshevist regime." [90]

There were certain qualifications to the general policy of limiting contacts between foreigners and Russians. Some foreigners found themselves more able than others to have closer relations with Soviet citizens. In fact, in cases involving naturalized citizens, alien residents, or political émigrés from other countries, the Soviet authorities encouraged close contact with the Russian community rather than isolation from it.[91] Journalists such as Louis Fischer and Maurice Hindus, who had close Russian ties through birth and marriage, were able to meet Russians socially without difficulty, and Fischer was able to help others to do so. Some American and English students who studied in the Soviet Union also reported relatively close contacts with Soviet citizens. One young American scholar, Philip E. Mosely, believed that because he avoided all association with foreign diplomats and any regular association with foreign journalists, he was able to move more freely in Moscow life and to make many Russian friends easily.[92] Jacob Miller, studying at the academy which trained future Soviet planners, was permitted after some difficulty to stay at the academy's hostel. He commented that he had relatively free contact with the planning students, although the warmth of other associations changed rapidly over the first few months of his visit.[93]

The Russians who most feared contact with foreigners were the classes the Soviet government regarded with suspicion, such as the former Russian intelligentsia and bourgeois engineers. Maurice Hindus noted that the peasants were the least suspicious of foreigners because few of them bothered to visit the villages, and that the further one traveled from Moscow the more hospitable the Russian people became toward foreigners.[94] This is confirmed by the statements of several foreign residents in the more remote areas of the Soviet Union. The mining engineer John Littlepage and his family were invited into Russian homes in the mining town of Kochkar in the Southern Urals to celebrate the Russian Easter.[95] An American Quaker who worked as a doctor in the Marinsky District of Western Siberia was accepted into the Russian community.[96] Individual foreigners living in isolated areas appeared to have escaped suspicion even during some of the worst parts of the purges.

Another type of contact also seems to have been easy to establish. Foreigners reported being able to talk freely with people they chanced to meet on trains or in other transitory situations, such as waiting in line. People serving foreigners, when out of hearing of guides and interpreters were willing to comment about life in the Soviet Union.

Internal conditions caused variations in the contacts between foreigners and Russians. Generally, one can say that contacts were easier to maintain during the 'twenties and only gradually became strained as time passed. However, a decisive change took place after the death of Kirov in December, 1934. Many of the former scholarly contacts of an English economist had disappeared by 1932; each year that she visited the Soviet Union

after that she had to search for a new set of contacts.[97] Friends
began to tell her in 1934 that they could not visit her again.
American journalists and other foreign residents in the Soviet
Union from before Kirov's death to 1937 or later stated that
after 1936 the gap between the communities grew larger.[98]

Yet one finds that Russian citizens also shied away from foreign contacts during earlier periods. This was especially true
following trials which involved foreign specialists. A Russian
engineer told Margaret McCarthy about a ban on meetings
between foreigners and Russian technicians. Russians feared
such meetings, especially after the Shakhti Affair in 1928, which
implicated both German engineers and Russians in acts of industrial sabotage.[99] An engineer with Metro-Vickers noted that by
1930 the life of foreign specialists in the Soviet Union was made
difficult by the impossibility of free social contact with the technical intelligentsia. During the Industrial Party Trial in 1930,
he reported, almost every Russian engineer who had had contact with British engineers employed by Metro-Vickers was subjected to OGPU interrogation.[100]

Even during periods of calm between trials, however, people
have testified to strained relations with different sections of the
Soviet population. On the other hand, during parts of the purge
period, some foreigners were still able to carry on contacts with
Soviet citizens: foreigners studying in the Soviet Union during
1936 and 1937 reported close contacts with Soviet students.[101]
Both Edmund Wilson and Louis Fischer cited 1935 as a period
when there appeared to be more freedom than ever before
(which might have been due to the slow onset of the purges
after Kirov's death).[102]

The extreme variability in the Soviet atmosphere between
1924 and 1937 is testified to by the experiences of Dr. Samuel
Harper, who made trips to Russia between 1904 and 1939. In
1926 there was no limitation on his freedom of movement;
however, he inquired of people trusted by the authorities
whether a visit might cause trouble for old friends formerly
active in public life, and in several instances he refrained from

seeing them. During this trip he was able to get acquainted with some of the younger men and women in Soviet institutions— Komsomol or Communist party members—although he said he "scrupulously refrained from getting too friendly on a personal basis" since he felt they always were on guard.[103] In 1930, he remarked, "Conditions for my study and work were not altogether favorable, though I received every courtesy at the hands of the authorities." [104] He blamed this contradiction on the fear of technical experts and the intelligentsia of being caught talking to foreigners. Although VOKS failed to co-operate, in 1932 he was able to see his old friends more freely than in 1930, the result, he believed, of the improved political position of technical experts.[105] But by 1934 it was difficult, for the most part, to travel around Russia alone. He finally found the son of an old friend who was on leave from a responsible position in an industry of Central Asia and who agreed to accompany him on an independent trip. They were allowed considerable freedom in visiting villages Harper selected, but were criticized by a party secretary in one provincial town for visiting a few badly run villages, and later by party officials in Moscow for visiting another small, backward town.[106] Consequently, Dewey's comment, "What I learned from my experience in this matter (rendered typical by a variety of similar experiences) is the necessity of giving an exact dating to every statement made about conditions in Soviet Russia," is a sound one.[107]

One exception to the general Soviet policy of limiting contacts between foreigners and Soviet citizens, organized social contacts, needs more detailed examination. To serve specific purposes the regime allowed—in fact encouraged—a certain number of planned relationships. Many of these were official and semi-official cultural functions such as rapprochement meetings, formal occasions such as teas for journalists, and lectures given by visiting foreigners to Soviet audiences. The wife of one engineer addressed a group of Chechen (in the Caucasus) women after the government had told them how their status would improve in a modernized economy. The husband spoke to a group of Russian school children.[108] Both talks probably served the propaganda ends of the Soviet regime vis-à-vis their own people, a matter which will be discussed in detail in the next chapter. The Soviet officials also attempted to get foreign engineers to attend the functions of clubs for Soviet specialists such as the Dzerzhinsky Club, or to attract the foreign specialists into "social activities." [109] A foreman at Dnieprostroi (site of a hydroelectric dam on the Dnieper River) complained to a visiting American writer of his despair at the fruitless attempts to interest American engineers in "social" work.[110]

Thrown on their own resources, the American colonies of experts tried several times to organize their own clubs, but each time they were thwarted by the government. In 1930 Alexander Gumberg suggested to Hugh Cooper that an American Club be formed in Moscow with Spencer Williams, representative of the American-Russian Chamber of Commerce, as secretary. He suggested that the club be used for conferences and discussions, and that Russian engineers and business executives connected with American work be allowed to become associate members. This, he said, would increase the opportunity for Russian and American specialists to meet away from the place of work and away from the supervision of Soviet officials. Soviet living quarters had been too small and crowded for such contact, and Soviet citizens hesitated to visit the home of foreign engineers.[111]

A. Choumak, manager of the American section of the USSR Chamber of Commerce for Western Trade, raised strenuous objections to the plan. Choumak wrote Gumberg that such a club would not create closer contact but would lead to estrangement between foreign specialists and Soviet engineering and technical circles.[112] As an alternative, Choumak urged Americans to join the foreign section of the Dzerzhinsky Club. Williams agreed that the tone of Choumak's communication symbolized Soviet hostility to any plan that would divest Soviet officials of control over contacts between Russians and foreigners.[113]

Walter Duranty, who was drawn into another venture by

foreign specialists to form a club, believed that Russian suspicion toward all clubs not under their control was due to the belief that they "had been nothing but pretexts for political activity of subversive character." [114] He reported that "the Western idea of a club as a purely social and non-political organization simply cannot penetrate the Russian mentality." The specialists, however, ignored the unsuccessful experience of the journalists in forming a club and elected a committee to confer with the authorities. The latter at first "welcomed the idea enthusiastically and spoke of clubrooms and canteens for American goods at cost prices, of magazines and books, of bridge and tennis." But, when the committee began to press for a decision, the Russians suggested that the specialists join the Russian Business and Engineers Club.[115] A joint meeting of Americans and Russians was subsequently described by Anna Louise Strong in a letter to the *Industrial Gazette*.

> I have attended many meetings in Russia, but I never saw anything so futile as this evening in the Business Club. First, the president didn't speak a word of English, nor did the principal speaker, Rudini. After some argument, an American vice-president was elected who didn't speak Russian. Then Rudini made a speech for an hour and a half about what sort of a club Americans ought to form, how the Germans had formed one, how the Americans ought to get organized, and then they would have a club and tennis and dancing and even golf.[116]

The *Industrial Gazette* commented that, "Miss Strong quite correctly condemns the handling of the meeting of American specialists. We await from the Soviet Business Club a concrete program of collaboration with foreigners." [117]

Certain Russian citizens, probably for purposes of surveillance, were assigned to associate with foreigners. Eugene Lyons stated that several Russians whom he befriended in earlier years continued to come around by official order after general social contacts had been reduced.[118] Several other foreign residents said that, although social relations became exceedingly difficult by 1936, certain foreign office officials and ballerinas were assigned to be friendly to foreigners.[119] But as early as 1926, the German journalist Paul Scheffer expressed a belief that all Communists were instructed to seek permission from the party for any prolonged association with foreigners. Other Russians were encouraged by Soviet authorities to entertain visitors, to show them around—"but not more than once."[120] Sometimes, in order to meet their commitments to foreign educational foundations, Soviet authorities even gave foreign residents permission to live with Russian families while studying or doing research.[121]

Finally, Soviet authorities created straw men to whom foreigners were given direct access. To combat rumors of a Trotskyist army in the Ukraine, the head of the Associated Press Bureau in Moscow, William Reswick, was invited to investigate. At an all-night party in his honor in Odessa, a man introduced as Leplevsky (cited by Reswick as commander-in-chief, according to the *New York Times,* of the Trotskyist army) came to his table to testify that "Trotskyism was dead in the provinces."[122] Reswick learned that the man was only a "Red Army officer of low rank who had at one time served under Trotsky"; other officers at the gathering insisted they had no other Leplevsky on the Army roster.

A similar case may have occurred during the visit of the British Trades Union delegation of 1924. Friedrich Adler, a noted Austrian Socialist, criticized the report they later produced, alleging that the Menshevik placed at the disposal of the delegation, to create the impression that free contact could be had with all factions in the Soviet Union, had recently gone over to the Bolsheviks.[123]

Censorship

Reports of the extent of censorship controls on journalists must be judged according to the perspectives of the different newsmen and Soviet officials. Maxim Litvinov, at a tea for foreign newsmen, expressed disbelief when faced with charges that the Soviet regime practiced censorship. After Walter Duranty had pointed out the Soviet censor, Litvinov replied: "Oh, . . . you can hardly call that censorship. That is just an effort to protect you gentlemen from misinformation in your news." [124] While Eugene Lyons was pro-Soviet, he felt that censorship was mild and regarded the censors as helpful in terms of saving him "from cabling implied criticisms of the Soviet regime into which [he] had been betrayed by an extravagant adjective or a too literal reading of the news." [125] Later, as his views changed, he found censorship to be a different, a more restrictive matter. William Henry Chamberlin experienced a similar change of attitude. In *Soviet Russia* (1931) he reported that, "the news censorship is not severe, as censorships go, and shows a slow but steady tendency toward giving the foreign journalist increasing latitude in conveying impressions as well as facts." [126] However, he did note that some items had been dispatched "in a delayed and weakened form." In *Russia's Iron Age* (1934) he appeared to be more disturbed by the number of rules restricting newsmen and described some of them in detail.[127] Both Lyons' and Chamberlin's changing evaluations were affected by the tightening of regulations during the famine years of 1932–33 to prevent the press from seeing the desolate countryside, but their changed personal attitudes toward the Soviet Union were the chief reason for a departure from their early attitudes toward censorship.

Techniques of censorship varied from stringent restrictions to psychological measures. News dispatched by wire was generally subject to approval by the censor; news sent by mail was free from this, although the journalist was subject to sanctions by the Soviet regime if it found the published dispatch unfavorable. During the famine of 1932–33 members of the foreign press corps could not leave Moscow without first submitting a detailed itinerary and obtaining permission from the Commissariat for Foreign Affairs.[128] While relative freedom was again allowed in late 1933, by 1936, as we have seen, the regime began to place actual hindrances on free travel by requiring journalists to submit an out-

line itinerary which the Foreign Commissariat and other Soviet
agencies would use to warn the chairmen of local soviets on the
route.[129]

Despite occasional easing of restrictions, there was an official
censor throughout this period. Prior to 1929 he was Theodor
Rothstein, chief of the Soviet Press Department of the Commissariat for Foreign Affairs.[130] He was followed in that post
by Jean Arens, an important GPU man. An English journalist
believed that since Rothstein was not a party man of importance, he may have feared rebukes from the GPU for being too
lenient toward correspondents, and thus antagonized the press
by excessive rigor in small matters.[131]

Paul Scheffer commented that the fist of Soviet censorship was
usually concealed under a glove of velvet. The press authorities
strove to create the impression that the Soviet government was
not afraid of the truth. In the 'twenties, in its desire to see the
press of all nations represented in Moscow, it gave visas to jour-
alists who were known to be skeptical of the Communist regime.[132] After the decree sanctioning the deportation of Nikolai
Basseches, a German journalist, was signed by the Politburo, Jacob
Podolsky, assistant director of the Press Department, intervened
with Litvinov and G. G. Yagoda (NKVD chief, 1934–36) to attempt to get the order reversed. Though Podolsky personally disliked Basseches, he felt that if he was expelled "the world would
say that Moscow tolerated only those correspondents who were
pro-Soviet and banished all others." [133] Stalin's sensitivity to this
possibility led to his successfully pressuring the Politburo to re-
verse the order at its next session.[134]

Scheffer felt that the art of Soviet censorship was "the art of
telling three-quarters, a half, still smaller fractions, of the truth;
the art of not telling the truth in such a way that the truth
would be made apparent to a thoughtful reader; or conversely,
the art of telling the whole truth up to the point where its negative
or positive significance would become apparent." [135] A concert-
ed attempt was made first to quiet the reporter's conscience
by disguising the true function of the censor. If this was not

successful, official approval would be withheld until the reporter, pressed for time, had to yield.[136]

Even more important, self-censorship was exercised by journalists to guarantee renewal of their visas. Permits to reside in the Soviet Union were granted foreigners for a maximum period of six months, and the foreigner who left the country even for a short time had to reapply for an entrance visa.[137] The government kept voluminous records on the views of all journalists. Some negative attitudes were tolerated, but if one wanted to remain in the country, only a mild negativism. The shift in Chamberlin's view of the USSR may be partially explained on this basis: when he was writing *Soviet Russia,* he was also doing the research for his monumental history of the Russian Revolution, which he wanted very much to complete; *Russia's Iron Age* was published after he had left the country permanently, while he was in the final phases of writing the history. Released from the threat of visa withdrawal, he perhaps felt freer to adopt a more critical attitude toward the Soviet Union.[138]

Harassment of Concessionnaires and other Foreign Agencies

The regime tried to exert control over foreign residents and agencies by means ranging from mild attempts to interfere in their affairs through active harassment to the "show" trials involving both foreigners and Soviet citizens. One example of interference involved the American-Russian Chamber of Commerce, which, late in 1929, became dissatisfied with the work of its Moscow representative, Charles Smith, and decided to replace him. Smith, according to Spencer Williams, was an elderly man who lacked initiative.[139] However, he was well disposed toward the regime and the Soviet Chamber of Commerce sent the American-Russian Chamber a telegram protesting the proposed action, noting that replacement of Smith would create an adverse impression.[140] Several years later, Smith's successor, Spencer Williams, discovered through a comical incident the Soviet attitude toward him. Because of the shortage of toilet paper, his chauffeur had presented him with carbon copies of old letters as a substitute. One set of papers turned out to be minutes of a meeting held two years before at the Soviet Chamber of Commerce. Peter I. Bogdanov, head of Amtorg, had been asked by the Western Department of the Chamber to hint to the American-Russian Chamber that it recall Williams, because he could not be so easily controlled as his predecessor. Bogdanov advised against this and apparently his advice had been accepted.[141]

Harassment of foreign specialists in the Soviet Union took many forms. Concessionnaires experienced the sudden withdrawal of operating advances, the imposition of heavy fines for minor infringement of regulations, and the stimulation of labor unrest among their Russian workers. The Harriman Manganese Concession had conflicts with labor unions over the types of clothing and dwellings provided for underground workers.[142] The German Drusag Concession (a sheep farm) was under continued harassment by the authorities, who fined its director and manager each 10,000 rubles for minor offenses against labor regulations.[143] This incident, added to many others such as a prolonged public trial involving the director, undermined discipline at the Concession. Apparently the regime hoped, without directly issuing termination decrees, to make further operations impossible. This interpretation seems consistent with a subsequent order dismissing all Russian employees of the Concession, who, the authorities claimed, were not on the electoral list, and substituting union employees whose qualifications for the job had yet to be proven.[144] Friction in the Lena gold fields between British concessionnaires and Soviet authorities appears also to have been caused partly by labor problems. The company claimed that it was subjected to "additional expenses through unexpected wage increases and to special losses through a strike probably artificially provoked by the Government itself." [145] Since the Soviet authorities did not generally seem much concerned with labor conditions in Soviet industry, the motivation of special interest taken in the matter in the foreign concessions arouses suspicion.

Other types of foreign firms operating in the Soviet Union were also harassed. Allan Monkhouse, an engineer for Metro-Vickers, complained that the Soviet authorities charged his firm an extremely high rent for an office in Moscow, and insisted that its books be open to public audit all the time.[146] Metro-Vickers also complained of Soviet interference in its relations with its Russian employees. In some cases the regime placed blame for such friction on the lower authorities. *Pravda* described as "petty and revolting methods" those actions taken when the manager of a Ural copper works cut off office supplies and removed the telephone of the McDonald Engineering firm.[147]

Such harassment, and the general GPU controls over foreigners were controls meant to restrict behavior. We have already described general police surveillance, the dossiers kept on foreigners by the GPU, and the entering and searching of rooms in the occupant's absence.[148] Several persons believed that the GPU was checking their whereabouts through phone calls: when the telephone was answered, the caller hung up. In addition, the GPU engaged interpreters, porters, and other Soviet citizens as spies. John Hazard, as a student in the Soviet Union, was given the "good advice" by Ambassador William C. Bullitt to tell the porter of the American Embassy what he was doing, to scotch speculative rumors in advance. The Embassy, Bullitt said, tried to get the most intelligent man available to work as porter so that his reports to the GPU would be factual and not fanciful.[149]

The trials involving foreigners, such as the Shakhti and Metro-Vickers trials, also appeared to be measures designed to restrict behavior. At the Metro-Vickers trial, Soviet authorities accused foreign specialists of gathering what appeared to the specialists "innocent" economic information. The publicizing, through public trials, of violations of the Soviet criminal code made foreign businessmen and engineers extremely cautious about gathering economic information.

The climate of suspicion generated by the charges of wrecking at both the Shakhti and Metro-Vickers trials caused a feeling of uneasiness among foreign engineers, who were afraid that they might be chosen as scapegoats.[150] For example, charges were leveled when machinery failed to operate, and foreign specialists were often accused of deliberately wrecking it.

INDIRECT CONTROLS TO PREVENT THE DISSEMINATION OF A NEGATIVE IMAGE

Mistranslation

A technique which served to create a false impression was inexact translation by the interpreters. An explicit assumption of Soviet ideology, according to Hadley Cantril, is "that an individual's thought and action are guided and molded by language and words and that, therefore, no inconsistencies or conflicts of meanings can be tolerated." [151] He quotes the book of two Soviet psychologists as saying, that "'through speech signals, a person acquires behavior norms and is guided by them in various life situations'" [152] Hence Soviet interpreters were under orders to use exact party terminology in their translations and to alter through mistranslation any communication that would interfere with the image the authorities hoped to disseminate.

Before her first job as an interpreter for the British Miners' delegation, Tamara Solonevich was told by the head interpreter to substitute politically precise terminology for the expressions used by the British trade union leaders in their speeches before Soviet audiences.[153] Miss Solonevich found this very difficult because she was not well acquainted with Marxist terminology (she had been able to obtain her job despite this political shortcoming because of a shortage of reliable interpreters during the early years of the Soviet regime). She also found it difficult to hew to the line of Marxian analysis and class stuggle in all her explanations of Soviet life to the delegation.[154]

Numerous examples showing that Soviet interpreters deliberately mistranslated speeches or conversations between Russians and foreign visitors can be cited. Andrew Smith tells how a foreign visitor to Elecktrozavod asked a Soviet worker how much the man paid for food. The interpreter in translating the answer of two rubles, thirty kopecks, conveniently left out the ruble denomination.[155] A visitor who understood Russian spotted a similar mistranslation while observing the Soviet oil fields at Baku in 1936 with a delegation of American businessmen connected with the oil industry. One man asked the Russian manager how long it took to drill an 800-meter well; the manager replied an average of from four to six months, but the Soviet guide said that he would tell the group from three to six weeks.[156]

Boris Silver, a Belgian Socialist who had spent time in Russia before the Revolution and knew the language, visited his sister-in-law and her husband in 1933. They lived on a *kolkhoz* often visited by Intourist group tours. Once the director of the *kolkhoz* addressed a group on the subject of "the advantages of co-operative farming and modern implements." Silver observed that "the chairman, who translated the speech, must have been sure that none of the audience understood Russian and that no one on the platform understood English." [157] It took forty minutes to translate a twenty-minute speech because the chairman padded it with percentages, statistics, geographical descriptions, and the activities of the Communist Party in his area.

Sometimes the political organizer took over the responsibility of the interpreter, as happened to Miss Solonevich and the British Miners' delegation. When she hesitated to translate a message from Russian workers alerting the delegation to the deceptive nature of their welcome, the political organizer took the paper and read "It is our miners sending you greetings, Comrade. They regret that you will not stop here." [158]

In these instances, mistranslations merely created wrong impressions; in other cases involving foreign businessmen, mistranslations, and delays or failures to translate reports into Russian, were used to sabotage work. The 1926 Ford delegation found it difficult to have translated and disseminated their report, which reflected unfavorably upon Soviet handling of tractors.[159] John Littlepage, who was hired by a top Soviet official to suggest improvements in Soviet gold mining, found that many of the recommendations of American engineers were never translated.[160] *Pravda* once described the resistance of Soviet managers at the Ural Copper Works to innovations proposed by foreign specialists; part of what it termed "an underground war against the new project and its author," consisted of sabotage of the specialists' reports by inaccurate translations from English.[161] Evidently some of the reports and recommendations originally requested by the Soviet government were sabotaged by subordinate officials.

Several engineers complained about a lack of interpreters competent to translate technical work, even though "practically the entire success of a foreigner's work in the Soviet Union depends on the ability of his interpreter." [162] An American engineer, working for the Archer-Wheeler Company in the Soviet Union, was told by his interpreter that she was often forbidden to provide him with certain information, and that his questions put her in a difficult position.[163] A former Soviet citizen knew an American engineer in the USSR who had two interpreters, NKVD women, who had instructions not to translate anything the American might say which the Russians were not supposed to hear, and vice versa.[164]

Although they sometimes lost patience with their interpreters and guides, many visitors were aware that the latter were always under suspicion just because they came into contact with foreigners. One American woman believed her interpreter to be intimidated: the American had wanted to give her some extra stockings as a gift, but the guide insisted that if she wore them she would fall under suspicion.[165] Other guides and interpreters feared punishment, both if they violated orders in satisfying tourists' requests and if their charges complained about them to Intourist. Tamara Solonevich tells of a new Intourist guide who without thinking explained to the person she was guiding that her salary of 300 rubles a month was not equivalent to $150 because the Soviet ruble was not actually worth half a dollar. The disclosure of the real worth of the ruble cost her her job and ultimately led to her arrest.[166]

Official Provision of Information

The problem of foreigners obtaining precise information about Soviet society was a two-sided one: on one hand visitors were bombarded with statistics they had not even requested; on the other hand, it was difficult to get certain types of information that foreigners needed to assist them in their work or in their efforts to obtain an accurate view of Soviet reality. A member of the early Ford delegation noted that the Russians were found to be "converts to the religion of planning . . . 'mad entirely on the subject of charts, diagrams, mathematical tables, etc.' " [167] But foreigners were also interested in this aspect of society and, as Spencer Williams remarked, "they took Soviet statistics too seriously. They thought what the Soviets hoped they would think, that what was on paper would be true in a very short time." [168] However, when one asked for information beyond that freely given, difficulties ensued. Silas Axtell reported that although nine-tenths of the information that the American trade union delegation of 1927 received consisted of official statistics, he found it difficult to get first-hand information on such subjects as agriculture.[169]

Foreign journalists in the Soviet Union often had substantial problems in getting information. Interviews with the higher Soviet officials were rarely given, and only after a written list of questions had been submitted in advance.[170] Stalin seldom gave interviews, and when he did, he used them to restate the ideas expressed in party resolutions. Eugene Lyons said that most of the news about Russia that appeared in the foreign press was culled from the Soviet press, with about 25 per cent being the product of "official handouts, the mendacities of paid tipsters and his [the reporter's] own fertile imagination." [171] Those few reporters with ties to Soviet society of marriage or birth were able perhaps to get a little more.

Little information came directly from Soviet institutions and organizations. The officials who received the journalists were often afraid to talk alone with newspaper men, calling in a second or third person to witness the interview. The more general practice, Walter Duranty's assistant testified, was to require submission of a written questionnaire, to which written answers were promised at some later date. Most of the questionnaires were then filed away and never answered.[172] In one case when Duranty and his assistant called at the offices of several Soviet organizations to get statistics on the exportation of cereals from the USSR, the information was said not to be available. The American-Russian Chamber of Commerce, proved to have the information in great detail and had received it from the very organizations to which the journalists had originally applied. The Chamber informed the newsmen that the government had already telegraphed the data abroad for general distribution.[173]

Difficulties which arose in the foreign business concessions in the Soviet Union were blamed by non-Soviet sources on the lack of prior information that foreign businessmen could obtain about Soviet conditions. A. A. Joffe, a Soviet official, was criticized in an editorial in a German newspaper for alleging that foreign concessionaires knew all about the objects of the concessions (i.e., the development of Soviet natural resources) before the contracts were signed, and that they had received exact information about the concessions.[174] According to the editorial, even if the concessionaires had had this information, it would not have been enough. "Anyone desirous of establishing a large concern with a huge amount of capital must be able to personally satisfy himself as to the economic conditions of the country on the spot itself . . . ." The writer contended that "this is the weak point, however, for the Soviet government is afraid to a sometimes almost comic extent to admit anybody into the country for the purpose of gaining information." [175] Paul Scheffer also agreed that inadequate knowledge by concessionaires of the conditions under which the concessions had to be worked was responsible for some of the difficulties encountered.[176] The severity of restrictions on gathering economic information in the Soviet Union was seen in its extreme form in the Soviet trials of foreigners (Shakhti Affair and Metro-Vickers) who thought they were gathering harmless information available freely in other countries.[177]

Immigration Policies

The final set of indirect controls that must be discussed in the chapter is immigration policy. Although by and large Soviet authorities welcomed foreign specialists and workers to the Soviet Union, they attempted to control the flow. In this effort they were impeded by Intourist, which sold one-way tourist tickets to foreign workers, telling them that they could find work after their arrival in the Soviet Union, although jobs were not always available.[178] Foreign specialists were also affected by the lack of co-ordination between the trading corporations which hired them and the institutions in which they were supposed to work; consequently, invited specialists frequently spent long hours of idleness.[179]

To remedy the situation concerning foreign workers, the authorities issued in early 1932 a series of orders, some of which created a Kafkaesque confusion. One order directed that no foreigner with a tourist visa could have his visa extended until he had a regular job, and that no regular job could be given to a foreigner on a tourist visa unless the individual had extended the visa for residence.[180] Soviet tourist organizations abroad were ordered to sell one-way tickets to Russia only to persons definitely employed. They were also ordered not to promise employment there. A new department for the regulation of immigration within the Commissariat for Labor was set up, headed by Michael Borodin.[181] Yet, as noted earlier (see p. 71), enough loopholes were left in these regulations to enable someone coming to Moscow without employment, but possessing a badly needed skill, to find work. The earlier order relating to residence permits was altered to allow the issuing of such permits to qualified workers for whom jobs could easily be found.[182] An

American who had had some training as a welder, after some difficulties over visa regulations, was finally assigned a job at Magnitogorsk and signed a contract.[183]

Little seems to have been done to remedy the lack of coordination in policy on foreign specialists except to publicize the situation. In an article appearing in *Voprosy Truda* (*Questions of Labor*), A. Kilinskii recommended that the foreign specialists from abroad be allowed to enter the country only after having received notice of contract confirmation by central authorities.[184] Yet one could not always be sure that the contract had been confirmed even after being told that it had. In 1934, an American specialist was hired in Los Angeles for a position and assured that as long as his services were satisfactory he would receive no less favorable treatment than that provided for in the original contract. On his arrival in the USSR he was told that this contract had not been confirmed; he found that in practice he suffered losses in salary.[185]

DECEPTION BY THE REGIME TO PROMOTE A POSITIVE IMAGE

Presentation of Models

At one end of the scale, Soviet authorities showed the best that they had and urged their guests to generalize from those unrepresentative conditions. A Communist leader of a British labor delegation remarked that the areas which the delegation was permitted to visit, such as the vicinity of the southern oil fields, contained good housing. "These," he said, "the delegates were allowed to visit freely and then swallowed the yarn that these townships were typical of all Russia." [186] Walter Citrine told his guide that though he wanted to see some of the poorer housing as well as the modern, he was not being directed to it. When he commented that he doubted whether delegations were shown the poorer conditions, his guide claimed that they "knew perfectly well what the bad conditions were like in Russia. What they required to know was what the Russians were aiming at. That was the purpose of the delegations; to see what the Socialist State was really doing." [187]

This attitude is indicative of the concept behind the term "socialist realism" as applied to Soviet literature. Andrei Zhdanov has stated: "Soviet literature must be able to show our heroes, must be able to look ahead to our tomorrow. This will not be Utopia, for our tomorrow is already being prepared by planned, deliberate work today." [188] Thus, the only realistic literature serving party interests, and the only exhibits suitable to show foreign delegations, were those that pictured things not as they were but as they ought to be according to party concepts. The result was to disseminate a distorted image of Soviet society in which the progress shown on paper was greater than the real progress.

Another example of the Soviet attempt to have the foreigner generalize from the best was even more misleading because it ignored class distinctions which actually existed. Members of a British labor delegation who were visiting the mines of the Donbas (i.e., the Don Basin) were taken to a changing-room for men who were going down into the mines. In each booth the group found a soft chair, bath or shower, pegs on which to hang clothes, clean towels, and soap. "We were told," said interpreter Tamara Solonevich, "that this was a workers' bathhouse. Afterwards, I learned that this bathhouse was especially for the director, his assistant, and the staff engineers. For the workers there existed other bathhouses, dirty and cold huts, and by no means at every pit. It seems that only 30 per cent of all mines in the Donbas have bathhouses for the workers." [189] Another visitor, who understood Russian, commented that he had a difficult time getting permission to visit workers' homes. Whenever he asked to do so, the Soviet authorities would take him to the homes of engineers and *stakhanovites*, which differed quite radically from those of ordinary workers.[190]

Maurice Hindus tells an interesting anecdote about Bernard Shaw's visit to the Soviet Union. He met Shaw during the latter's stay in Russia, and Shaw expressed to him a desire to see a collective farm. Hindus knew of one such farm which, although small, was well run by Russians who had lived at one time in America. The Commissariat for Foreign Affairs had planned a visit to a large state farm; it did not know of the farm Hindus suggested and had the Commissariat for Agriculture check it. The farm proved to have only two tractors. The Commissariat for Foreign Affairs, displeased, told Hindus that they wanted to show Shaw a farm with fifty tractors. They became still angrier when he refused to persuade Shaw to forget his suggestion. The entire entourage finally went to the collective farm Hindus had suggested; Moscow officials found it so excellent that it became a part of the standard Intourist itinerary.[191]

Plainly, the authorities hoped to impress foreign visitors by showing them one example of a highly mechanized agricultural settlement, perhaps not realizing that a well-run but smaller settlement might better testify to Soviet agricultural progress. Here was one failure of Soviet techniques of deception. But these models, however atypical, were at least functional prototypes and hence quite different from another technique of deception: the actual construction of façades to be dismantled when their purpose was fulfilled.

The Potemkin Village

The Potemkin Village was one of the regime's most controversial techniques. The term comes down from the time of Catherine the Great, whose Minister, G. A. Potemkin, erected the façades of entire villages along her route to the Crimea to convince her that her colonization policy was being implemented. During the present century, the term "Potemkin Village" has been more loosely used to include guiding visitors to the best areas of the country; showing "models" which, although not erected specifically for foreigners to see, did not reflect the general state of affairs; and actual creating of façades similar to those of Prince Potemkin.

The extent and the nature of the preparation preceding the visit of an important individual or delegation has always been a question. Louis Fischer said "that if a manager of a hotel knew fifteen Americans were coming, he knew he would have to do his best. Local patriotism and pride were involved as well as orders from above."[192] But evidence reveals that a great deal of deliberate preparation took place preceding the arrival of important foreigners.

Other activities which come a bit closer to the original Potemkin Village consisted of changes in everyday routines. Before the visit of former French Premier Edouard Herriot to Kiev, the authorities ordered the residents to clean the streets and repair the pavements.[193] A similar order preceded the visit of a May 1 trade union delegation to Elektrozavod in Moscow; an American Communist who was working there related that a *subbotnik*, or extra "voluntary" work period, was called the day before the visit to clean up the place.[194] A similar "cleaning-up" was also called at the Kharkov Tractor Plant before the visit there of another delegation.[195]

A problem which troubled Soviet authorities in the 'twenties and 'thirties was the existence of large numbers of beggars and *bezprizornye*—homeless, wild children who roamed city streets day and night. They could hardly be a feature of a humanitarian society without unemployment. So the authorities tried to remove the beggars and *bezprizornye* from the streets during visits of important foreigners and delegations. A young American girl living with her parents near Tiflis reported hearing of an occasion when government officials removed all such children from the streets before a prominent American and his party were expected in Moscow.[196] Others saw this done in Kiev before Herriot's visit [197] and in Moscow and Kharkov before the November festivities and other visits of foreign delegations.[198] Anne O'Hare McCormick, wondering "why a government so good at rounding up political suspects" let homeless children roam around, was told by her guide, "they could not be 'co-

erced.' " [199] Yet during the celebration of the Tenth Anniversary
of the Revolution, when foreign labor delegations and other
visitors flocked to Moscow, she noticed that the authorities
rapidly cleared the streets of the capital. When a member of
a British labor delegation, who had heard about the *bezprizornye*,
brought up the subject after not observing any evidence of them,
she was informed by the guide that this question was "very greatly exaggerated and really was a case of capitalist lies; furthermore, the enquiring delegates were invited to inspect the streets
and homes." [200]

Several foreign Communists described as harsh the measures
taken by Soviet authorities in regard to those removed from the
streets. An American Communist learned from some beggars
who eventually returned that they had been loaded on trains
and trucks and transported out of the city.[201] Vidor reported
that the wild children were sent to homes and temporary con-
centration camps.[202] A German writer who visited one of these
places remarked that it had an inadequate staff and that the
children lived under conditions of neglect.[203]

Before the arrival of delegations, the government would issue
a decree reducing food costs or opening up some new service
for Russian workers. Before the 1927 celebrations *Pravda* announced the opening of several new hospitals; [204] and the next
year it reported the opening of 350 new schools in the Leningrad
area.[205] Butter disappeared from the shops and restaurants before
the festivities, a British resident worker recalled, only to reappear
on the day the delegations arrived in town.[206]

In addition, Soviet officials actually erected façades, which
they dismantled after the visitors departed. The German correspondent Theodore Seibert, who was living at a Russian hotel,
describes how the management told the Russian tenants to seek
other accommodations during the visit of the First German Labor
Delegation. The next day, the journalist was surprised to see several vans arrive "laden with fine furniture, with strips of carpet
which were laid down in the previously bare passages." He was

further astonished when the coarse bed linen and towels were replaced by articles of much better quality. . . ." [207]

James Abbe, the American photographer, sent on a trip into the Ukraine by the Moscow Director of Amtorg to disprove rumors of famine, was amazed at one discovery he made. At the bottom of a mine shaft which he had been invited to descend, ". . . like a mirage, was a brilliant, electrically lighted Red Cross Station, cross and all, with a trained nurse in spotless white uniform, instruments in boiling water and a hospitable-looking operating table." Based on a knowledge of previous experiences, Abbe commented that "the Bolsheviks have learned to be prepared." [208]

An English worker who witnessed a visit by twenty-five Italian aviators to Odessa in 1929 reported that the local soviet installed electric lights in the peasant huts for the occasion. Kiosks were erected to sell foodstuffs of good quality at low prices only to the aviators; "the peasants in the vicinity were warned by the local authorities that under no circumstances were they to attempt to purchase anything from these kiosks." [209] Electricity was provided for many additional homes in Kiev during the visit of Herriot. [210] During both the Herriot and the Bernard Shaw visits, special food was transported by air and rail to places where the guests would stop. [211] Because Shaw was a vegetarian the authorities had to exert extra effort to provide fresh vegetables for him during a period of famine.

Finally, to illustrate the literal meaning of the concept Potemkin Village, one must turn to the factories and farms listed on the visitor's itinerary. A former American consular official who served in the Soviet Union related to me what two Italian-Americans who worked on a *kolkhoz* visited by many foreign tourists had told him. On visiting days the party either gave them good clothes, or told them to get out of the way while political officials dressed up as farmers. [212] At this place as well as at many factories, the visitors would be given a sumptuous meal. For the farm workers there was the pleasure of watching the production, and the chance to eat food which never appeared on ordinary days.

The impresssions of foreign residents, including journalists, are almost unanimous in considering these Soviet efforts at deception as one big show. Eugene Lyons said, "They showed the best, but what was presented as typical was in fact atypical." [213] William Chamberlin commented that "there was a greater attempt to create impressions. In other countries, it is true, the more favorable sides are also exhibited, but in Russia there was a more intensive effort to show them." [214] An American embassy official, Charles Thayer, who served in Russia during the 'thirties remarked that "the difference between tourism there and in the United States was that while we take them to the best, there are no attempts to prevent people from seeing the worst. The technique of dazzling is part of the Russian passion for theater, a component of nationalism and natural pride." [215] Thayer also added that "an inferiority complex is the other side of the coin and the reason for cutting off foreign contact with shabbiness and the worst." [216] Louis Fischer agreed with this: "The average show put on by a Soviet manager," he said, "was far different from that put on by his American counterpart. The latter would not have to hide anything . . . Soviet propaganda directed toward foreigners was based on a feeling of their own inadequacy and inferiority." [217] All these men agreed that tourism in the Soviet Union was far different from that elsewhere during the 'twenties and 'thirties, although some of them also tried to understand the situation which motivated the Soviet authorities to produce spectaculars.

At times even some Soviet intellectuals were irritated by this compulsion. Walter Duranty, in a *New York Times* article, cited a remark made by Ilya Ehrenburg in *Izvestia,* criticizing the "show put on for visitors, especially in the so-called foreign hotels of Soviet Russia." Ehrenburg's comments were motivated by an experience he had had at the Hotel National: told one morning that he could not have his tea, Ehrenburg "looked around and discovered they were having a sort of dress rehearsal for the arrival of 300 American tourists." He criticized the staff of the hotel for trying to create a false atmosphere of the kind reflected in émigré cabarets in Paris or New York.[218]

Controls on foreigners ranged, then, from devices peculiar to the Soviet—the fraction, the political organizer, and the "show trial"—to ones employed by other closed societies—the Potemkin Village and press censorship. In different ways the controls operated to prevent foreigners from penetrating behind the façades erected by the regime, while at the same time they created a series of illusions to convince foreign visitors that their experiences were not being manipulated.

Through the use of the Communist fraction and the political organizer, the Soviet authorities attempted to steer the delegations. The fraction, being more disciplined and decisive than other delegation members, was able to influence the process of opinion formation in directions desired by the Soviet regime.

Such techniques as the Potemkin Village, selection of an itinerary from a prearranged list, and the creation of false impressions through mistranslations by interpreters rested on certain assumptions of human gullibility and lack of a critical sense to penetrate beneath Soviet-erected façades. Soviet authorities were convinced that at the very time that foreigners were being manipulated, they could be made to believe that they were arriving at conclusions independent of external direction. Just as Hitler recognized the potency of the "big lie," the Soviet regime realized that the more preposterous the façades, the more likelihood that visitors would be taken in, for they would find it incredible that a country at the stage of development of the Soviet Union would go to such lengths in attempts to fool foreigners. Who would believe he was being deceived by GPU men and political officials posing as ordinary workers? Who would imagine that electricity was temporarily installed in peasant huts solely to impress foreign visitors?

Direct and indirect controls operated to limit foreign contacts with Soviet citizens. Devices like currency control and group tourism were augmented by the more direct techniques of providing separate facilities for foreigners and creating an atmosphere hostile to the promotion of close relations between peoples. This atmosphere was created by harassment of Russians who had what the regime considered to be excessive contact with foreigners and by surveillance of the activities of foreigners who had close relations with Russians. At the same time that the regime was discouraging spontaneous relationships independent of political control it was substituting a certain amount of controlled contact under political supervision, such as inviting foreign engineers to join Soviet clubs.

Although the Soviet regime used propaganda techniques primarily to prevent foreigners from probing behind the image that the Bolsheviks hoped to disseminate, it was not above attempting to restrict behavior by coercion: harassment of foreign firms and attempts to interfere with their operations; surveillance of the activities of foreigners through various GPU controls; and accusing foreigners of sabotaging Soviet industry. Since trials for sabotage were obviously for show, and since few of the foreigners received extended sentences, even if found guilty, their main effect was to create an atmosphere of fear which inhibited contacts between foreigners and Soviet society. The requirement of visa renewal served to restrain journalists from being entirely forthright in their observations unless they were ready to leave the USSR.

It may be concluded that Soviet tactics were designed to handle each situation with a certain amount of flexibility so that foreigners would be confused about what the real situation was in the Soviet Union. Hence the removal of barriers to free investigation when the pressure against them got too strong and the allowance of a limited amount of access to what was normally inaccessible. But, the important thing was that behind all the mechanisms was felt the controlling hand of the regime, manipulating contacts between foreigners and Soviet society.

Of all the techniques used to manipulate the experiences of

foreigners in the Soviet Union, which proved most useful? One must remember, first of all, that the regime hoped to disseminate a favorable image of Soviet Russia while limiting to a minimum the amount of genuine, free contact with Soviet society and Soviet citizens. In order to maintain limited contact, Soviet authorities often found it necessary to compromise their major objective; harassment of foreigners and many of the less subtle control techniques could not help to disseminate a favorable image.

The techniques which proved most useful to the Soviet Union were those that worked in fertile soil. By flattering visitors when visitors valued recognition, the authorities indirectly promoted the regime. The emphasis on the future in Soviet propaganda created a favorable impression among foreign intellectuals who were depressed with the present world: while some admitted that the Soviets had not yet reached Utopia, they were quick to add that they believed the Bolshevik regime was constantly looking toward the future and was well along the road to constructing a better society. The models that visitors viewed were not regarded as showpieces, but as the symbols of a new civilization.

Other visitors were not disturbed by Soviet showmanship because they had come to the Soviet Union to see a show. Generalizing from their own relatively comfortable position as privileged tourists, they could not understand how other visitors could talk about conditions of famine, poor transportation, and crowded lodgings. Thus, the regime found that providing its guests with superior accommodations netted returns.

Control techniques which created an illusion of freedom were relatively effective. Few had the time or inclination to analyze the situation and ponder the questions of whether the freedom of movement was fulfilled by an independent walk in the vicinity of the hotel, or whether free choice of an itinerary was fulfilled by being able to choose among several items suggested by authorities. The financial controls and those inherent in group tourism infuriated the few but passed unnoticed by the many.

Since the usefulness of a technique did not require 100 per cent effectiveness, the Soviet Union found these techniques useful because they guaranteed that the tourists would see only the most favorable side of the Soviet Union. The Communists were aiming at some kind of favorable equation which most effectively promoted the regime at the least cost to a closed society. Even if its techniques had mixed results, the regime felt it had succeeded as long as only a minority was alienated.

Such coercive devices as censorship and harassment of foreign firms and engineers were not designed to improve the Soviet image. But they were effective in limiting foreign activity, and since only a minority was affected, the cost was not very great. Journalists, although reacting negatively to censorship, wanted to remain in the country and so submitted. The 1928 Shakhti trial affected only one group of foreign engineers and the regime was quick to disassociate individuals and their firms in the accusations. By the time the Metro-Vickers trial took place, the period of opportunity for foreign endeavor in the Soviet Union was nearly ended.

What do Soviet techniques reveal about the regime? They reveal that a closed society fears spontaneity even when it stems from sympathizers. Political organizers and fractions were deemed necessary even within sympathetic labor delegations. The techniques reveal that the regime was ready to sacrifice its favorable image when it believed such a vital interest as secrecy of data was being challenged, and that techniques of coercion remained available for use when techniques of persuasion and propaganda failed. The centralization of resources in a totalitarian state enable it to influence and manipulate foreigners in a way that government in a free society cannot even attempt to follow, since in most cases the powers of government do not extend into the sphere of entertainment of foreign visitors.

6

Utilizing Foreigners for Propaganda

I have tried to show that foreigners were encouraged to visit and to work in the Soviet Union because they were a source of technical skills and a potential means of disseminating a favorable image of the country abroad. In a more specific sense, however, foreigners were made to serve the propaganda ends of the Soviet regime, both internally and externally. The Soviet authorities required their foreign guests to give both personal and group testimony, in the form of prepared resolutions and reports of the advantages of living in Soviet society. Journalists were used as channels of promotion for particular projects. Publicity given the visits of foreigners in the Soviet Union strengthened the regime internally, vis-à-vis its own people, as well as externally in relation to the rest of the world.

What were made to appear as spontaneous expressions of good will were, for the most part, manipulated by the Soviet regime and other Communist organizations. Study of the resolutions of good will and support shows how faithfully most of them reflected the precise Soviet preoccupations of the period, and how often they used Marxist-Leninist language.

RESOLUTIONS AND TESTIMONIALS

One finds in the different testimonials various promises to combat

159

the danger that then most worried the Soviet Union, whether physical attack by an "imperialist" power or editorial attacks of "fascist" editors. Evidence of Soviet manipulation of these testimonials comes from accounts of former Communists and of individual foreign visitors or residents who became suspicious when they found their names signed to statements they never made. Tamara Solonevich, a Soviet interpreter attached to the Commission on Foreign Relations, asserted that resolutions, especially those signed by labor delegations, originated in the secretariats of the Comintern and Profintern.[1] Information received by the American legation in Riga, Latvia, from the Estonian Foreign Office reported that all protests against accusations of forced labor, including those by foreign specialists, were prepared in the Secretariat of the Communist party.[2]

Fred Beal, in *Proletarian Journey*, described how he channeled the rebellious drives arising from the poor living conditions of the foreign workers at Kharkov into expressions of indignation at capitalist society. In the end they signed resolutions which Beal had drawn up that "proclaimed to the world the wonders of Socialist Construction, the solving of unemployment and the fight against the kulaks and the wreckers, agents of imperialist powers trying to sabotage the Workers' Revolution."[3] Beal went on, "We threw in a few cheers for our leader Stalin and condemned the complainants as Fascists."[4] Bolshevik papers which catered to foreigners, such as the *Moscow News,* termed "absolutely necessary" the task of organizing the social opinion of the English and American specialists, who "must not come and go, leaving no trace either on Russia or on themselves."[5]

The Soviet authorities were well aware that after a man had signed his name to a resolution, he would be unlikely to disclaim it on his return home. In some cases, visitors would sign or lend their names to statements as a gesture of good will. Spencer Williams, a member of the American business delegation of 1929, when questioned about the accuracy of statements attributed to him and other members of the delegation, replied that the statements were not accurate. No one had protested, however, since the general mood was "let's diffuse a spirit of good will." [6] An American engineer reported that many Americans signed various statements denying the existence of forced labor without any knowledge, positive or negative, of the conditions described, and without question or examination of the statements. [7] Other resolutions were signed in order to get economic advantage or permission to leave the Soviet Union. Asked to state his position "should capitalist Europe declare war on the Soviet Union," Liam O'Flaherty signed, "I'll make war on capitalist Europe with every means in my power." He had only eight rubles in his pocket and suspected that Soviet largesse would be forthcoming if he signed. [8] James Abbe admitted that in order to get a permit to leave the country he had signed an affidavit which stated that he had seen no hunger and no forced labor. "I knew that [the statement] was not true, but I signed the thing to get out." [9]

Several people asserted that they openly refused to make such testimonials. An American agricultural economist was approached by Soviet authorities one day and asked to "right up" [sic] a derogatory article in an Iowa agricultural journal on Soviet agriculture, written by another agricultural economist who had worked in the Soviet Union. He refused to do so. [10] John Waters, an American who had worked for the Grain Trust, was asked by a Soviet official to sign a statement written in Russian. When he asked for a translation, the official hedged. Translated, it proved to read: "We engineers, specialists and workers of Germany, America and other countries working in the industrial and economic enterprises of the Soviet Union resent the slanderous lies circulated by the press of the various countries regarding the so-called 'COMPULSORY LABOR' alleged to exist in the USSR." [11] The statement closed with: "Not one of the undersigned has witnessed any so-called 'forced labor' in any branch of Soviet industry." [12] Waters refused. George Burrell reported that the group in Grozny refused to sign prepared statements that they had observed no forced labor in Russia because they had witnessed such labor.[13] An American engineer at Chelyabinsk also described how Soviet officials urged him to make statements placing Soviet conditions in a favorable light; he refused.[14]

In some cases the Soviet officials exerted considerable pressure on individuals to sign the resolutions. Solonevich tells how the officials accompanying the British Miners' delegation were instructed to see to it that the delegation struck out as little as possible from the original draft of a resolution which was so inflated with revolutionary sentiment that even its authors knew it would not be adopted verbatim.[15] At the same time they were to prevent the delegation from inserting any points critical of the Soviet system. The sessions in which the political organizers worked on the delegation took place in the sitting room of the delegates' luxurious train hotel.[16] The work of the Communist fraction during the meeting has already been described (see pp. 113–14). After the political organizer had failed to get the delegation leaders to disown the Labour party leaders in the resolution, he went on to the next point—a pledge to help overthrow the British government. Since all that he could obtain from the delegation leaders were promises to think matters over, sessions marked by incoherent speeches and the flowing of cognac continued over several days. The delegates never gave way on these points, though they did subscribe to much praise of Soviet success. Further, they tried to include some criticism of Soviet conditions, but except for a point about sanitation in the Donbas, their criticisms were not included in the final draft of the resolution.[17]

Vodka and other types of liquor must have been used as effective lubricants to "spontaneous" revolutionary sentiments in other cases as well. A member of a youth delegation to the Soviet Union commented on the liquor available aboard the Soviet ship which transported that delegation as well as an adult delegation to Russia. "The crew gave us parties and we gave them parties in return, at which enthusiastic speeches and fervent declarations of brotherhood were exchanged." [18] A member of the Communist fraction of the adult delegation remarked that the fraction was able to obtain signatures for grandiose resolutions on the Revolution after the delegation members were well fed and full of drink.[19]

Another case involving resolutions by foreigners appears to be even more suspect. The *American Federationist*, official magazine of the AFL, reprinted in 1925 an interview that John Turner, a member of the British Trades Union delegation of 1924, gave to a special correspondent of the *New York Daily Forward* (the Yiddish *Vorwarts*), a Jewish Socialist paper.[20] *The Daily Forward* correspondent first drew attention to the fact that the major London papers had carried daily cable reports from Russia which included long quotations from the columns of *Izvestia* and *Pravda* filled with praise for Soviet conditions, attributed to the British delegation. However, he pointed out, the official labor papers, the *Daily Herald* and *New Leader*, had not published a single word directly received from the delegates, except in regard to the Zinoviev Letter (a forged letter in which the Comintern gave instructions to the British Communist party on its tactics in the election). The speeches reprinted by the other papers had been almost exclusively those of A. A. Purcell and John Bromley (two delegates known for their Soviet sympathies before they left for Russia), except for an interview which appeared in the *Manchester Guardian*, alleged to have been granted by Turner and laudatory toward the USSR. In the interview granted to the *Daily Forward* correspondent Turner said that he was surprised when the *Manchester Guardian* published the interview alleged to have been granted by him; he was especially surprised, since the interview praised the Soviet Union, a sentiment which differed from his real feelings.[21] Turner was sure that the interview printed in the *Guardian* had been obtained by a representative of *Izvestia* from Benjamin Tillet, another delegate, probably at a railway station, where requests for interviews and autographs were regularly made of delegates. He told the *New York Daily Forward* correspondent:

> I don't know what he [Tillet] said to that representative of *Izvestia*. All I know is that I was approached later and asked for

my autograph, which I granted without any suspicion. But it [*Izvestia*] had paid someone to photograph that signature of mine and attach it to Ben Tillet's interview under my own name, in order to create the impression that I had made those statements.[22]

A German musician, Heinz Unger, who spent considerable time in the Soviet Union working for the government, testified to being the subject of a faked interview by the *Moscow Daily News*. After several Soviet pianists had received honors at international conferences, Soviet papers stressed Stalin and Soviet education as the causes of the musicians' success. In a statement solicited from Unger, he had stressed innate talent and the Russian heritage. The interview which finally appeared omitted this reference and attributed to him only statements which praised the Soviet conservatories and academies.[23]

DELEGATION REPORTS

In addition to prepared resolutions, signed before they left the Soviet Union, many delegations published reports after they returned home. It is more difficult to assess the amount of Communist manipulation involved in these reports, but there is evidence to indicate its existence. Communist sources seem to have taken a great interest in the production and distribution of these reports. Among the documents seized by the British Home Office in its 1925 raid on Communist Headquarters in London was a letter to the secretary of the Agitprop Department of the Comintern.[24] The letter, dated May 21, 1925, declared that the party was continually carrying on agitation for the widest possible popularization of the report of the British delegation to the USSR. Another document seized, the "Plan of Work of the Agitprop Department of the Executive Committee of the Communist International for the Next Half Year" included "assistance with the publication of the report of the British [1924 Trades Union Congress] Delegation." [25]

A French Communist trade union paper, *La Vie Ouvrière*,

covered the trip of the British delegation in detail and printed selections from its report before the report was published in Britain. The paper called the report "one of the most important documents that one can find at the present time in order to realize the exact situation in Soviet Russia." [26] A Soviet source cited the significance of the report, relating it to the subsequent formation of an Anglo-Russian Committee of Trade-Union Unity which promoted closer relations between the British and Soviet proletariat. [27]

Although the report was praised in some non-Communist circles, Friedrich Adler, the Austrian Socialist leader, criticized it from the point of view of European Socialism. His criticism was partially concerned with the authorship of the volume: Adler claimed that only the preface in the printed report had originated solely with the delegation and bore no signatures but theirs; the conclusion bore the signatures of both the delegates and advisors. "The whole report," said Adler, "however, originates with the advisory delegates, and the greater part of it is the work of George Young." [28] Earlier in the book Adler had revealed that the sympathies of the three advisory delegates, George Young, H. G. Grenfell, and A. R. McDonell, were extremely pro-Soviet: "Grenfell had for a long time been regarded as having intimate relations with the Soviet Embassy in London." [29] Adler believed that Young alone had written two-fifths of the report, and another two-fifths with the assistance of McDonell, who had written three chapters alone, while Grenfell was the author of the chapter on the Red Army. "The precise fault that must be imputed to the Delegation as such," said Adler, "is that it attempts to relate travel experiences which could not by any means be accessible to it. This is done by trying to make it appear that the Delegation can accept responsibility for the literary product of the advisors." [30]

Some evidence of Communist manipulation is also present in the report of the major American trade union delegation of 1927. The role of the American Communist party in the formation of the delegation was discussed above, on pages 47–52. To have the delegation produce a favorable report was a part of the Communist plan from the very beginning.[31] Benjamin Gitlow has said that, after the Purcell tour failed to produce any money, the Comintern informed the American Communist party that the costs of preparing the report, as well as the cost of sending the delegation to Russia, would be paid by Moscow (although, as has been pointed out, sums of money for the trip were in fact contributed from other sources). Gitlow named Robert Dunn, a member of the delegation's technical and advisory staff and secret party member, as the real director of the delegation. According to Gitlow, Dunn, "in collaboration with Communist International and American Communist Party representatives, drafted the report. . . . Every word of it was then edited by the Party. . . . The report . . . was nothing but a rehash of what we of the Communist Party had been saying in defense of the Soviet Union. . . ."[32]

The report was favorable to Russia. But after interviewing Paul Douglas, a member of the advisory staff of the delegation, and examining information independent of the report, I find there were differences of opinion among delegation members, which Gitlow seems to have glossed over. When the delegation passed through Poland on its return from Russia, several members talked to the Associated Press representative in Warsaw. Delegate John Brophy of the United Mine Workers told the correspondent that, while a decision by the delegation to speak only through James Maurer and Albert Coyle limited his freedom of expression, his impressions of the trip "were about 'fifty-fifty' in regard to things he liked and disliked."[33] Douglas in the interview conducted at that time "intimated that his report of conditions would differ materially from that of Maurer, but that he was not at liberty to speak about them until after the report of the party as a whole had been published."[34] A third member of the delegation, James William Fitzpatrick, President of the Actors and Artists of America, stated that the intellectuals in the group "would not subscribe to the opinion of Mr. Maurer as to conditions in Russia." [35] Later, in a letter to the *New York Times*, Fitzpatrick voiced complete disagreement with the interim report which was published immediately after the delegation returned to the United States.[36]

An interview by a foreign service official at the American Embassy in Berlin with Professor J. Bartlett Brebner, another member of the advisory staff of the delegation, confirms dissension among the delegates. Brebner, after being asked "if the whole labor delegation could agree upon a common report of what they saw," said that "he expected that the final document would include minority reports on a good many points." He was aware of disagreement "on the question of religious freedom under the Soviets." [37] A Catholic delegate felt strongly that religion was being oppressed and would insist upon presenting his views.

Despite these evidences of considerable dissent beneath the surface, only one delegate, Silas Axtell, discussed publicly and in detail why he believed the report was a fraud: ". . . While many of the facts reported were consistent with my own observation, yet the whole report was written with such a solicitous and affectionate regard for the welfare of the dominating group in Russia, whose guests we had been, and the impression from reading the report was so different from the one that I had received, I could not possibly subscribe to it." [38] He believed it was impossible for any group to get much definite and reliable information in thirty days about a country as large as Russia.

The contrast between the highly favorable tone of the final report and the dissent among individual delegates suggests some manipulation in its production; but a definitive statement about the extent of manipulation is impossible.[39] One can be more definitive about the reports of the various rank-and-file delegations which visited the Soviet Union: according to an oral source, formerly high among the leadership of the American Communist party, the reports produced by these delegations were the product of Communist efforts.[40]

One other type of report, which was published by the Co-operative Publishing Society of Foreign Workers in the USSR, needs to be discussed. These reports, with titles like *American Workers in the Soviet Union* or *Foreign Workers in a Soviet Tractor Plant*, glorified the life of the foreign workers in Soviet society.[41] According to a former Comintern worker, the Co-operative Publishing Society had nothing to do with the genuine activities of foreign workers; it functioned only to publish propaganda material in foreign languages, often written by foreign Communists, primarily for the benefit of European Communist parties which could no longer do so themselves.[42]

EXTERNAL PROPAGANDA

In addition to influencing the reports produced by delegations and books written by individuals, Soviet authorities used foreigners in other ways to promote the regime. Despite a statement by one journalist that Soviet officials "neither regarded them as spies and enemies, nor exerted much effort to court or propagandize them," Soviet officials sponsored several press junkets up the Volga and through Central Asia in order to highlight certain wonders of Soviet society, such as the opening of the dam at Dnieprostroi.[43] This trip, and the first trip into Central Asia on the trans-Siberian railroad, were events which lent themselves well to written descriptions and to photographs. Soviet authorities also invited foreign correspondents to a party dedicated to the opening of the tourist season in 1934.[44] The journalists were the principal guests, for the regime believed that they "could influence tourists to spend their money in Russia."

Publicity given the visits of foreigners in the Soviet Union also served to promote the Soviet regime. Reporters and photographers attended the arrival, journey, and departure of each important foreign guest or delegation, in some cases asking the visitors for their impressions before they had even seen the country.[45] Soviet papers publicized international congresses held in the Soviet Union, cultural rapprochement parties, and the activities of foreign specialists and workers within the country. For example, as we have seen, the government insisted that Dreiser arrive in the Soviet Union for the November festivities so that the regime could announce his arrival in connection with them.[46]

An example to illustrate the extent to which the Soviet regime was willing to distort a minor altercation in order to focus attention on a major propaganda theme was the publicity given the alleged beating of an American Negro worker by two white American southerners at a Stalingrad restaurant. The Soviet newspaper *Trud* ran a series of articles on the incident and subsequent trial, editorially describing the affair as an "outgrowth of race prejudice in the United States and other capitalist countries" and stressing the need for "reeducating foreigners employed in the Soviet Union in an international spirit." [47] Stating that "Soviet power will in no case permit the methods of race hatred which prevail in the countries of capitalism to be inculcated by anyone in our land of the Soviets," a further issue described in detail re-education work being undertaken by the Central Committee of Metal Workers who planned to send English-speaking propagandists to Stalingrad. The same issue also carried reports of indignation meetings held in various places throughout the Soviet Union in reaction to the beating.[48]

Trud later reported the trial, emphasizing the testimony of witnesses that the attack was due to race hatred and that Lewis, one of the white southerners, was "not only a drunken rowdy but a fascist." Headlines read "The Whole System of Capitalism Before the Courts," and "Lewis and Brown—Agents of American Fascism." [49] Those who attended the trial, however, reported that newspaper accounts of both it and the incident were inaccurate.[50] They also noted that *Trud* could hardly be called a disinterested observer: before the trial began the paper had stated that the forthcoming trial had been mentioned at the Fifth Congress of the Profintern and that it had called at its office a meeting of the Negro delegates to the Congress. At this meeting a further conference between Negro delegates, *Trud* employees, and some white American delegates was arranged, and an American Negro Communist, James Ford, who was a member of the Executive Bureau of the Profintern, was appointed conference chairman.[51] Four propaganda themes to be stressed during the trial were agreed upon:

1. The theme of mobilizing "the attention of the world proletariat around the decision of the Soviet court on the deed of two 'fascist' Americans who had managed to gain admission to the Soviet tractor works."
2. The theme of "self-determination for Negroes in the capitalist world."
3. The theme of the "labor correspondent movement among Negro workingmen of capitalist countries."
4. The theme of "contact between workmen at Soviet enterprises" and Negro workmen at American and African enterprises.[52]

During the special conference, the value of the incident for revolutionary propaganda among American Negroes was stressed. In addition to noting this pre-trial conference, observers of the trial claimed that propaganda on racial equality had been disseminated among Americans at Stalingrad for some time before the incident. Thus, the conduct of *Trud* demonstrated that even before the actual trial took place, the Soviet regime viewed it as a focus for a general campaign of propaganda.[53]

An American columnist who attended the trial agreed, stating that there had been little friction between Negro and white workers at Stalingrad. The brawl had taken place along the Volga River after the three men involved had all been drinking. The correspondent believed that the trial, which distorted the actual facts, was really a trial of the American racial system and had little to do with the actual incident.[54]

INTERNAL PROPAGANDA

While this trial was apparently part of a larger campaign of international propaganda, it also served to remind Soviet citizens of the regime's claim that racial prejudice existed only in capitalist societies. Other incidents and activities involving foreigners in the Soviet Union were also used in the service of internal propaganda goals. A member of a British business delegation believed that "the prestige accruing from the visit of a British delegation was obviously used to strengthen the Soviet officials before the Russian people." [55] This was also probably true of the favorable statements made about the regime by visitors.

While the sabotage trials of Soviet citizens and foreigners attracted world-wide attention, many observers felt that they were tailored primarily for domestic consumption. Walter Duranty of the *New York Times*, commenting on the Shakhti Affair, wrote that the real purpose of the public trial (which he called a "demonstration") was "to acquaint the mass of the Russian people with the circumstances of the case and, as a minor consideration, to apportion the exact degree of guilt and fix the penalties. . . . The picked 'audiences' at these trials automatically became channels for spreading, at a given moment determined by the authorities (i.e., Stalin), certain views and opinions which the said authorities wished to have impressed upon the nation." [56] Duranty noted that foreign observers, puzzled by the apparent willingness of the accused to admit their guilt, were unaware that the accused were not brought into court until the alleged guilt had been established by preliminary inquiries.

The public was also mystified as to why the Soviet regime should care to implicate Germans at the very time that German-Soviet trade negotiations were progressing nicely. But, as William Chamberlin put it, during the trials of foreign engineers "propaganda ran ahead of the more prudential considerations" of not angering the West at a time when trade and credits and diplomatic recognition were desired.[57] Louis Fischer remarked in an interview with the author that "Chicherin was enraged over the Shakhti Affair, but the GPU had its own views and intentions." [58] These statements indicate that agencies of government advocated different policies toward foreigners; the Commissariat for Foreign Affairs was aware of the effect that poor treatment of foreigners might have on diplomatic and trade relations with the West, while the GPU subordinated everything to the internal considerations characteristic of a closed society.

The trials appeared to serve the domestic propaganda ends of arousing the Russian people to the potential danger of foreigners and of explaining to Russian citizens the failures of Soviet industry to fulfill its quotas. Duranty believed that much of the damage and loss which led to the Shakhti Affair was due to the fact that the Russians mistakenly considered themselves competent to install and manipulate intricate German machinery without German aid. The American Embassy in Berlin supported this conclusion, saying that it was known that German engineers found that the machinery installed in the Donetz without their help was "in a deplorable state due to the neglect of workmen and more especially to mismanagement higher up." [59] While John Littlepage believed that a great deal of industrial sabotage, of which some could not be carried on "without the complicity of highly-placed Communist managers," was going on in Soviet mines, he did agree that it would call for a "very wise man indeed to determine [the difference] between so-called wrecking and plain ignorance." [60] The police were so anxious to make a good showing that, said Littlepage, they reported every little blunder in every industry as evidence of sabotage.

A second crisis involving foreigners, which served an internal propaganda function, took place in 1933, when several representatives of the British firm Metropolitan Vickers were implicated in charges of sabotage in electric power plants. They were accused of gathering secret information relating to defense and utilizing it to the detriment of the state, and of bribing certain employees of the power stations to carry out counterrevolutionary wrecking activities.[61] One of the British engineers arrested, Allen Monkhouse, believed that Metro-Vickers was used as a scapegoat because it "was one of the few organizations which had engineers working in electric power supply undertakings in every important industrial area of the U.S.S.R." [62] Thus Soviet errors in the electric power industry could be concealed by imputing such errors to a conspiracy by a foreign firm working in the Soviet Union.

I have already described the excessive publicity and other attention given to foreigners. Through these excesses, the Soviet regime built up in Communist circles the reputation of individual foreigners as great social thinkers, sympathetic to the current of world history represented by Soviet Communism. But once these individuals became critical of the Soviet Union, the wrath of the Soviet and international Communist propaganda machine descended on their heads, and a deliberate campaign was begun to discredit them before pro-Soviet audiences.

A good example of this strategy is the case of André Gide. Long known for his pro-Soviet sympathies, Gide returned from the Soviet Union in 1936 sadly disillusioned with Communist society. He had courteously remained quiet about his first doubts while still in Russia, expressing his true feelings only after he returned to France.[63] Books about the Soviet Union written by Communist sympathizers during 1936 and 1937 devoted their last chapters to attacks on Gide.[64] According to a former Russian citizen, who was told the story by a Comintern official, Soviet authorities urged the German-Jewish novelist Lion Feuchtwanger to write a favorable book about the Soviet Union, specifically challenging Gide's conclusions.[65] The attacks of Soviet and Communist-appointed critics were so severe that Gide felt forced to write another book explaining again why he could no longer praise the Soviet Union.[66] The Soviet citizens who were aware of what was going on during this literary battle cynically watched the spectacle of Feuchtwanger's visit to the Soviet Union and his interview with Stalin. A satirical verse on Feuchtwanger and Gide circulated in official circles.[67]

Treatment similar to that given Gide after his reversal of position was given Panait Istrati, a Balkan author, once regarded by Soviet officials as a person who would refute "capitalist lies." Such cases suggest that intellectuals were regarded by the Soviet regime as useful to them in many different ways but not as intellectuals with critical faculties and the ability to make realistic, perceptive appraisals. Any favored intellectual who suddenly became a critic of the regime was then discredited in an attempt to prevent other people from following his example. Essentially, regardless of the actual views and opinions and actions of foreigners, their presence in the Soviet Union was used for propaganda purposes.

7

The Realization of Soviet Objectives: Success or Failure?

We have examined the Soviet objectives leading to a policy of encouraging foreigners to visit and work in the USSR and the various techniques and controls utilized to manipulate their experiences while there. Now we must assess the success or failure of the Soviet regime in its endeavors both to disseminate a favorable image of the country and to utilize the technical skills of foreign specialists and workers. There are several degrees of success. First, the regime could have successfully projected a positive image of Soviet society and thereby secured some or all of its foreign policy objectives. Second, the Soviet Union could have satisfactorily met its goal of disseminating a positive image yet failed to achieve some or all of its foreign objectives because of factors beyond its control. Third, there might have been no way to prove a cause-and-effect relationship between the projection of a favorable image and the attainment of particular foreign objectives. Fourth, failure to project a favorable image might or might not have affected the attainment of foreign objectives.

THE IMAGE OF THE "REVOLUTIONARY FORTRESS"

As we have seen in Chapter 2, the positive image that the Soviet regime wanted to disseminate was multi-faceted. Basically, it was

175

the image of a dynamic, non-radical society which promised a better future for all its citizens. Toward the visiting labor rank and file, however, the Soviet regime projected instead the image of Soviet society as a "revolutionary fortress" of the world proletariat.

First, the regime hoped to promulgate the image of a thriving society owned and managed by the working classes. Soviet authorities attempted to persuade visiting workers that the spread of Communism to their own societies would produce similar conditions, but that the chances for the spread of Communism rested first of all with the defense of the Soviet Union as the home base. Thus, the dissemination of the particular image of a successful USSR served the broader Soviet purpose of obtaining worker support for defense of the country. Evidence of some success in attaining this objective is to be found in the resolutions and reports put out by the delegations, and in a report published by the Communist Youth International, asserting that the reports of young British Social Democrats aided the formation of the "United Front of the British young workers against the attacks of British Imperialism against the Soviet Union." [1]

However, since so much of the evidence testifying to Soviet success in projecting the image of the "revolutionary fortress" was obvious Communist propaganda, it is impossible to assess with certainty the extent to which each member of the labor delegations actually agreed to defend the Soviet Union. It is possible that the USSR successfully projected the image and obtained positive support for the idea that defense of the home base was necessary. But the question of whether or not the workers would have actually fought for the Soviet Union is moot, since the invasion which had been feared by Russia did not materialize until 1941 and under conditions far different from those imagined during the earlier war scares.

A second objective that it was hoped might be served by this image of Russia more directly concerned the expansion of Soviet Communism. The Communist authorities hoped that the visiting workers would see with their own eyes that the proletariat was capable of building a new type of society, and would return home ready to work for the overthrow of their own governments and the installation of the dictatorship of the proletariat. Again, the resolutions and reports put out by the delegations imply that the projection of the image was successful. Workers pledged to work for a united international labor movement under Profintern control, an accomplishment which the Soviet regime believed would assist the expansion of Communism. But the uncertainty remains.

Communist authorities stressed the activities of the delegations after they returned home as evidence that the messages of the delegates were reaching large groups of workers. The report of the Tenth Congress of the British Communist party mentioned that the members of a visiting delegation had addressed over 2,000 meetings, at which approximately 250,000 people were present.[2] Twenty-two thousand copies of the sixpenny report of the delegation were said to have been sold. Members of a co-operative who visited Russia gave positive reports to members of their organization upon their return. A special report of the Communist party noted that the Co-op Department of the party had, through these activities, extended its influence into the Co-operative movement.[3] A report by the British National Committee of the Friends of Soviet Russia described similar events in France, with returning French delegates addressing more than a thousand meetings of trade unions, Socialist clubs, and co-operatives.[4]

The Communist International asserted that the Czech Communist party was able to utilize in the press the reports of a Czech delegation of co-operative members. It further asserted that visits and reports by both the British and Czech delegations were most useful for Communist propaganda among the masses because a majority of the delegates were known to be Social Democrats.[5] A Communist Youth International report stated that the publications of the various delegations "gave a great impetus to the [young] workers to follow the example of the Russian young workers and to carry on the United Front at home. . . ."[6]

In Britain, the publication said, the reports of young Social Democratic workers strengthened the left wing in the Guild of Youth, the youth organization of the Independent Labour Party.

All these statements seem to indicate that delegates returning home from the Soviet Union carried out successfully the role that the Soviet regime had hoped they would play—dissemination of a particular image of the Soviet Union as part of a technique to expand Communist influence among Social Democratic workers. However, again it must be stressed that it is difficult to make a definitive judgment on the success of Soviet objectives solely on an examination of Communist sources. The evidence indicates that many of the delegation reports and resolutions were not produced by the entire delegation, but by the Communist fraction, or by the Communist International, or by one of the Communist parties. Furthermore, criticism of the composition of labor delegations is also found within Communist sources. This criticism leads one to believe that even though the Soviet regime might have successfully projected a positive image to delegates, because of the make-up of some delegations, the extension of Communist influence was only partially achieved.

We have already indicated the great attention paid to composition of the delegations by the Communist parties and national chapters of the Communist-front Friends of the Soviet Union, in order to suggest that workers of all types and affiliations expressed interest in the Soviet Union.[7] All the organizations involved in the selection process attempted to mask the fact that they were under Communist control but their attempts were not adequate to prevent their coming under fire from Communist authorities. Local front bodies were warned to refrain from other party activities. The Friends of the Soviet Union in the British Dominions as well as the British chapter itself were criticized for a "tendency to forget on far too many an occasion the super-Party character of the FSU and its work."[8] Local units of the American chapter were criticized for committing such errors as establishing joint headquarters with Communist party sections, campaigning for Communist political candidates, and participating in Communist election rallies.[9] Two members of the British Committee of FSU resigned in 1929 because the secretary of the Committee was appointed by the Communist party without consulting anyone on the Committee. They also resented the fact that the secretary used circulars which tended to identify the organization with the Communist party and Minority Movement.[10]

The Friends of the Soviet Union were also criticized for appealing to a narrow public. During a meeting in Moscow, the national secretaries of FSU chapters were told that as long as their organizations had the reputation of being branches of the Communist party, they would appeal only to Communists and sympathizers.[11] Their work was criticized for duplicating the work of the party; they were told to seek new audiences. However, despite the continued criticism, the organizations never seemed to develop into the mass societies they were supposed to be. O. Piatnitskii ascribed the failure of such organizations to the excessive centralism which existed in all Communist mass work and to the failure of Communist parties to consolidate their influence.[12]

Judging from all these criticisms, one doubts whether the traditional labor movement was greatly influenced by the activities of these labor delegations. Evidence indicates that in many cases it was impossible to get delegations with non-Communist as well as Communist members. A report of Comintern activities criticized the French Communist party for having sent a delegation of co-operative members entirely composed of Communists which, the report said, "could not produce the desired effect." [13] The report laid the blame on inadequate preparation and the small amount of Communist infiltration into the co-operative movement.

The Moscow conference of the national FSU secretaries also criticized the errors in mass work that resulted in too few delegates being elected directly from the factories, and too few representatives of important industries being included in the delegations. The publication of the Profintern pointed out that

the revolutionary press, particularly the press of the revolutionary trade union opposition, practically without exception underestimated the work of the delegations. "The question of election
of delegates, of their visit to the USSR, of the return of the
delegates and their reports," said the article, "was insufficiently
brought out in the revolutionary trade-union press." [14] The article
argued that the Communist parties were not taking sufficient
advantage of the campaigns of the returned delegates to recruit
Social Democrats, syndicalists, unorganized workers, and other
members of the delegations into the Friends of the Soviet Union
and the revolutionary trade unions. It went on to say, "The movement must make the sending of delegations, their election, their
reports on their return, a political campaign to win the masses
from the influence of social-fascism and win new sections of the
working class for Communism." [15] All of this indicates that even
though the Soviet regime achieved some success in indoctrinat-
ing the members of the labor delegations, the delegations were
not representative enough of the entire labor movement to have
much effect on extending Communist influence beyond certain
radical labor circles.

Another reason for the failure of the Soviet regime to attain
its broad objective among the rank and file concerns the problem
of the "objective conditions." Karl Kreibich, in *Communist International,* had spoken about both the objective and subjective
preliminary conditions necessary before a successful Communist
revolution could take place. The objective condition was the
deepening crisis of capitalism; the subjective condition was the
recognition by the proletariat that the only way to its salvation
lay through social revolution.[16] The absence of the objective
condition in the United States, even during the Great Depression,
has been pointed out by Irving Howe and Lewis Coser. Ultra-
leftism and the "united front from below" never had any real
relation to American life; the politicization by the Communist
party of every bread-and-butter struggle of American workers
led to a rejection of Communist leadership by rank-and-file labor.
Howe and Coser remark that "so self-destructive were the Com-

munist policies in the trade unions during the Third Period [1928–1934] that even the Party press had occasionally to acknowledge the more glaring stupidities." [17]

Thus, one must conclude that with regard to rank-and-file labor the Soviet regime probably achieved some small success in projection of the image of the USSR as a "revolutionary fortress," but because of the composition of the delegations visiting Russia and the situation of the labor movement in the West, the favorable image did not contribute, despite Communist assertions of success, to extending Communist influence in the traditional labor movement.

THE IMAGE OF THE "GOOD SOCIETY"

The second facet of the image the Soviet regime wished to disseminate was that of a non-revolutionary society where laborers were better off than elsewhere. They hoped that the image of a "good society" for workers would appeal more than the image of a "fortress of world revolution" to the few labor leaders whom the regime was able to attract and to certain groups of intellectuals interested in the cause of labor. By toning down the revolutionary emphasis, the regime hoped to decrease the distrust of Soviet objectives displayed by the labor leadership, thus facilitating the breaking down of barriers to Communist penetration of the movement. The regime also hoped to convince those interested in labor conditions that recognition of and stable diplomatic relations with Soviet Russia would be desirable.

The reports produced by several delegations of labor leaders and intellectuals testify to Soviet success in disseminating the view that labor was well off in the Soviet Union. The report of the British Trades Union delegation of 1924 concluded that, in the opinion of the delegates, the housing, education, and supplementary advantages that the real wages of the Russian worker provided were "in many respects better than those obtained by labour elsewhere in Europe." [18] The delegation also asserted in its report that "the Russian workers are the ruling class of Russia. They enjoy the rights of a ruling class." [19] The report of the 1927

American trade union delegation to the Soviet Union claimed that "it is not an exaggeration to state that in no country since the world war have the industrial wage earners made the relative progress which has recently been made in Russia." [20]

The reports of the American and British delegations apparently had some effect on public opinion. Meno J. Lovenstein declared that the reports of the British and American trade union delegations "constituted milestones in the change of opinion" in the world toward more balanced attitudes regarding Russia.[21] Soviet sources attributed the formation of the Anglo-Russian Committee of Trade Unions to the visit of the British delegation, and they attached great significance to the delegation's report.[22] The Anglo-Russian Committee lasted only for a short while, however, dissolving in 1927 when Britain broke diplomatic relations with the Soviet Union.

The individual dissents to the American trade union delegation report, and evidence we have already examined which pointed to the manipulation of both the British and American reports by Communist authorities leads one to question whether the dissemination of an image of a society favorable to labor was entirely successful. Interestingly enough, the Soviet authorities admitted that the British delegation, which represented the Trades Union Congress, had come to the Soviet Union with its mind completely made up about trade union unity.[23] Negative comments about conditions in the Soviet Union, made by labor leaders such as Walter Citrine and David Dubinsky after returning from their individual trips, reinforces the doubts.[24]

Because the AFL regarded the American delegation as hostile to the best interests of labor, it is doubtful whether the delegation's report did anything to decrease that organization's distrust of the USSR. However, the report probably did have some impact among intellectuals who professed an interest in labor's position in the world. Although the American delegation argued in favor of diplomatic recognition of the USSR it is not definitely known whether the report had any influence on government policy. To some extent then, the Soviet regime was successful in promoting an image of a society beneficial to labor, but it was probably more successful in influencing intellectuals than labor leaders. In Britain, because for a short time those favoring closer relations between Soviet and British labor movements dominated the Trades Union Congress, Soviet intentions were under less suspicion in the traditional labor unions than in America.

In this context, the Soviet regime attempted through the use of personal testimony to combat the rumors of famine in Russia after the massive Soviet collectivization drive in 1930–31.[25] Through the use of such propaganda techniques as distributing films of a picnic feast between foreign workers and pseudo-Volga Germans and treating Friends of the Soviet Union delegations to sumptuous feasts, the Soviet regime hoped to demonstrate that the rumors were false. They were especially aided in this endeavor by the assertions of George Bernard Shaw, who bragged that, although his friends loaded him with provisions, warning him that there was no food in Russia, he threw them away in Poland before he entered the Soviet Union because he knew that the talk of famine was all a lie.[26] Of course, the Soviet authorities responded by seeing that fresh vegetables followed Shaw wherever he stopped in the Soviet Union.[27]

THE IMAGE OF THE "FATHERLAND OF THE WORKING CLASS"

A third facet of the image the regime wished to disseminate depicted the USSR as a land of opportunity for all foreign workers and more specifically a place of asylum for those members of the proletariat who had to flee their own countries because of political persecution. By publicizing the activities of foreign workers in the Soviet Union, the regime hoped to attract the attention of other workers outside the country, especially those dissatisfied with their present positions. The idyllic conditions of labor in the Soviet Union, as portrayed in the material put out by the Co-operative Publishing Society of Foreign Workers in the Soviet Union and disseminated through the publications of Communist-front organizations and the advertising of Soviet trade delegations, probably convinced a number of foreigners that the Soviet Union was indeed a land of opportunity, and many flocked to Russia with great hope. However, once in the Soviet Union, they found the food poor, the working hours long, and the standard of living generally very low.

The conditions of the political émigrés belied the image of "the fatherland." Many foreign observers testified that groups like the Schutzbunder were welcomed to the Soviet Union, fêted, and given the best that the Soviet regime had to offer foreigners. But after the émigrés had served the initial propaganda ends of the Soviet regime by allowing the USSR to be portrayed as a haven for the oppressed, they were subjected to the same conditions as Soviet workers. As we have seen, some who were able to avoid Soviet prison camps or recruitment into the International Brigade decided to return to Austria, despite the knowledge that long prison terms awaited them there.[28]

The difficulty that the Soviet Union had in integrating foreign workers into Soviet society testifies to the failure of the regime to convince foreign workers to submit voluntarily to Soviet plans. While the *Moscow Daily News* boasted of the large number of foreign workers who were involved in Russian activities and organizations, letters to the editor criticizing the poor management of activities for foreign workers continued to appear. During 1930, 1931, and 1932, the periodical *Partiinoe Stroitel'stvo* reprinted resolutions adopted by the Central Committee of the All-Union Communist party criticizing deficiencies in party and trade union work among foreigners. An article appearing in February, 1931, asserted: "We, the Party organizations first and foremost, did nothing towards explaining to the Americans what the proletarian dictatorship actually signified, what were the conditions of our constitution, what the five-year plan represented, what were the tasks of Americans in the U.S.S.R., etc." [29] There were claims that Communists paid insufficient attention to political and educational work among foreign workers. Resolutions accused the trade unions of having done little to draw foreign members into labor union work, socialist emulation, and shock brigades.[30] An article in September, 1932, cited what it called an "absolutely erroneous opinion that foreign workmen cannot understand our difficulties because they are 'petty-bourgeois,' " and called this a "defeatist attitude." The article went on to say that local organizations must develop further mass political work in order to help foreign workmen rid themselves of the vestiges of petty-bourgeois attitudes.[31]

One of the activities that the *Moscow Daily News* boasted about was the involvement of foreigners in Soviet elections. However, other evidence casts doubt on the extent of such activity. A worker at Stalingrad stated that in order to avoid trouble a great number of Americans had registered to vote, but that they did not actually take part in election meetings.[32] This comment was confirmed by an assistant to Walter Duranty, who reported that most workers did not regard the campaign seriously, since it was quite evident that candidates had been selected in advance—on the basis of their acceptability to Soviet officials.[33]

While much of the criticism cited above is of Soviet organizations for not performing their work among foreigners correctly, it also suggests that many of the foreigners refused to co-operate with the plans of the authorities. Soviet confirmation of the fact that attempts to involve foreigners in election activity ended in failure at Stalingrad indicates more directly that the foreigners resisted integration.[34] The large number of individuals who tried to get in touch with the American Embassy to re-establish their citizenship, once the Embassy was opened in 1934, is also evidence that Soviet efforts to integrate foreigners were not successful. Apparently the image of Russia as a land of opportunity for foreign workers had little appeal to those foreign workers who spent extended periods within the country.

THE IMAGE OF THE PROGRESSIVE, HUMANITARIAN SOCIETY

The fourth facet of a positive image of the Soviet Union depicted the country as a humanitarian society—the chief world center of all progress, spiritual cultivation, and enlightenment, which enabled all classes to enjoy a better life. And the Soviet regime reaped its richest propaganda harvest, especially among intellectuals and middle-class bourgeoisie, with this image of itself. Soviet success here rested on three factors: first, the preconceptions held by foreign intellectuals about the Soviet Union; second, these intellectuals' vulnerability to Soviet propaganda techniques which made them feel important; and third, their limitations as critics in attempting to evaluate the situation.

The tragedy of the intellectuals during the first third of the twentieth century, their disillusionment with Western civilization and their attraction to Communism and Soviet Russia, has been well documented in recent critical studies as well as in their own memoirs.[35] Even before the Great Depression intellectuals had condemned modern Western society for failing to provide ideals to which they could dedicate their lives. They were attracted by the idea that "the Communists mean it." As Irving Howe and Lewis Coser put it, there was "belief in some ultimate Reality that the Communists alone had been able to penetrate; the implicit assumption that by adopting the pose of ruthlessness the Party was proving its claim to a deeper seriousness."[36] The Soviet Union seemed to be a gigantic social laboratory, operating on the principles of human dignity and equality and creating "a new civilization" which would benefit mankind. Raymond Aron, speaking of the French intellectuals and Soviet Russia, asks: "How could the progressive intellectuals refuse to offer their talents to a State which proclaims the true doctrine, to the building up of a society which conforms with the hopes of revolutionary rationalism and which is generous to experts and men of letters—*providing they obey?*"[37]

One of the most sensational cases of conversion was that of Sidney and Beatrice Webb, who believed that in Communism they had found a new civilization. To the Webbs, Marcel Liebman has commented, a planned and orderly society was an essential element of Socialism; hence they were pleased with Russian planning, inaugurated as a system with the first Five-Year Plan in 1928, because this was one of their suggestions which appeared to be well on the road to realization in at least one country.[38] Malcolm Muggeridge has said of the Webbs and people like them: "The people who came to the Soviet Union wanted so passionately to see certain things in being that they could not see anything different. They were not liars. You just could not change their minds with facts." [39]

Men like John Dewey and George S. Counts, who before their respective Soviet trips had not succeeded in getting the American school system to adopt their ideas on modern education, were amazed to find many of these ideas being accepted in the Soviet Union, at least in several of the model schools they were taken to see. Thus, when Dewey was questioned about being shown models, he answered that they were "show-places in the sense that they were well worthy of being shown. I hope they were the best of their kind, so as to be representative of what the new regime is trying to do; there is enough mediocrity everywhere without travelling thousands of miles to see it." [40] Burton Holmes reacted in much the same way to his tour: "I did not ask to see the slums. I do not seek the slums of other foreign cities. Why should I seek them here? I see enough of dilapidation and poverty all over town." [41] Thus, the mental outlook of the visitors was conducive to the appeal of the Soviet concept of "Socialist Realism." These people were fascinated by the idea of planning for the future and did not care to see what they believed was solely the heritage of the Tsarist past.

Vast numbers of the visitors came to see what they wanted to see, to find corroboration of views previously held and opinions previously expressed. They looked through prisms which filtered in only acceptable visions. They were searching so desperately for an ideal that they rarely questioned what they were shown. This is the only possible explanation, for example, for Frankford Williams, the American psychiatrist who wrote several books and articles on the absence of mental illness in the Soviet Union (e.g., *Russia Fights Neuroses*) when in reality the atmosphere created by the accelerated tempo of industrialization was not conducive to sound mental health.[42]

Their overwhelming interest in the Five-Year Plan and production percentages, in a post-1929 world marked by economic dislocation, also caused many intellectuals to overlook the more oppressive political features of the Soviet system. Economic democracy appeared to be a more important value than political democracy, and the intellectuals were ready to accept the Soviet class analysis of Western political democracy. Thus, many intellectuals agreed with the conclusions of the British Trades Union delegation report, that although the dictatorship of the proletariat under the Communist party denied in principle individual political liberty, "government authority by a minority can be judged best by results. It is with these results, not with the political philosophy of Russian Communism, that these reports are mainly concerned." [43]

Yet some people with another type of preconception were also vulnerable to Soviet propaganda techniques. Many of the most virulently anti-Soviet foreigners left the Soviet Union less vigorously opposed than they had been when they arrived, after seeing that the Soviet Union could not be as bad as some of the stories told about it abroad. The critical visitor was, of course, especially apt to modify his opinion after being the recipient of privileged treatment.

Intellectuals, then, were influenced by both positive and negative preconceptions. They were also influenced by propaganda techniques which made them feel important, and this second major factor cannot be underestimated. To an objective observer, the Soviet granting of contracts and cash advances to mediocre authors for the publication of unfinished books and articles would seem likely to have aroused at least some suspicion of Soviet motives. Arthur Koestler intimated, however, that the vanity of the budding author quickly dissipated all suspicions. [44]

Most foreigners, in addition to their preconceptions and vulnerability to favorable treatment, lacked the tools by which to evaluate objectively Soviet society. Most of them did not have a knowledge of the Russian language or of Russian life under Tsarism. Since, as I have suggested earlier, some of them had never seen factories or crèches before, they lacked even nonspecialized measuring rods by which to evaluate those observed in the Soviet Union. A diplomat at the American Legation in Riga, speaking of an American business delegation which visited the Soviet Union in 1929, remarked that "it is sufficient to say that if some of the delegates quoted had prepared themselves for their visit by even a cursory study of economic conditions in Soviet Russia, and if they had been able carefully to study the Soviet press during the course of their visit, they would probably have expressed themselves somewhat differently, even though desirous of appearing appreciative to their hosts." [45] Paul Douglas, speaking of the American trade union delegation of 1927, commented that "they did not know what weak spots to investigate." [46]

The desire for comfort also proved to be an effective check on critical investigation. If one were persistent enough to gain the privilege of independent travel, it was possible to get a truer picture of the Soviet Union, but most tourists were glad to submit to their guides without a fuss. Jay Darling wrote that "every traveller in Russia becomes aware, the moment he wanders from the tender care of the 'Intourist,' that something devastating has happened to the management of the magnificent old hotels. . . ." [47] Intourist brought reasonable comfort to travel and so most people stayed with Intourist.

Soviet success in projecting a positive image of itself as a humanitarian society brought the regime many dividends. Libraries and bookstores were filled with books by prestigious authors who extolled the great successes of the Soviet Union. The *Soviet Union Review* cited a number of books yielding "no ammunition for the fantastic stories circulated in the United States that production in the Soviet Union comes from convict or forced labor." [48] The editor of a collection of statements by foreign visitors regarded a book like *Dreiser Looks at Russia* as a weapon in the struggle then going on in the literary world where the "enemies of the Soviet state" were using literature in order to defame the Soviet Union.[49]

Other dividends for the Soviet Union included the willingness of prominent intellectuals who had visited the Soviet Union to lend their names to such Communist-front organizations in America as the Friends of the Soviet Union, the Cultural Relations Society, the League of Professional Writers, the League Against War and Fascism, and to their foreign counterparts. In 1935 a Congress of Peace and Friendship with the USSR was held in London. Skillfully steered by a few competent Communist party members, it was attended by a galaxy of well-known individuals from almost all walks of life.[50] Members of the scientific and artistic professions, just returned from short tours of the Soviet Union and convinced that Russia was successfully implementing the private dreams of scientists and artists, addressed the assembly. Nathan Glazer noted similar reactions among intellectuals on the American scene (to a lesser extent his remarks also pertain to Western Europe). "The Communist Party," according to Glazer, "had always spoken of itself as the 'vanguard of the proletariat' though it had enormous difficulties in realizing this extravagant slogan. But, from the middle thirties to the early fifties, the period of its greatest size and influence, the Party was rather more successful in becoming the 'vanguard of the intellectual and professional workers.'"[51]

Thus Soviet success in disseminating a positive image among many foreign intellectuals and professions enhanced the reputation of the USSR and Communism within these circles. In the United States the USSR, perhaps, scored a more specific victory: that of helping to create a more favorable atmosphere for official recognition of the Soviet Union. It is true that many diplomatic sources credit increased Japanese aggression in Asia and the resurgence of Germany as the factors that motivated recognition.[52] According to this interpretation, the American government hoped that Japanese aggression could be halted if both the United States and Russia maintained a common front. However, the success of the Soviet Union in managing to disseminate to intellectuals and businessmen the image of itself as a nonradical, dynamic, and humanitarian society (as we will see) contributed to a climate of opinion in which the decision to recognize Russia, even if based on other circumstances, was facilitated.

Not all intellectuals and members of the middle class were deluded about the nature of Soviet society. Without more information on individual personalities, however, it is hard to determine why some intellectuals did succumb to Soviet propaganda techniques and some did not. Many did at one time but realized later the extent of their delusions. The evidence of such conversions and eventual disillusionments is available in the large body of material known as the "Literature of Disenchantment." [53] Perhaps those people who had to actually work in the Soviet Union under conditions marked by inefficiency and restrictions saw through the image of the progressive society. Journalists like Eugene Lyons and William Chamberlin, who were initially quite pro-Soviet, underwent radical changes in opinion after living in Russia.

One reason for disillusion was the prosaic but common reaction to the drabness and inefficiency of Soviet life. Many who visited and lived in the USSR complained about the inefficiency of Soviet organizations which catered to foreigners. The American students who attended the Anglo-American Summer School at Moscow University unanimously criticized the administrative arrangements and the management of the project in Moscow.[54] They believed that administration was complicated by the failure of the Russian authorities to make adequate preparations, thus preventing the smooth functioning of classes and excursions for several days after the Summer School was scheduled to open. For example, they learned that many of the professors were uninformed of the services they were expected to render the school until the very week it opened. The students believed that "none of them [professors] had been given an adequate understanding of the type of information which would be most acceptable to their classes." [55]

While the activities of VOKS as they were described on paper seemed impressive, there were more than a few complaints about the actual operation of the agency. One visiting journalist described his contact with a representative of VOKS:

> I found her very agreeable and willing and went away thinking life would be made easy for me. I soon found, however, that the Society for Cultural Relations was practically useless. All my suggestions came to naught, and I could only see under their auspices what I could just as well see without their assistance.[56]

Professor Samuel Harper complained in 1932 that VOKS not only failed to help him obtain the schedule of interviews he wanted but also prevented him from going ahead on his own.[57] Harper claimed that as a result of this failure to secure for him the contacts he had requested, he did not see many Soviet officials. The main criticism of VOKS appeared to be its slowness in operation. One British economist acknowledged that only her persistence netted her any help from the organization.[58]

While some people were annoyed by the inefficiency, others were more disturbed by the restrictive nature of the regime— the many places they found closed to investigation, the controls on genuine contact with the Soviet population, and the censorship. Some of the foreign engineers and journalists saw evidence of forced labor which they refused to keep silent about. Those who had contact with Russian citizens like the engineer Walter Rukeyser and Dr. Samuel Harper expressed anguish at their friends' misfortunes in the hands of the GPU. Rukeyser wondered why the GPU demonstrated its methods to him shortly before he and his wife returned to the United States.[59] Individuals who were ready to forsake comfort for independent investigation became irritated at the negative characteristics of group tourism. Those who were able to undertake independent investigation and travel were able to compare what could be seen on one's own initiative with what was shown to members of guided tours. Journalists and foreign specialists were in the best position to perceive the extent of the gap between image and reality in the Soviet Union.

Finally, a much smaller group of foreign visitors refused to acknowledge that the Soviet Union had made any type of progress. These people were so violently anti-Soviet from the beginning that their preconceptions blinded them from seeing another aspect of Soviet reality—that progress was being achieved, slowly and painfully, in the Soviet Union.

THE IMAGE OF A PROMISING COMMERCIAL OPPORTUNITY

Soviet success with foreign businessmen was based on a somewhat different constellation of factors. To the business community, the Soviet Union attempted to appear as an economically thriving society with potential as a market for the products of capitalist industry and as a field for application of Western industrial techniques. This particular image appealed to many Western businessmen in their search for profit, especially after 1929 when domestic markets and job opportunities diminished. The fact that high Soviet officials were willing to talk with visiting businessmen lent credibility to Soviet intentions, and so the Soviet Union was highly successful in projecting the image.

Beginning in 1929, relations between the Soviet Union and foreign business circles rose to new heights, resulting in a sharp rise in Soviet import of goods necessary for industrialization and in the signing of many technical assistance contracts.[60] A 1930 list published by Amtorg listed forty-three American companies which had concluded technical assistance agreements with the regime or who were doing contract work for it. The list included such firms as Du Pont de Nemours, Ford Motors, International General Electric, RCA, and Sperry Gyroscope. German firms included AEG (Allgemeine Elektrizitaets Gesellschaft), Orga-Metall, and Drusag (Deutsch-Russischen Saatbau A.G.,). England was represented by Metropolitan-Vickers.[61]

While trade increased with Great Britain and the United States during 1929 and 1930, long-term credit from these countries was for the most part unobtainable. However, in 1931, the Soviet regime did obtain a long-term credit arrangement with Germany for the purchase of industrial equipment, which resulted in the regime's favoring to a much greater extent than before imports from Germany at the expense of other Western nations until Soviet imports from all countries declined in 1932.[62]

The Soviet regime desired economic assistance for its own sake, but Soviet authorities also hoped that closer economic relations would lead to the resumption of diplomatic relations with Great Britain and recognition by the United States. The regime seemed willing during 1929 and 1930 to trade with the United States without pressing too strongly for recognition, although visiting business delegations were told that the potential of the Soviet market would only reveal itself completely after the renewal of relations or recognition. Nevertheless, the degree of influence exercised by the business communities in Great Britain and the United States on diplomatic policy toward Russia is difficult to determine. For example, one cannot establish a definite cause-and-effect relationship between the visit of British businessmen to the Soviet Union in 1929 and the re-establishment of British-Soviet relations six months later. It is a fact that G. L. Piatakov attempted to convince the delegates that development of Russia as a market was dependent on the restoration of relations. The six-month interval between the visit and the resumption of diplomatic relations provides some grounds for thinking that the favorable report of the British delegation had some influence on the newly formed Labour government, but it must be added that this government had long favored the resumption of diplomatic relations with the Soviet Union.

The influence of business circles on the decision of the United States in 1933 to recognize the Soviet Union is even harder to assess. The American-Russian Chamber of Commerce and other business groups played an active part in the drive for recognition by the United States. The Board of Directors of the Chamber, which had opposed recognition in 1926, passed a resolution in May, 1933, reversing its stand. The resolution cited the "growing importance of the U.S.S.R. as a world power," and stated that the American government should support American businesses abroad, for the situation was such that they had to attain "equal opportunity with their European competitors or be reconciled to a very minor position in this trade for an indefinite time in the future with resultant incalculable loss to American business and labor." [63] By 1933, many American businessmen were well acquainted with Russia, having helped it through the first stages of its Five Year Plan, and most believed that, despite difficulties, it was possible to do business with the Russians.

As we have seen, diplomatic sources played down the role of the business community in the recognition decision. The historian Robert Browder concludes that although the United States government was not misled by the extravagant predictions of the Soviet regime and the American business community about increased commercial relations after recognition, it made no attempt before granting recognition to correct the exaggerated expectations of the public.[64] Although Moscow continued to use trade as bait, according to Browder, her real interest lay in a political rapprochement to meet threats from the Far East, an interest which by the time of recognition in 1933 coincided with the policy interests of the United States.[65] But American businessmen and intellectuals did help to create a climate of opinion favorable to the recognition of the Soviet Union.

However appealing the image of the market potential of the USSR was to visiting businessmen, foreign specialists who worked in the Soviet Union reacted with mixed feelings to the image of the country as a field for the application of Western industrial techniques. Although foreign specialists were specifically invited to the Soviet Union by top government officials and were given privileged accommodations, features internal to Soviet society created many problems.[66] The atmosphere of fear generated by the Shakhti and Metro-Vickers trials did not support the image of a society which welcomed foreign technical assistance.[67] Although many important Soviet officials recognized the need for foreign assistance and welcomed foreign specialists, other high officials, especially those associated with the police apparatus, placed a higher priority on sealing the society off from foreign contacts. This created friction among Soviet officials and between Soviet officials and foreign specialists. Its most dire result was the accusation that foreign specialists participated in sabotage against the regime, a situation which did not foster an atmosphere conducive to the best utilization of foreign technical experience.

The Shakhti trial involved some German engineers associated with AEG, a firm whose head was the earliest and most influential advocate of business with the Russians; it caused a rupture in German-Soviet trade relations until the verdict cleared the Germans.[68] The second trial involving foreigners concerned the firm of Metro-Vickers; the conviction of two British engineers in 1933 was followed by a British embargo on Russian goods until both men had been released.[69] There is some evidence to indicate that General Electric and several other companies as well ordered their engineers to leave Russia after this incident, since they were unable to get any assurance that failures in plant operations would not be called political sabotage.[70] However, one man who worked with General Electric declared that the firm ceased activities in Soviet Russia around that time because its work was completed.[71]

There seems to be a difference in opinion about the cause for removal and dismissal of foreign engineers after mid-1931. The Soviet authorities insisted frequently that they were dismissing only those who had misrepresented their qualifications.[72] Other engineers agreed with this statement for the most part, but did indicate that several qualified engineers were let go after their contracts were signed because changes were made in Soviet development patterns.[73] One specialist said that though the grounds given for his dismissal concerned the violation of certain Soviet directives, he was privately informed that the real reason was the reluctance on the part of the regime to make dollar payments on his contract because of a shortage of foreign currency.[74] Other engineers also testified to the breaking of contracts by the Soviet authorities because of the currency problem.[75]

Despite complaints and grievances voiced by foreign engineers and businessmen who worked in Russia or who did business with the Soviet regime, the McDonald Engineering Company's view is typical of the overall evaluation of the experience.

Our relations with the Russian Government were partly satisfactory and partly unsatisfactory. Knowledge of the unsatisfactory experience might be of assistance in knowing the point on which to be on one's guard in connection with commercial negotiations. I do not consider, however, that the unsatisfactory portion of our contact outweighs the satisfactory portion, nor am I unfavorable to doing business with Russia. I think simply that we should go in with our eyes open in every particular possible, and if this is done, I believe there are ways to work out satisfactory agreements.[76]

Men like Hugh Cooper who went in with their eyes open were able to arrange satisfactory conditions for their companies. The salary and accommodations for the top specialists were entirely adequate. Compared to Western society at that time, such employment offered purposeful opportunities to engineers looking for technological challenge and jobs as well as profit to businessmen.

CONCLUSION

We may say that the Soviet regime was partly successful in projecting its image among labor delegations, liberal intellectuals, and businessmen who visited Russia. For people who resided in the country for longer periods, however, the regime was far less successful because when tested against the hard facts of reality the image was found wanting.

Preconceptions which foreign visitors and residents held about Russia played an important role in influencing attitudes evolving from their experiences there. The influence of preconceptions was reinforced or weakened by other considerations. Favorable opinions which foreign writers held about Soviet civilization, for example, were reinforced by the publicity given their visits by the Soviet government and by offers of publication as well. Advantageous treatment for those visitors who started out with negative preconceptions changed their attitudes. The attitudes of those businessmen and engineers who were initally favorable to doing business with the Russians remained unaltered as long as they continued to believe that the advantages outweighed the disadvantages.

It is also interesting to note that attitudes both favorable and unfavorable changed after a lapse of time following a visit. Theodore Dreiser, for example, was somewhat critical of the Soviet Union immediately following his trip, but as time passed, he (because of other influences) revised his opinions of Soviet Russia.[77] So, although initial preconceptions may have contributed in many cases to influencing subsequent attitudes, they did not work in a total vacuum. Their impact was subject to modification by the actual experiences and influences subsequent to the visit.

In regard to the success of the Soviet regime in attaining its objectives, somewhat different conclusions may be drawn. The extent to which the short-range objective of national security was achieved was never really put to the test, since the USSR was not in danger of attack during this period. As far as the objective of stabler diplomatic relations is concerned, visitors to the Soviet Union did contribute to a climate of opinion abroad which would tolerate such relations. The more material objectives of the regime, such as the obtaining of technical assistance, limited credit, and increased trade, were quite successfully realized. The realization of Soviet objectives in utilizing foreign specialists and workers was less successful because of obstacles posed by the Soviet political climate and administrative inefficiency.

The long-term objective of the extension of Communism among the world proletariat was not realized through the indoctrination of labor delegations which visited the Soviet Union. These delegations were not truly representative of the labor movement in their own countries and were too closely associated with Communist organizations to have much influence among non-Communists. However, the regime was more successful among intellectuals and middle-class groups in enhancing the reputation of Communism and the Soviet regime. Under more favorable "objective" circumstances,[78] these favorable perceptions might have furthered the permanent growth of Communist influence.

With the assistance of people who went to the Soviet Union, Russia and Communism became major topics of discussion. The Soviet message was able to penetrate even into circles previously hostile to the USSR. This is not to say that in all cases people became less hostile, but there was greater access to a point of view that had previously been confined to a much smaller group of sympathizers. So, if a general aim of the Soviet Union could be said to be the penetration of non-Communist communication channels, the regime did achieve success.

8

Continuity and Change, 1924-1965

This book has been a study of the experiences of outsiders within a closed society, i.e., a society which attempts to limit contact between its citizens and foreign influences, whether foreign ideas or foreign visitors. Yet even a closed society must allow some degree of contact between its citizens and the outside world. I have here attempted to examine in depth one historical situation in which a totalitarian country opened its doors to foreigners in order to satisfy certain very important domestic and international objectives.

The main focus of my study has been on the conditions and circumstances under which this particular society encouraged foreign visitors and residents and on the mechanisms and techniques used to control the behavior of foreigners inside the country. The hypothesis was advanced that a totalitarian country would admit foreigners only for highly specialized reasons, that the ruling authorities would then attempt to minimize the psychological impact of these foreigners on a nation which knew only the image of the outer world presented by the rulers, that the authorities hoped that foreign visitors would spread a favorable image of the Soviet Union after returning home, and consequently, that they would manipulate the experiences of visitors so that they would not observe too closely the negative side of life within the country.

The findings summarized in the preceding chapters can be put in a broader perspective by comparing them with evidence from more recent periods, which may show the constant features of Soviet totalitarian policy. In 1955, after a period of eighteen years of almost total isolation, the Soviet Union once again began to encourage foreigners to visit the country. By that time the Soviet Union, although still a closed society, had undergone certain important political and economic changes. During the next several years it continued to progress in the direction of internal liberalization, although not always in a straight line. It is interesting to compare, then, some of the conclusions in this study of the treatment of foreigners in the Soviet Union during the period 1924–1937 with those reached by such Soviet specialists as Frederick Barghoorn and Edward Crankshaw, who have studied cultural diplomacy during the 'fifties and early 'sixties.[1]

The present study has indicated some of the reasons why a closed society encourages foreign visitors and residents. From an economic standpoint, the Soviet Union needed foreign credits and currency and the products of Western technology and skills. So it invited foreign businessmen and engineers to come to see for themselves the potentialities of the Soviet market and the job opportunities of Soviet industry. The regime also worked to attract large groups of semi-skilled naturalized Americans and Western Europeans, and alien residents of Russian and East European stock because they were valuable to the regime for propaganda reasons as well as for economic purposes. There were other objectives. Soviet Russia hoped that foreign visitors would serve as channels through which Communist influence would be extended throughout the West. The regime hoped that certain prominent personalities would serve as opinion leaders and help disseminate a favorable image in areas neutral or hostile toward Soviet Russia, to help achieve such objectives as recognition by the United States. At home, Soviet authorities hoped that the presence within the country of foreigners carefully manipulated by the regime would strengthen the position of the authorities in relation to the Soviet people.

Although the world situation and the position of Soviet Russia have changed considerably since the 'thirties, one finds in studying the pilgrimage to Russia, especially by citizens of underdeveloped countries in the years 1955–1964, amidst different emphases, a certain continuity of objectives. Some Soviet objectives which led to the encouragement of foreign visitors during the earlier period (such as recognition by the United States and technical assistance), had been satisfied by 1937. There have been virtually no long-term foreign residents in recent periods; at least, Barghoorn and other observers have not been able to make contact with them. Although the Soviet regime can still use the foreign currency brought by visitors, the primary purpose now served by opening the doors to foreigners is political. Eugene Lyons, long familiar with Soviet Russia, remarked: "Today the main motivation of the Soviet Union is to impress the world with its liberalism . . . the monetary side is secondary." [2] The Soviet Union is still attempting to promote a favorable image of itself, an image which stresses peaceful intentions, and social, economic, and cultural progress. During the 'twenties and 'thirties dissemination of a similar image served to help attain such specific objectives as recognition and economic aid; today such dissemination aims to promote the more general policy of peaceful coexistence.

In terms of the growth of Communist influence within the world today, a differentiation must be made between two groups of people: those living in underdeveloped parts of the world and those inhabiting the North American and non-Communist parts of Europe. During the late 'twenties and 'thirties, Soviet interest in the underdeveloped areas was minimal; Russia's attention was primarily directed toward the West. The year 1955 marked not only a major reopening of Soviet doors to foreign visitors, but also the beginning of the Soviet Union's earnest attempt to woo the people of the underdeveloped nations. By inviting foreigners from such nations to the USSR, the regime hoped to promote Soviet and Communist influence in those parts of the world.

In regard to visitors from Western Europe and the United States, recent Soviet objectives have been of a more limited nature. The Soviet Union hopes to extend its influence in the underdeveloped countries by convincing them that life in Soviet society is superior to life in the West. But the Soviet Union works to enhance its position in Europe and the United States by penetrating the walls of anti-Communism there in order to convince people that Soviet Russia truly aspires to a policy of peaceful coexistence.

Although a closed society may find it necessary to encourage foreigners to visit and settle in its country, it must manipulate them in order to promote a favorable image of itself and to minimize the psychological impact of foreigners on its citizens. The study of the 1924–1937 period has shown that the Soviet Union attempted to manipulate the experiences of visitors from the time they were invited to visit or reside in the Soviet Union until a considerable period after their return home. Within Soviet Russia, the mere presence of foreigners was used, regardless of their actual opinions, for propaganda purposes. Publicity given the activities of foreign visitors served the purposes of both internal and external propaganda.

Today, as one author puts it, "activities which for democratic societies are basically uncontrolled are within the Soviet style framework an essential ingredient of foreign relations and the conduct of diplomacy."[3] One question of considerable interest is whether the foreign visitor today has more freedom of movement than the visitor during the 'thirties. The answer varies from year to year. According to various sources, there appears to be a continuous process of tightening and liberalizing relations between foreigners and Soviet citizens.[4] Visitors have complained that many of the administrative aspects of Soviet travel exemplify inefficiency and obstructionism, and that a foreigner upon entry on Soviet soil becomes a prisoner of Intourist: "Unless he is a member of a specially-sponsored government tour, carefully worked out by top government authorities, the ordinary tourist to the Soviet Union has no status." He is treated as a "pawn of the Soviet state," rushed from place to place, given little opportunity to talk to Soviet citizens or to see things which are not part of a standard itinerary.[5] Yet other visitors have remarked that they have been amazed by the freedom allowed visitors in today's Russia. Edward Crankshaw comments on the conflict between "the image of the Yale Professor [referring to Frederick Barghoorn] who knows his Russia backwards, goes to great lengths to observe the rules and finishes up with a charge of espionage hanging over his head; or the image of the innocent tourist, who blunders about, pokes his nose into all sorts of odd corners, asks tactless questions and is never even reprimanded—even though he may go about slung like a Christmas tree with cameras and exposure meters." [6] Crankshaw believes that both images are right; however, the image of the professor is that of the real Russia, while the tourist's image is the image of display put on for his special benefit in certain selected places.

Publicity given the activities of foreign visitors within the Soviet Union still serves propaganda purposes. The Barghoorn affair probably served as a sharp warning to the Russian people not to get too friendly with foreigners. A different illustration of the use of the foreign presence is found in an article published in *Izvestia* for October 9, 1955, in which statements allegedly made by thirteen members of the House of Representatives who had visited the Soviet Union were used to create the impression that they were favorably impressed by the Soviet regime, "by the friendliness and peaceful intentions of the Soviet people, and by Soviet economic strength and progress, as well as by the value of the exchange of delegations in the strengthening of peace and the relaxation of tensions." [7] The article ended with a statement attributed to George M. Malone, one of nine senators who had accompanied the representatives. Malone, a senator not known for his friendliness to Russia, was supposed to have remarked that "the United States should concentrate on making

---

its own system work and stop interfering in other people's business." [8]

There are several differences between the people going to the Soviet Union today and those who went in earlier years that may lessen the opportunity for Communist manipulation of their experiences. The number of people going to the USSR from the West under the auspices of Soviet-controlled Communist front groups has been greatly reduced. Another great difference in foreign visitors stems from the cultural-exchange agreements negotiated by the Soviet Union with various countries, including France, Great Britain, and the United States. Under these agreements a certain number of foreign visitors from different cultural fields serve as official representatives of their governments and go to the Soviet Union to display the cultural achievements of their nations to the Russian people. The cultural-exchange programs have also provided for the exchange of scientific personnel, students, and young teachers selected by university organizations to study in the Soviet Union. While their experience abroad has not been totally free from obstruction on the part of the Soviet authorities, they have had greater opportunity to become acquainted with Soviet life than other visitors.[9] Guests of the Soviet Union under the cultural-exchange programs have been more purposeful visitors than the earlier ones. Since the visits have been arranged through negotiation on the state level, the Soviet regime realizes that every time it manipulates the experiences of these visitors for narrow political purpose, it endangers the continuation of a program it considers desirable as part of its propaganda campaign.

It can be said, using the terminology of Philip Selznick, that the Communists have used their organizational apparatus as a weapon in order to maximize their influence.[10] The study of the 1924–1937 period has illustrated that the maximum economic and psychological profit from the foreign presence in the Soviet Union could be reaped at the least cost to the integrity of the closed society by utilizing a vast assortment of organizational mechanisms. These mechanisms, characterized by specificity of function and clientele, worked to recruit foreigners to come to the Soviet Union and to control their activities within the country. A major organizational form was the front organization, a mechanism which attempted to disguise itself as a non-Communist association in order to attract the attention and co-operation of non-party members.

While some of the names of the organizations involved in the 1924–1937 pilgrimage to Russia have changed, in many ways the new organizations resemble the old, but they have been instructed to avoid a conspicuous association with foreign Communist parties. VOKS has become the State Committee for Cultural Relations with Foreign Countries, but it carries on many of the same activities. Today, along with the State Committee, there exists a Union of Soviet Societies for Friendship and Cultural Relations with Foreign Countries, which co-ordinates the activities of different foreign friendship societies existing within the Soviet Union and attempts to promote friendship societies in all the areas of the world. This function was formerly performed by VOKS and the International Association of Friends of the Soviet Union under the supervision of the Commission on Foreign Relations.[11] Since 1957, the State Committee has also performed the function of co-ordinating the various official Soviet cultural-exchange programs with foreign countries. One organization which has changed neither name nor methods is Intourist, which, judging from the comments of tourists who have had contact with it, continues to exert a restrictive influence on foreign travel within the Soviet Union.

Although the International Association of Friends of the Soviet Union no longer exists under that name, new front organizations like the World Federation of Trade Unions have taken over some of its functions. During the early 'fifties, a number of new peace organizations were founded as fronts for international Communism in order to carry out the Stalin Peace Policy. Other front organizations such as the World Federation of Democratic Youth and the International Union of Students have jointly sponsored the International Youth Festivals. While many of these organizations do not exist primarily for the purpose of promoting travel to the Soviet Union, a by-product of their work probably consists of encouraging interest in what is going on inside Russia.

The centralized resources of a totalitarian state permit it to use a variety of techniques to manipulate the experiences of foreigners. During the 'twenties and 'thirties Soviet techniques ranged from pampering foreign visitors to restricting their freedom of movement and contacts. Techniques of control also varied from those which subtly controlled the movement of visitors while giving them an illusion of freedom to the coercive techniques of censorship and the harassment of foreign firms and individuals.

Even though many present-day visitors to the Soviet Union have remarked on their amazement at the freedom allowed visitors, every one of the manipulative techniques described as existing in the 1924–1937 period can be illustrated by contemporary incidents. Foreign tourists have found it tiring to be rushed about without rest from one sight-seeing tour to another. Restrictions on travel throughout the Soviet Union still remain, although they have been liberalized from time to time. Elaborate regulations on sale of gasoline and the requirement that, in most cases, motor tourists be accompanied by guides have served to limit severely the mobility of travelers. The average tourist may be surprised and pleased at not being obviously followed about, but, as one writer notes, "there is no need for the police to waste specialized manpower on him; they know he cannot get far. In the hotel his movements and, above all, his visitors are watched by the floor superintendents. . . . His movements outside are reported on by Intourist, and his longer excursions by Intourist drivers." [12] With the permanent residents, the net draws much closer: there are greater restrictions on the movements of newspapermen than on the movements of the ordinary tourist. [13]

The pampering of certain foreign visitors is not restricted to

Asians and Africans but is intensified in their case. In order to impress representatives of the underdeveloped areas who attended the Moscow Youth Festival in the summer of 1957, these delegates were given "their own dining halls, with waiters and candlelight service," while delegates from Western Europe and the United States were given "cafeteria-type meals." "Display windows of large Soviet stores showed mixed white and Negro dummies and the dummies of black-skinned children were used to display the best of Soviet wearing apparel." [14]

The display windows are larger today. Russia has more to show than it did in the 'twenties and 'thirties. The government is anxious to impress visitors with its liberality. But, as in the earlier period, the game of delays or excuses delivered with a smile is played if a visitor wants to see a place where Intourist thinks he ought not to go. One writer on the Soviet Union cites several examples. Some British schoolteachers were eager to see a Soviet elementary school and asked their guide if she could take them there. The guide responded that if they had asked in advance, it could have been arranged, but it couldn't be done at the moment. When the schoolteachers replied that they had asked in advance, the guide was silent. One tourist asked to see a factory; the guide answered that this would be possible in Leningrad. Leningrad came, but there was no factory. When several people vigorously protested, the guide remarked that she had been seriously reprimanded for the request.[15] Despite these incidents, most visitors to Russia have found travel conditions somewhat freer than expected. The guided tour is still the pattern, but there is a little more opportunity to communicate with people and to get to know the country.

During the late 'twenties and 'thirties, the Soviet regime achieved remarkable success in disseminating a favorable image to those whose stay in the Soviet Union was limited and who lacked the tools necessary to probe beneath the Soviet façade. Economically, the Soviet regime did quite well in obtaining the machinery and technological skills it wanted, and to a lesser extent, the credit. Psychologically, through the use of foreign visitors, a climate of opinion was created which facilitated the renewal of diplomatic relations by Great Britain and recognition by the United States.

This climate of opinion revealed the regime's success in enhancing the reputation of the Soviet Union and Communism among intellectuals and middle-class groups. It did not succeed so well with workers, because the workers' delegations which visited the Soviet Union were not at all representative of major sectors of the European and American labor movement.

The Soviet regime still has considerable success in impressing its favorable image upon foreigners. The decrease in the number of foreign residents who stay for long periods has perhaps resulted in more superficial observations on the part of foreigners today. As one writer says:

> Short trips abroad always lead to generalisations. Even a country where one can move about freely and independently must be carefully studied before one can begin to understand it. How much more complex then is the understanding of a country as tightly buttoned-up as the Soviet Union—despite or possibly because of the assistance of Intourist! It leaves most of its visitors only the choice of sticking to their old clichés, or of devising new ones which only years of unhindered travelling could eventually correct— although, by then, the Soviet people and the Soviet Union could well have changed again several times over.[16]

Since many a casual visitor's preconception of the Soviet Union is somewhat favorable, a short visit to the USSR under the auspices of Intourist does little to change attitudes. Even one who comes to the Soviet Union prepared to be suspicious of what the Soviet regime has to show him may be pleasantly surprised that the Russia he sees is quite different from what he imagined. Because the Soviet policy of peaceful coexistence evokes spontaneous support from the Soviet people, the regime finds that it is much easier to persuade visitors of its good will today than it was during the 'thirties and later years of Stalin's reign. On the one hand, preconceptions play a role in influencing impressions similar to the role they played during the 1924–1937 period. On the other hand, preconceptions today show less bias than they did during the 'twenties and 'thirties because now-adays visitors to the Soviet Union from the West are not so violently for or against the regime.

The superficial impressions of most foreigners, resulting from shortened periods of residence in the Soviet Union are counter-balanced by the observations of visitors, especially those from the academic world, who are far more sophisticated about Soviet and Communist techniques than were their peers thirty years ago. They are able to recognize some of the achievements of the Soviet regime without ignoring the darker side of the picture. The greatest dividends for the Soviet regime come from the visits of people from the underdeveloped areas of the world. While the Westerner can easily see that the material standard of living in the Soviet Union does not match that of the West, the visitor from an underdeveloped area regards it as vastly superior to that in his country. Since many of the visitors from underdeveloped areas have been the nationalist leaders of those areas, their visits to the Soviet Union have at least temporarily resulted in the enhancement of Soviet influence through the signing of various technical assistance, loan, and trade agreements.

The manipulation of visitors by a Communist regime involves a wide range of contacts which are susceptible to political control. Liberalization of contacts and of investigation is permitted in order to promote a favorable image. But when such a policy interferes with the interests of a closed society, a tightening up of restrictions and regulations takes place.

However, there are certain features of totalitarian control which remain constant. Totalitarian regimes show a tendency to indoctrinate rather than to educate. This approach extends to their contacts with foreigners as well as to their treatment of their own citizens. There is only one "proper view of reality," and the authorities are convinced that individuals need help and guidance in order to understand this. A second feature of totalitarian control is the omnipresence of politics. All contacts between a closed society and the outside world are subject to political exploitation. Frederick Barghoorn notes that cultural diplomacy, "the manipulation of cultural materials and personnel for propaganda purposes," is a branch of intergovernmental propaganda that "has been much more highly developed by communist states than by non-communist countries. . . ."[17]

In terms of organizations and techniques, a study of both the pre-World War II period and the post-1955 period indicate a certain continuity of form and method. These organizational mechanisms and techniques may be peculiar to the Russians or to Communists, or to all totalitarian countries. Such a distinction would have to be made through comparative studies.

As long as the Soviet Union can minimize the amount of free contact between foreigners and Soviet society, the opening of its doors to foreign visitors tends to enhance its image abroad. Although the effort to manipulate foreign visitors may be costly in material terms, such costs have in the past been more than offset by material and propaganda gains. The cessation of visits from foreigners during the war years was a practical necessity; however, Stalin's continuation of a policy of discouraging foreign visitors did not redound to Soviet advantage. The policy of earlier years, readopted by Khrushchev after Stalin's death in 1953, represented a far more rational alternative.

Future Soviet policy toward visitors from abroad is difficult to predict. The present regime tends to follow Khrushchev's policy of encouraging such visitors. And as long as such a policy continues to serve political purposes—in this case the programs of peaceful coexistence and the wooing of Asian and African nationalists—the Soviet Union will probably continue to practice it. However, even though from time to time the USSR may liberalize restrictions and controls, as long as it remains a closed society it will continue to control, to a lesser or a greater extent, the activities of foreigners within the country.

Notes
Bibliography
Index

Notes

CHAPTER 1: THE CLOSED SOCIETY AND FOREIGN GUESTS

1 Societies are sometimes classified as open or closed according to the freedom allowed the individual to use his critical faculties while he is in the society. An open society is a pluralistic one which guarantees citizens both theoretical and *de facto* freedom of expression, association, and movement.

2 Claire Selltiz *et al., Attitudes and Social Relations of Foreign Students in the United States* (Minneapolis: University of Minnesota Press, 1963). The book brings together a series of studies on cross-cultural education performed under the auspices of the Committee on Cross-Cultural Education of the Social Science Research Council. Another study published in 1965 is based on a symposium held at George Peabody College for Teachers, October 22–24, 1964. See Stewart Fraser, ed., *Governmental Policy and International Education* (New York: John Wiley & Sons, 1965).

3 Harold R. Isaacs, *Emergent Americans; A Report on Crossroads Africa* (New York: John Day, 1961). Crossroads Africa was a service project conceived as an effort to involve growing numbers of young people in a close personal relationship with their counterparts on the African continent.

4 Howard P. Smith, "Do Intercultural Experiences Affect Attitudes?" *Journal of Abnormal Social Psychology,* 51 (Nov., 1955): 469–77. The intercultural experiences in the study included the Experiment in International Living, the Quaker

Voluntary Service Group, and tours undertaken through the United States National Student Association.

5   Frederick C. Barghoorn, *The Soviet Cultural Offensive* (Princeton, N.J.: Princeton University Press, 1960).

6   Carl J. Friedrich and Zbigniew K. Brzezinski, *Totalitarian Dictatorship and Autocracy* (New York: Frederick A. Praeger, 1961), p. 9.

7   Alfred G. Meyer, *Leninism* (New York: Frederick A. Praeger, 1962), p. 81.

8   Hadley Cantril, *Soviet Leaders and Mastery Over Man* (New Brunswick, N.J.: Rutgers University Press, 1960), p. 57.

9   Elihu Katz and Paul F. Lazarsfeld, *Personal Influence* (Glencoe, Ill.: The Free Press, 1955), p. 32.

10 Tamara Solonevich, *Zapiski Sovetskoi Perevodchitsy* (*Diary of a Soviet Interpreter*), (Sofia, Bulgaria: Golos Rossii, 1937), p. 34.

11 See Paul Kecskemeti, "The Soviet Approach to International Political Communication," *Public Opinion Quarterly*, 20 (Spring, 1956): 304, on the motivation behind Soviet external communications.

12 Katz and Lazarsfeld, *Personal Influence*, pp. 325–26.

13 Carl I. Hovland, Irving L. Janis, and Harold H. Kelley, *Communication and Persuasion* (New Haven, Conn.: Yale University Press, 1953), pp. 19–22.

14 Quoted in Barghoorn, *The Soviet Cultural Offensive*, p. 37.

15 Katz and Lazarsfeld, *Personal Influence*, pp. 68–69.

16 Cantril, *Soviet Leaders*, p. 57.

17 Muzafer Sherif and Carolyn W. Sherif, *An Outline of Social Psychology*, Rev. ed. (New York: Harper & Bros., 1956), p. 40.

18 Walter Lippmann, *Public Opinion* (New York: Macmillan, 1960), p. 81.

19 See Sherif and Sherif, *Outline of Social Psychology*, pp. 44, 98–99, for material on the subject of perception relevant to this study.

20 The Sixth World Congress of the Communist International, held in the summer of 1928, is the source of the forecast. According to Isaac Deutscher (*Stalin: A Political Biography* [New York: Vintage Books, 1960], p. 404) the forecast was authorized by Stalin. The Communist International, which consisted of representatives of the Communist parties in different countries, was

set up in 1918 as an instrument of Soviet policy designed to extend and to control the world Communist movement and to allow the Soviet foreign office to carry on ordinary diplomatic relations with foreign countries until the world revolution was completed. Stressing the autonomy of the Soviet foreign office and the Communist International, the Soviet government was able to carry on simultaneously two ultimately contradictory policies.

21 The doctrine of "socialism in one country" was first formulated by Stalin in the autumn of 1924 to counter Trotsky's doctrine of "permanent revolution." Stalin argued that the Soviet Union could complete the building of socialism without the preliminary victory of the proletarian revolution in other countries. He boasted that Russia, relying on the great assets of her raw material and people, could industrialize despite her isolation in a capitalist world.

22 Kecskemeti, "Soviet Approach to International Political Communication," p. 305.

23 George F. Kennan, *Russia and the West under Lenin and Stalin* (New York: Mentor Books, 1962), p. 266.

24 Interview with Fischer, Jan. 21, 1963.

25 It is difficult to set a date for the abatement of the flow of foreign visitors into Russia. As late as April 25, 1938, the head of Intourist stated that the Soviet Union intended to continue further to develop foreign tourism. See Decimal Files, Department of State, 861.111 Intourist/67, memorandum on Intourist services, April 26, 1938. Frederick Barghoorn states (*Soviet Cultural Offensive*, p. 47) that travel to Russia was still continuing on a considerable scale during the summer of 1939. But after reading almost all available memoirs of foreign visitors and residents in the Soviet Union during the mid- and late 'thirties, I believe that the pilgrimage to Russia for all purposes except for some very specific diplomatic reasons had stopped by the end of 1938, not to be renewed until 1955. See Louis Fischer, *Men and Politics* (New York: Duell, Sloan & Pearce, 1941), p. 433. Furthermore, Barghoorn (p. 74) notes 1955 as the first startling expansion of the Soviet cultural exchange program. See also Ernest J. Simmons, "Negotiating on Cultural Exchange, 1947," *Negotiating with the Russians*, Raymond Dennett and Joseph E. Johnson, eds. (New York: World Peace Foundation, 1951), pp. 248–49, on the difficulties of obtaining visas in the very early postwar period.

CHAPTER 2: OBJECTIVES AND THE SOVIET IMAGE

1 Hadley Cantril, *Soviet Leaders and Mastery Over Man* (New Brunswick, N.J.: Rutgers University Press, 1960), p. 16.
2 I. Stalin, *Sochineniia* (*Works*) (Moscow: Institut Marksa-Engelsa-Lenina, 1947), VII: 284.
3 U.S. Congress, House of Representatives, Committee on Foreign Affairs, Subcommittee No. 5 on National and International Movements, Supplement 1, "100 Years of Communism, 1848–1948," *The Strategy and Tactics of World Communism*, 80 Cong., 2 sess. (1948), p. 128.
4 Communist Party of Great Britain, *Reports, Theses and Resolutions of the Eighth Congress of the Communist Party of Great Britain, October 16–17, 1926* (London: CPGB, 1927), p. 76.
5 The Communist International, *The Communist International Between the Fifth & the Sixth World Congresses, 1924–8* (London: CPGB, 1928), p. 101.
6 Communist Party of Great Britain, "Political Report of the Central Committee," *The New Line: Documents of the Tenth Congress of the Communist Party of Great Britain, January 19–22, 1929* (London: CPGB, 1929), p. 27.
7 *Imprecorr*, Nov. 17, 1927, p. 1442.
8 Liam O'Flaherty, *I Went to Russia* (New York: Harcourt, Brace, 1931), pp. 216–17. Lement Harris, "An American Workman in Russia," *Outlook and Independent*, 157 (Feb. 25, 1931): 317.
9 *Soviet Union Review*, May, 1929, pp. 82–83.
10 *Moscow Daily News*, May 26, 1932, p. 3.
11 William A. Williams, *American-Russian Relations, 1781–1947* (New York: Rinehart, 1952), p. 238.
12 B. Vinogradov, *Deciat' Let Kapitalisticheskogo Okruzheniia SSSR* (*Ten Years of the Capitalist Encirclement of the USSR*) (Moscow: Institut Mirovogo Khoziaictva, 1928), p. 114.
13 Jan Valtin (Richard Krebs), *Out of the Night* (New York: Alliance Book Corp., 1941), p. 368.
14 CPGB, *Reports, Theses and Resolutions . . .* , p. 76.
15 *Labor Unity*, April, 1932, p. 25.
16 *Imprecorr*, May 28, 1931, p. 518, citing an article from *Trud*.
17 Decimal Files, Department of State, 861.00B/348, negotiations with the Delegations of German and Swedish workmen in Moscow and Leningrad, Aug. 17, 1925, p. 1.
18 *Pravda*, May 8, 1936, p. 6.
19 *Imprecorr*, Dec. 31, 1928, p. 1763.

20 Interview with Charles Thayer, Feb. 13, 1963; Interview with John N. Hazard, Dec. 10, 1962; William Reswick, *I Dreamt Revolution* (Chicago: Henry Regnery, 1952), p. 235.

21 Allan Nevins and Frank Ernest Hill, *Ford—Expansion and Challenge, 1915–1933* (New York: Charles Scribner's Sons, 1957), p. 674.

22 Circular advertising 1929 trip, in American-Russian Chamber of Commerce Files, in Alexander Gumberg Papers, State Historical Society of Wisconsin Library, Madison.

23 Anne O'Hare McCormick, *The Hammer and the Scythe* (New York: A. A. Knopf, 1928), p. 268.

24 Stalin, *Works*, VII: 351.

25 *Pravda*, Nov. 4, 1927, p. 1.

26 Karl Kreibich, "The Delegations to Russia," *Communist International*, 5 (Jan. 1, 1928): 17.

27 *Ibid.*

28 A. Abolin, "The Development of the Soviet Trade Unions," *RILU Magazine*, No. 1–2 (Jan. 15–Feb. 1, 1932), p. 99.

29 Decimal Files, Department of State, 861.00B/608, translation of article from *Sputnik Moprovtsa*, No. 7 (April 1–15, 1931), n.p.

30 Benjamin Gitlow, *I Confess* (New York: E. P. Dutton, 1940), p. 294; William Z. Foster, *History of the Communist Party of the United States* (New York: International Publishers, 1952), p. 259; Interview No. 8, Dec. 18, 1962. Gitlow remarks that the delegation went to the Soviet Union in 1926. However, because of difficulties encountered by those planning the trip, the delegation did not actually go to the Soviet Union until the summer of 1927. See American Trade Union Delegation to the Soviet Union, *Russia after Ten Years* (New York: International Publishers, 1927).

31 See Chapter 5.

32 *Pravda*, June 3, 1934, p. 5.

33 Kreibich, "Delegations to Russia," p. 18.

34 *Soviet Union Review*, Dec., 1928, p. 189.

35 Neal Wood, *Communism and British Intellectuals* (London: Victor Gollancz, 1959), pp. 124–25.

36 *Ibid.*

37 Eugene Lyons, *Assignment in Utopia* (New York: Harcourt, Brace, 1937), p. 367.

38 H. J. Freyn reply in answers to questionnaire on Forced Labor in the Soviet Union, in American-Russian Chamber of Commerce

Files; John Scott, *Behind the Urals* (Cambridge, Mass.: Houghton Mifflin, 1942), p. 88.
39 Interview with John Scott, Nov. 21, 1962.
40 *Soviet Union Review*, May, 1929, pp. 82–83.
41 *Ibid.*, June, 1927, p. 92. Amtorg was a Soviet trading organization in the United States which served as intermediary between Americans interested in doing business with Russia or working in the Soviet Union, and the Soviet government.

CHAPTER 3: THE CAMPAIGN TO WOO FOREIGNERS

1 Alfred G. Meyer, *Leninism* (New York: Frederick A. Praeger, 1962), p. 98.
2 *Ibid.*, p. 52.
3 *Ibid.*
4 Philip Selznick, *The Organizational Weapon* (Glencoe, Ill.: The Free Press, 1960), p. 78.
5 Great Britain, Home Office, *Communist Papers—Documents Selected from Those Obtained on the Arrest of Communist Leaders on the 14th and 21st October, 1925*, Cmd. 2682 (London, 1926). (Cited hereafter as *Communist Papers.*) Unlike the Zinoviev Letter and the documents published in *British White Paper, Russia No. 2* (1927): *Documents Illustrating the Hostile Activities of the Soviet Government and the Third International Against Great Britain*, Cmd. 2874 (London, 1927), following the Arcos raid, the authenticity of these documents, as far as I can see, has never been challenged. Both Henry Pelling, *The British Communist Party: A Historical Profile* (New York: Macmillan, 1958), p. 34, and Louis Fischer, *The Soviets in World Affairs* (New York: Vintage Books, 1960), p. 458, note the documents without questioning their authenticity. Likewise, a Communist leader, Tom Bell, in his book, *The British Communist Party: A Short History* (London: Lawrence & Wishart, 1937), p. 108, also cites the existence of the documents and the circumstances under which they were taken from Communist party headquarters without challenging their authenticity.
6 "A Plan of Work of the Agitprop Department of the ECCI for the Next Half Year," *Communist Papers*, p. 10. The introduction to the "Plan" attributes (p. 8) the marginal comments to Bell.
7 Letter, May 21, 1925, *ibid.*, p. 14.
8 I. G. "Krepnet zhivaia sviaz s proletariatom vsego mir" ("Strong

vital ties with the proletariat of the entire world"), *Mezhduna-rodnoe Rabochee Dvizhenie*, No. 16 (April 20, 1932), p. 5.

9   Tamara Solonevich, *Zapiski Sovetskoi Perevodchitsy* (*Diary of a Soviet Interpreter*) (Sofia, Bulgaria: Golos Rossii, 1937), p. 36.

10   *Ibid.*, pp. 36–37. See also, A. Rudolf (Raoul Lazlo), *Pourquoi j'ai quitté l'URSS*, La Documentation Anti-Communiste du CILACC, No. 10–11 (1935), p. 7.

11   *Pravda*, 1926: Oct. 8, p. 3; June 10, p. 3; British National Committee to Send a Workers' Delegation to the USSR, Nov., 1927, manifesto announcing a delegation selection meeting. See Russia files of Trades Union Congress Reference Library, London.

12   *Trud*, Sept. 28, 1927, p. 1. International Red Relief was created in 1923 and was directed first by Clara Zetkin, then by Elena Stassova. It proclaimed its aim to be "to accord assistance to all victims of the revolutionary struggle." Although many of its activities were similar to those performed by International Workers' Relief, an organization founded in 1921 by Willi Munzenberg, the two groups were separately organized and directed by different people. MOPR is the abbreviation for the Russian chapter of International Red Relief. The initials MOPR stand for Mezhdunarodnaia Organizatsiia Pomoschi Bortsam Revoliutsii (International Organization for Assistance to Militants of the Revolution). The Russian initials for International Workers Relief are MEZHRABPROM. See Gunther Nollau, *International Communism and World Revolution: History and Methods* (London: Hollis & Carter, 1961), p. 154, *n.* 5.

13   *Daily Worker*, Dec. 12, 1925, p. 2.

14   Decimal Files, Department of State, 861.00B/446, report concerning the proposal of the All-Union Council of Trade Unions to form an International Workmen's Information Bureau, Nov. 20, 1926.

15   *Ibid.*

16   *Ibid.*

17   *Imprecorr*, Nov. 17, 1927, p. 1442.

18   *Pravda*, Oct. 20, 1927, p. 7.

19   *Ibid*, 1927: Oct 27, p. 4; Nov. 10, p. 7.

20   *Imprecorr*, Nov. 17, 1927, p. 1442.

21   *Ibid.*, Nov. 24, 1927, pp. 1485, 1490.

22   *Pravda*, Nov. 15, 1927, p. 1.

23   V. Iarotskii, "Kongress druzei SSSR" ("Congress of Friends of the USSR"), *Vestnik Truda*, No. 11 (Nov., 1927), p. 123.

24 Karl Kreibich, "The Delegations to Russia," *Communist International,* 5 (Jan. 1, 1928): 19.

25 *Ibid.*

26 *Imprecorr,* Jan. 12, 1928, p. 50.

27 Interview with Reeves, March 22, 1963

28 *Imprecorr,* Nov. 17, 1927, p. 1442.

29 *Ibid.,* May 31, 1928, p. 533.

30 *Le Vie Ouvrière,* Jan. 6, 1928, p. 2.

31 "Debate on Report—The Immediate Tasks of the Communists in the Trade Union Movement, 12th Session, 6th ECCI Plenum, March 2, 1926," *Imprecorr,* March 25, 1926, p. 351.

32 Communist International, *The Struggle against Imperialist War and the Task of the Communists: Resolution of the Sixth World Congress of the Communist International, 1928* (New York: Workers Library, 1932), p. 66.

33 Communist Party of the United States of America, "Tasks in the Struggle Against Hunger, Repression and War—Resolution of the 13th Plenum of the Central Committee, CPUSA," *The Communist,* 10 (Oct., 1931): 832.

34 *Soviet Russia Today,* Jan., 1934, p. 5.

35 *Imprecorr,* Aug. 28, 1930, p. 835.

36 Friends of Soviet Russia, *Hands Off Soviet Russia: Report of the Cologne Conference of Friends of Soviet Russia* (London: British National Committee of FOSR, 1928), p. 21.

37 Communist Party of Great Britain, "Political Report of the Central Committee," *The New Line: Documents of the Tenth Congress of the Communist Party of Great Britain, January 19–22, 1929* (London: CPGB, 1929), p. 28.

38 Friends of Soviet Russia, *Hands Off Soviet Russia,* p. 18.

39 *Imprecorr,* May 31, 1928, p. 534.

40 *Ibid.,* June 7, 1928, p. 575; *Pravda,* May 29, 1928, p. 2.

41 Friends of Soviet Russia, *Hands Off Soviet Russia,* p. 2.

42 *Pravda,* May 29, 1928, p. 2.

43 *The Worker,* Feb. 28, 1930, p. 3.

44 *Pravda,* Oct. 24, 1933, p. 1.

45 Nemzer, "The Soviet Friendship Societies," *Public Opinion Quarterly,* 13 (Summer, 1949): 269

46 Solonevich, *Zapiski Sovetskoi Perevodchitsy,* p. 37.

47 *Pravda,* Oct. 8, 1926, p. 3.

48 *Soviet Russia Today,* Jan., 1934, p. 10.

49 *Ibid.,* Feb., 1934, p. 14.

50 British National Committee to Send a Workers' Delegation to the USSR, Nov., 1927.

51 *Pravda,* July 24, 1926, pp. 2, 4.

52 Friends of Soviet Russia, *Hands Off Soviet Russia,* p. 22. See also: Communist Youth International, *The Communist Youth International: Report of Activity between the Fourth and Fifth Congresses, 1924–28* (London: CPGB, 1928), p. 36; *Pravda,* Oct. 8, 1926, p. 3; *Workers Life,* Sept. 13, 1929, p. 1. (*Workers Life* was a publication of the Minority Movement, the British Section of the Communist Profintern.)

53 *Communist Youth International,* pp. 43–44.

54 *Workers Life,* Sept. 13, 1929, p. 1.

55 *Soviet Russia Today,* Feb., 1934, p. 14.

56 Margaret McCarthy, *Generation in Revolt* (London: William Heinemann, 1953), pp. 71–73.

57 *Ibid.,* p. 72.

58 *Ibid.,* p. 74.

59 *Soviet Russia Today,* Feb., 1934, p. 14.

60 *Workers Life,* Sept. 13, 1929, p. 1.

61 *Pravda,* Oct. 11, 1927, p. 5.

62 Benjamin Gitlow, *I Confess* (New York: E. P. Dutton, 1940), p. 294.

63 Interview No. 8, Dec. 18, 1962.

64 Lovestone to Walsh, Jan. 30, 1926, in Frank P. Walsh Files, New York Public Library.

65 Lovestone to Walsh, Feb. 8, 1926, *ibid.*

66 Walsh to Lovestone, Feb. 15, 1926, *ibid.*

67 *Daily Worker,* Dec. 11, 1925, p. 2; Jan. 27, 1926, p. 1.

68 Interview with Douglas, Feb. 5, 1963; letter from Douglas to author, Sept. 29, 1967.

69 Philip Taft, *The AFL from the Death of Gompers to the Merger* (New York: Harper & Bros., 1959), p. 430.

70 *Ibid.*

71 "Statement of the Executive Council of the American Federation of Labor, June 28, 1926," as cited in Taft, *The AFL . . . ,* p. 430. See also American Federation of Labor, *Proceedings of the Forty-Sixth Annual Convention* (Washington, D.C.: AFL, 1926), p. 271.

72 Taft, *The AFL . . . ,* p. 430; AFL, *Proceedings . . .* (1926), pp. 263, 271, 279.

73 *Ibid,* p. 271.

74 *Ibid.*

75 "Comment by Matthew Woll on an American Trade Unionist's Interview with Stalin," *Current History*, 27 (Feb., 1928): 692.
76 Interview with Douglas, Feb. 5, 1963; letters from Douglas to author, Sept. 29, 1967, and Jan. 23, 1968. The meeting with Coyle took place in New York at the Pennsylvania Hotel. Douglas stresses that Coyle's reputation was excellent at that time.
77 Gitlow, *I Confess*, p. 295.
78 Interview No. 8, Dec. 18, 1962.
79 Gitlow, *I Confess*, p. 297.
80 *Daily Worker*, Dec. 15, 1925, p. 3; 1926: Jan. 28, p. 1; March 5, p. 3.
81 Coyle to Walsh, March 12, 1927, in Walsh Files.
82 American Trade Union Delegation to the Soviet Union, *Russia after Ten Years* (New York: International Publishers, 1927), p. 10.
83 Interview with Douglas, Feb. 5, 1963; letter from Douglas to author, Sept. 29, 1967.
84 Anne Washington Craton to Walsh, Dec. 17, 1927, in Walsh Files.
85 Coyle to Walsh, June 7, 1928, *ibid.*
86 John Brophy, *A Miner's Life* (Madison, Wis.: University of Wisconsin Press, 1964), p. 220.
87 Interview No. 8, Dec. 18, 1962.
88 *Soviet Russia Today*, Feb., 1934, pp. 14–15.
89 *Imprecorr*, Jan. 12, 1928, p. 50.
90 *Ibid.*, May 15, 1930, p. 428.
91 Gitlow, *I Confess*, pp. 294–95.
92 Walsh to Lovestone, Feb. 8, 1926, in Walsh Files.
93 *Ibid.*
94 Walsh to Lovestone, Feb. 15, 1926, *ibid.*
95 British National Committee to Send a Workers' Delegation to the USSR, Nov., 1927.
96 "Comment fut designé à Vallaures un délegué pour la Russie Soviétique," *Les Cahiers du Bolchevisme*, 5 (Aug., 1930): 796.
97 McCarthy, *Generation in Revolt*, pp. 69–70.
98 *Communist Youth International*, p. 33.
99 *Ibid.*
100 *Ibid.*, p. 34.
101 *Ibid.*
102 *Ibid.*
103 *Ibid.*
104 Interview with Thomas, Dec. 27, 1962.

105 Andrew Smith, *I Was a Soviet Worker* (New York: E. P. Dutton, 1936), p. 19. See also U.S. Congress, House of Representatives, Special Committee on Un-American Activities, *Hearings on Investigation of Un-American Propaganda Activities in the United States,* 76 Cong., 1 sess. (1939), p. 6986.
106 Smith, *I Was a Soviet Worker,* pp. 19, 24–25.
107 *Investigation of Un-American Propaganda Activities,* p. 6987.
108 *Der Socialistische Bote,* Feb. 5, 1927, cited by Joseph Douillet, *Moscow Unmasked,* trans. A. W. King (London: Pilot Press, 1930), p. 34.
109 Solonevich, *Zapiski Sovetskoi Perevodchitsy,* p. 36; Rudolf, *Pourquoi j'ai quitté l'URSS,* p. 7.
110 Solonevich, *Zapiski Sovetskoi Perevodchitsy,* p. 35.
111 *Ibid.,* pp. 116–17; Smith, *I Was a Soviet Worker,* p. 20; *Investigation of Un-American Propaganda Activities,* pp. 6987–88.
112 Elizabeth Bentley, *Out of Bondage* (New York: Devin-Adair, 1951), p. 113. See also *Investigation of Un-American Propaganda Activities,* pp. 4544, 4751, 4802–5, 4836, 4896–901.
113 Interview No. 8, Dec. 8, 1962.
114 Nollau, *International Communism and World Revolution,* p. 155.
115 Decimal Files, Department of State, 861.00B/608, translation of two articles from *Sputnik Moprovtsa,* March 16–31, 1931, and April 1–15, 1931; *Pravda,* June 3, 1934, p. 5; Oct. 20, 1927, p. 7.
116 Liam O'Flaherty, *I Went to Russia* (New York: Harcourt, Brace, 1931), p. 222.
117 *Ibid.,* pp. 259–60.
118 *Soviet Union Review,* Sept., 1927, p. 126.
119 *Ibid,* April, 1928, p. 57.
120 *Ibid.,* Sept., 1929, p. 143; *Soviet Russia Today,* Nov., 1935, p. 12.
121 Nemzer, "Soviet Friendship Societies," p. 271; Eugene Lyons, *Assignment in Utopia* (New York: Harcourt, Brace, 1937), p. 62.
122 *VOKS Weekly News Bulletin,* Sept. 1, 1928, cited by Ruth Emily McMurry and Muna Lee, *The Cultural Approach* (Chapel Hill, N.C.: University of North Carolina Press, 1947), p. 111.
123 *Soviet Union Review,* Sept., 1927, p. 126.
124 *Ibid.,* p. 127.
125 *Soviet Russia Today,* Nov., 1935, p. 13.
126 *Soviet Union Review,* June, 1929, p. 106.

127 Statement for Press, April 7, 1954 (not issued), in Files of the Anglo-American Institute of 1st Moscow University, Institute for International Education, New York City; *Moscow News,* July 11, 1935, p. 7.

128 "A Plan of Work of the Agitprop Department of the ECCI for the Next Half Year," *Communist Papers,* p. 10.

129 *Soviet Culture Review,* Oct. 25–Nov. 7, 1931, as cited by Mc-Murry and Lee, *The Cultural Approach,* p. 117.

130 *Soviet Union Review,* April, 1928, p. 58.

131 *Ibid.*

132 *Ibid.,* June, 1927, p. 100.

133 First Annual Report of the Society for Cultural Relations, 1924–25, London, England, p. 1, in Library of the British Museum.

134 *Ibid.,* p. 3; *Soviet Union Review,* June, 1927, p. 100.

135 O'Flaherty, *I Went to Russia,* pp. 257–58.

136 *Soviet Union Review,* Dec., 1929, p. 196.

137 *New York Times,* Nov. 22, 1933, p. 8.

138 Ruth V. Morse, "Russia's Four Hundred," *Survey Graphic,* 26 (April, 1937): 234–35.

139 Other Soviet organizations, including the Soviet Academy of Science, the Union of Soviet Writers, and the Bureau of Revolutionary Literature, invited and entertained visiting intellectuals.

140 Report by Alexander Gumberg on the 1929 Delegation to the Soviet Union, Oct. 19, 1929, Circular describing purpose of delegation, in American-Russian Chamber of Commerce Files, p. 2, in Alexander Gumberg Papers, State Historical Society of Wisconsin Library, Madison.

141 Interview with Williams, Part II, Dec. 6, 1962.

142 Decimal Files, Department of State, 861.00/11004, memorandum on interview with Mr. B., representative of E. W. Bliss Co., Dec. 3, 1926, p. 2.

143 U.S. Congress, House of Representatives, Special Committee to Investigate Communist Activities in the United States, *Hearings,* 71 Cong., 3 sess. (1930), Part 1, Vol. 5 (Dec., 1930), p. 37.

144 *Ibid.,* p. 38.

145 The Soviet authorities often used the word "specialist" in regard to ordinary workers in order to create the impression that foreign bourgeois specialists were forsaking their background to become loyal Bolsheviks. As will be discussed in Chapter 4, Soviet authorities generally overvalued the qualifications of foreigners.

It is quite difficult to determine the total number of foreign specialists and workers in the Soviet Union during the period of study, since different sources give conflicting estimates even when they are considering the same time periods. The problem is further complicated by the use of different categories, such as workers, specialists, technicians, engineers, and mechanics, by each source. The figures for all nationalities range from 1350 to 6000 during 1929–30, and from 4500 to 10,000 during 1931–32. The figure that seems to be mentioned most often is 4000–5000 during 1931. See figures released by Amtorg in *New York Times,* June 6, 1931, p. 9; figures cited at the 16th session of the All-Union Communist Party-Bolshevik as found in *Mezhdunarodnoe Rabochee Dvizhenie,* No. 29–30 (Oct., 1930), p. 15; also figures cited by V. Rabovskii, representative of VTsSPS, *ibid.,* No. 31–32 (Nov., 1930), p. 21; see also *Soviet Union Review,* Jan., 1931, p. 7. In March, 1931, a director of the Supreme Council of National Economy declared that about 5000 foreign specialists and workmen were then employed in Soviet industry. See M. Gurevich, *The Five Year Plan* as cited in Max Beloff, *The Foreign Policy of Soviet Russia, 1929–41,* 2 vols. (London: Oxford University Press, 1947), I: 31, *n.* 1. Another official of the Supreme Economic Council gave the figure as 5000 foreign-born engineers, workers, and technicians. See *Imprecorr,* Dec. 3, 1961, p. 1121.

For the same reasons, it is just as difficult to determine how many American specialists and workers were in the Soviet Union. In addition, Soviet authorities classified as American any laborer who had worked in the United States and used American methods and tools. The figures for American specialists and skilled workers in the Soviet Union range from 1000 to 2000. Most sources seem to indicate that they were outnumbered by those of German nationality. Figures cited in the *Soviet Union Review,* Jan., 1931, p. 7, and figures released by Amtorg in the *New York Times,* June 6, 1931, p. 9, mention 1000 American engineers and technicians. An earlier diplomatic dispatch from Riga mentioned the figure of 2000 American technical men in the Soviet Union. See Decimal Files, Department of State, 861.-5017LC/200, Nov. 28, 1930. Senator William E. Borah noted in a speech reported in the *Congressional Record,* March 3, 1931, that over 2000 experts from the United States were employed in the USSR as technical experts and employees of American corporations. See *Congressional Record,* Vol. 74, 71

Cong., 2 sess., p. 7113. The *Moscow News,* April 8, 1932, p. 1, mentions 1700 American specialists and workers in heavy industry. Finally, the *Journal of Commerce and the Commercial,* April 26, 1937, p. 20, notes that 1500 Americans participated in Soviet industrial expansion under the first Five-Year Plan, 1928–32, as cited in Andrew J. Steiger, *American Engineers in the Soviet Union* (Pamphlet Series No. 3, Russian Economic Institute, 1944), p. 4.

146   "Rules for Contracts with Foreign Engineers," *British-Russian Gazette and Trade Outlook,* 6 (Nov., 1929): 38.

147   Decimal Files, Department of State, 861.602/261, translation of resolution on Council of Labor and Defense dated August 24, 1934, on The Procedure in Concluding Contracts with Foreign Specialists.

148   A. Kilinskii, "Ob usloviiakh truda inostrantsev v SSSR" ("On labor conditions for foreigners in the USSR"), *Voprosy Truda,* No. 1 (Jan., 1931), p. 76.

149   "O khode vypolneniia direktiv TsK po rabote s inostrannymi rabochimi" ("On the manner in which the directives of the Central Committee pertaining to work with foreign workers are being carried out"), Postanovlenie TsK VKP (b) ot 23 Marta 1931 goda (Enactment of the Central Committee of the All-Union Communist Party-Bolshevik, March 23, 1931), *Partiinoe Stroitel'-stvo,* No. 7 (April, 1931), p. 75.

150   *Ibid.*

151   John D. Littlepage and Demaree Bess, *In Search of Soviet Gold* (New York: Harcourt, Brace, 1938), p. 9.

152   Interview No. 1, March 29, 1963.

153   Interview No. 2, Feb. 12, 1963; Decimal Files, Department of State, 861.5017LC/422, memorandum on conversation with Mr. K., alien resident of U.S., Feb. 19, 1932, p. 2.

154   Nathan Glazer, *The Social Basis of American Communism* (New York: Harcourt, Brace & World, 1961), p. 38.

155   *Ibid.,* p. 41.

156   Decimal Files, Department of State, 360p.1115 Casper, Michael/10, memorandum on conversation with American worker employed by the Soviet government, May 12, 1931, pp. 2–4.

157   *Ibid.,* 861.5017LC/574, memorandum on interview with Finnish-American, Dec. 9, 1932, p. 1; 861.5017LC/591, memorandum on interview with Mr. W., Finnish-American, Feb. 7, 1933, p. 1; 861.5017LC/413, memorandum of conversation with Finnish-American, Jan. 15, 1932, p. 1.

158 *Ibid.*, 861.5017LC/659, memorandum on talk with Mr. T., Finnish-American, May 5, 1933, p. 2.

159 *Ibid.*, 361.11 Employees/228, memorandum on conversation with an alien resident of the U.S. on the activities of Tractor and Auto School, Brooklyn, March 18, 1932, p. 5.

160 *Ibid.*, pp. 3–5.

161 Gitlow, *I Confess*, p. 301.

162 Decimal Files, Department of State, 861.111 American Passports/16, letter from Special Agent, Department of State to Agent in Charge, New York, Feb., 1928, p. 1.

163 *Ibid.*, 861.55/29, Report on Trend of Migratory Movements in Russia, March, 1935, p. 19.

164 *Ibid.*, 861.111 American Passports/16, letter from Special Agent, Department of State to Agent in Charge, New York, Feb., 1928, p. 1.

165 *Ibid.*

166 Gitlow, *I Confess*, p. 301.

167 Mira Wilkins and Frank Ernest Hill, *American Business Abroad: Ford on Six Continents* (Detroit: Wayne State University Press, 1964), p. 213.

168 Charles E. Sorenson, *My Forty Years with Ford* (New York: W. W. Norton, 1956), pp. 194–95.

169 Allan Nevins and Frank Ernest Hill, *Ford—Expansion and Challenge, 1915–1933* (New York: Charles Scribner's Sons, 1957), p. 680.

170 *Ekonomicheskaia Zhizn'*, June 9, 1927, p. 4.

171 *Ibid.*, Sept. 14, 1929, p. 2.

172 *Ibid.*, Sept. 29, 1929, p. 3.

173 Decimal Files, Department of State, 861.5017LC/365, memorandum on talk with Mr. G., naturalized American at Stalingrad, Nov. 17, 1931, p. 1; *New York Times*, March 6, 1932, Sec. III, p. 4.

174 Smith, *I Was a Soviet Worker*, p. 38.

175 *Ibid.*, p. 39; Decimal Files, Department of State, 861.5017LC/422, memorandum on conversation with Mr. K., alien resident of the U.S., Feb. 19, 1932, p. 14.

176 See Chapter 5, pp. 147–48.

177 "O khode vypolneniia direktiv TsK po rabote s inostrannymi rabochimi" ("On the manner in which the directives of the Central Committee pertaining to work with foreign workers are being carried out"), p. 75.

178 "O sostoianie raboty s inostrannymi rabochimi i spetsialistami" ("On the state of work with foreign workers and specialists"), Postanovlenie TsK VKP (b) ot 16 Aout 1931 goda (Enactment of the Central Committee of the All-Union Communist Party-Bolshevik, Aug. 16, 1931), *Partiinoe Stroitel'stvo,* No. 18 (Sept., 1931), p. 56.

179 *Moscow News,* 1931: Jan. 6, p. 7; Jan. 11, p. 7.

180 Louis Fischer, *Men and Politics* (New York: Duell, Sloan & Pearce, 1941), p. 233.

181 Decimal Files, Department of State, 861.5017LC/166, memorandum on interview with Moscow correspondent of *London News Chronicle* and *London Sunday Times,* April 8, 1930, p. 3.

182 Arthur Koestler, *The Invisible Writing* (New York: Macmillan, 1954), p. 63.

183 Walter Arnold Rukeyser, *Working for the Soviets* (New York: Covici-Friede, 1932), p. 31.

184 V. P. Artemiev and G. S. Burliutsky, "International Activities of the Soviet Organ of State Security after World War II," *The Soviet Secret Police,* Simon Wolin and Robert M Slusser, eds. (New York: Frederick A. Praeger, 1958), pp. 332–33. See also Paul V. Harper, ed., *The Russia I Believe In: Memoirs of Samuel N. Harper, 1902–1941* (Chicago: University of Chicago Press, 1945), p. 149; Victor Kravchenko, *I Chose Freedom* (New York: Charles Scribner's Sons, 1946), p. 185; John Wynne Hird, *Under Czar and Soviet: My Thirty Years in Russia* (London: Hurst & Blackett, 1932), p. 52.

185 Travel Brochure, The Open Road, New York Public Library.

186 The following material is taken from the interview with John Rothschild, May 14, 1963.

187 Percy M. Dawson, *Soviet Samples: Diary of an American Physiologist* (Ann Arbor, Mich.: Edwards Brothers, 1938), p. 425.

188 Interviews with Philip E. Mosely, Nov. 19, 1962; with Maxwell Stewart, Jan. 29, 1963.

189 Interview with Rothschild, May 14, 1963.

190 *Ibid.;* and interview with Maurice Hindus, March 5, 1963. Several answers were obtained to the question "Who designed the itinerary?" asked of different individuals who were involved with the Open Road. One American journalist noted that until 1935 he had complete power to set the itinerary. Many of the leaders of the Open Road, although not Communists, were sympathetic to the Soviet Union, and were probably allowed considerable discretion.

191 Interview with Rothschild, May 14, 1963.
192 News Release, June 18, 1930, American-Russian Chamber of Commerce Files, in Alexander Gumberg Papers. See also *Soviet Union Review*, March, 1927, p. 56.
193 Captain A. H. Mitford, "The Russian-British Chamber of Commerce and its Functions," *British-Russian Gazette and Trade Outlook*, 6 (July, 1930): 202.
194 Interview with Williams, Part 1, Nov. 27, 1962.
195 Statement for Press by IIE, April 7, 1954 (not issued), p. 1, in Anglo-American Institute of 1st Moscow University Files.
196 *Ibid.*
197 *Ibid.*, p. 3. See also I. V. Sollins, "A New Venture in International Education," *IIE News Bulletin*, 9 (Dec., 1933): 4.
198 Institute of International Education, Sixteenth Annual Report of Directors, 1934–35, pp. 11–12, in New York Public Library.
199 Ernest Remnant, "The British Industrial Mission to Russia," *English Review*, 49 (July, 1929): 37.
200 Meyer, *Leninism*, p. 52.

CHAPTER 4: INDULGENCE AND INTEGRATION

1 André Gide, *Afterthoughts on the U.S.S.R.*, trans. Dorothy Bussy (New York: Dial Press, 1938), p. 59; R. H. S. Crossman, ed., *The God That Failed: Six Studies in Communism* (London: Hamish Hamilton, 1950), p. 193.
2 Interview with Thomas, Dec. 27, 1962.
3 Helen Dreiser, *My Life with Dreiser* (New York: World Publishing, 1951), p. 163. See also The Communist International, *The Communist International Between the Fifth & the Sixth World Congresses, 1924–8* (London: CPGB, 1928), pp. 107–8.
4 Dreiser, *My Life with Dreiser*, p. 164.
5 *Ibid.*, p. 166.
6 *Ibid.*, p. 168.
7 William H. Chamberlin, *Russia's Iron Age* (Boston: Little, Brown, 1934), pp. 333–34.
8 *Soviet Union Review*, April, 1927, p. 72.
9 Ben Robertson, Jr., "Our Sailors Sleep in the Palace of the Czar," *Scribner's Magazine*, 91 (May, 1932): 298–99.
10 Charles E. Sorenson, *My Forty Years with Ford* (New York: W. W. Norton, 1956), p. 200.
11 Tamara Solonevich, *Zapiski Sovetskoi Perevodchitsy* (*Diary*

of a Soviet Interpreter) (Sofia, Bulgaria: Golos Rossii, 1937), pp. 59, 64.

12 John Vidor, *Spying in Russia* (London: J. Long, 1929), p. 26.

13 Liam O'Flaherty, *I Went to Russia* (New York: Harcourt, Brace, 1931), p. 215.

14 Sorenson, *My Forty Years with Ford*, p. 199.

15 George A. Burrell, *An American Engineer Looks at Russia* (Boston: Stratford, 1932), p. 21.

16 *Soviet Russia Today*, Jan., 1934, p. 4.

17 Memorandum on Entertainment of American Business Delegation, Tiflis, Aug. 4, 1929, in American-Russian Chamber of Commerce Files, in Alexander Gumberg Papers, State Historical Society of Wisconsin Library, Madison.

18 I. Stalin, *Sochineniia* (*Works*) (Moscow: Institut Marksa-Engelsa-Lenina, 1947), VII: 283.

19 Andrew Smith, *I Was a Soviet Worker* (New York: E. P. Dutton, 1936), p. 25.

20 Charles M. Muchnic, "A Businessman's View of Russia: Letters from an American Executive," *Harper's Magazine*, 159 (Sept., 1929): 437.

21 William J. Robinson, M. D., *Soviet Russia as I Saw It* (New York: International Press, 1932), p. 48.

22 Walter Citrine, *A Trade Unionist Looks at Russia* (London: Trades Union Congress General Council, 1935), p. 14.

23 Edmund Wilson, *Red, Black, Blond and Olive* (New York: Oxford University Press, 1956), p. 293.

24 "John Dewey in Russia," *Survey*, 61 (Dec. 15, 1928): 349.

25 Crossman, *The God That Failed*, pp. 65–66.

26 Sorenson, *My Forty Years with Ford*, p. 202.

27 Eugene Lyons, *Assignment in Utopia* (New York: Harcourt, Brace, 1937), p. 328.

28 John Scott, *Behind the Urals* (Cambridge, Mass.: Houghton Mifflin, 1942), pp. 90–91.

29 Sorenson, *My Forty Years with Ford*, p. 197.

30 William C. White, "Americans in Soviet Russia," *Scribner's Magazine*, 89 (Feb., 1931): 176.

31 Burton Holmes, *The Traveler's Russia* (New York: G. P. Putnam's Sons, 1934), p. 10.

32 Gide, *Afterthoughts on the U.S.S.R.*, p. 58.

33 O'Flaherty, *I Went to Russia*, p. 218.

34 Lyons, *Assignment in Utopia*, p. 218.

35 *Soviet Russia Today*, Jan., 1935, pp. 14–15.

36 Crossman, *The God That Failed*, p. 65.
37 *Ibid.*, p. 66.
38 See Chapter 3, p. 60.
39 *Soviet Union Review*, May, 1930, p. 85.
40 Sidney I. Luck, *Observation in Russia* (London: Macmillan, 1938), pp. xv–xvi.
41 Decimal Files, Department of State, 592.4A17/95, general statement by Mr. W. on Urals Excursion of XVII International Geological Congress in Moscow, 1937, Aug. 26, 1937.
42 See Chapter 3, pp. 76–77.
43 Statement for Press, April 7, 1954 (not issued), p. 1, in Anglo-American Institute of 1st Moscow University Files, Institute for International Education, New York City.
44 *Moscow News*, 1934: Jan. 27, p. 1; Aug. 11, p. 5; "Seeing Red; Russia Attracts Students," *Review of Reviews*, 92 (July, 1935): 70.
45 Statement for Press, April 7, 1954 (not issued), p. 2, in Anglo-American Institute of 1st Moscow University Files.
46 Interview with Bolsover, March 21, 1963.
47 Interview with Mosely, Nov. 19, 1962.
48 Geroid T. Robinson, *Rural Russia under the Old Regime* (New York: Macmillan, 1949).
49 John S. Curtiss, *Church and State in Russia, 1900–1917* (New York: Columbia University Press, 1940).
50 Interview with Hazard, Dec. 10, 1962.
51 *Ekonomicheskaia Zhizn'*, May 25, 1929, p. 5.
52 *Ibid.*, April 8, 1926, p. 3.
53 A. Kilinskii, "Ob usloviiakh truda inostrantsev v SSSR" ("On labor conditions for foreigners in the USSR"), *Voprosy Truda*, No. 1 (Jan., 1931), p. 76.
54 Decimal Files, Department of State, 861.5017LC/354, memorandum on interview with Mr. P., a Negro American, expert employee in Amo Plant, Sept. 25, 1931, p. 1.
55 *Ibid.*, 861.5017LC/468, memorandum on conversations with several American mining engineers employed in Soviet Russia, May 13, 1932, pp. 11–12.
56 *Ibid.*, 861.5017LC/364, memorandum on talk with wife of naturalized American citizen employed at Kharkov Tractor Plant, Nov. 9, 1931, p. 1; 3611.11Employees/133, information from International Migration Service based on conversations with a boy, July 24, 1931.

57 Scott, *Behind the Urals,* p. 86; Soviet Union Review, Jan., 1930, p. 14.
58 Scott, *Behind the Urals,* p. 86.
59 Interview No. 2, Feb. 12, 1963; interview with John Scott, Nov. 21, 1962.
60 Decimal Files, Department of State, 861.5017LC/287, memorandum on talk with American consulting engineer, June 28, 1931, p. 13; 861.5017LC/568, memorandum on conversation with Mr. M., who had been at Kramkombinat at Kramatorsky, No. 22, 1932, p. 14.
61 *Ibid.,* 861.5017LC/348, memorandum on talk with Mr. U., representative of Westinghouse Electric and Manufacturing Co., Sept. 29, 1931.
62 *Ibid.,* 861.5017LC/454, memorandum on conditions in Russia, April 12, 1932, p. 16.
63 Various sources testify to the poor conditions of specialists on individual contracts. Two engineers employed by Oglebay Morton to furnish technical advice in Soviet mining areas stressed that people working under individual contracts did not have the protection or advantages secured by those employed by American engineering firms with a chief engineer in Moscow to see that the contract was carried through. See Decimal Files, Department of State, 861.5017LC/347, memorandum on talk with two American engineers employed by Oglebay Morton, Oct. 14, 1931, pp. 8–9. Both Walter Duranty and Margaret Bourke-White noted that the superior conditions of the engineers affiliated with Hugh L. Cooper was due to the fact that Cooper had the energy and foresight to see that the contract was drawn up with special care and that payments in gold were guaranteed beforehand. See Walter Duranty, *USSR* (New York: J. B. Lippincott, 1944), p. 140, and Margaret Bourke-White, *Eyes on Russia* (New York: Simon & Schuster, 1931), p. 84.
64 "The State Syndicate of Retail Trade (GORT)," *VOKS,* No. 1 (1932), p. 181.
65 *New York Times,* July 12, 1930, p. 12.
66 *Soviet Union Review,* Feb., 1930, p. 32.
67 Heinz Unger, *Hammer, Sickle and Baton: The Soviet Memoirs of a Musician* (London: Cresset Press, 1939), p. 147.
68 John D. Littlepage and Demaree Bess, *In Search of Soviet Gold* (New York: Harcourt, Brace, 1938), p. 173.
69 Interview with Chamberlin, Jan. 30, 1963.

70 White, "Americans in Soviet Russia," pp. 171, 175.
71 Anne O'Hare McCormick, *The Hammer and the Scythe* (New York: A. A. Knopf, 1928), p. 269.
72 Louis Fischer, *Men and Politics* (New York: Duell, Sloan & Pearce, 1941), p. 221.
73 George S. Counts, *A Ford Crosses Soviet Russia* (Boston: Stratford, 1930), p. 137. Frederick Griffin, *Soviet Scene* (Toronto: Macmillan of Canada, 1932), p. 117.
74 F. Rubiner, "Rabota sredi inostrannykh rabochikh—zadacha vsei Partorganizatsii" ("Work among foreign workers—the task of the whole Party organization"), *Partiinoe Stroitel'stvo*, No. 17–18 (Sept., 1932), p. 18.
75 Ruth Kennell and Milly Bennet, "American Immigrants in Russia," *American Mercury*, 34 (April, 1932): 469–70.
76 *New York Times*, Aug. 24, 1931, p. 7.
77 Decimal Files, Department of State, 361.11Employees/228, memorandum on activities of Tractor and Auto School, Brooklyn, N.Y., March 18, 1932, p. 4.
78 *Ibid.*, 861.5017LC/469, memorandum on discussion with Mr H., former alien resident of U.S., May 27, 1932, p. 7.
79 Interview with Stewart, Jan. 29, 1963.
80 Decimal Files, Department of State, 861.5017LC/469, memorandum on talk with Mr. H., May 27, 1932, p. 8; 861.5107LC/643, memorandum on conversation with Mr. M., employed in Russia by Russian Nonferrous Metals Trust, April 4, 1933, p. 16; 861.5017LC/723, memorandum on conversation with Mr. M., employed at Chelyabinsk Tractor Works, Oct. 26, 1933, p. 2.
81 Interview with Spencer Williams, Part II, Dec. 6, 1962.
82 See Chapter 3, pp. 69–70.
83 Decimal Files, Department of State, 361.11Commune Colonists/4, translation of an article from Latvian paper *Latvis*, Dec. 23, 1928, p. 2.
84 *Ibid.*, 861.111American Passport/6, Report No. 89 covering the American passports of naturalized citizens, Nov. 21, 1927; 861.5017LC/11, memorandum on talk with Mrs. S., Oct. 11, 1928.
85 *Ibid.*, 361.11Employees/68, letter dated May 5, 1931, p. 2.
86 *Ibid.*, 861.5017LC/413, memorandum on conversation with Finnish-American émigré to Russia, Jan. 15, 1932, p. 3.
87 *Ibid.*, 360p.1115 Casper, Michael/10, memorandum on conversation with Mr. and Mrs. C., May 22, 1931, pp. 5–7.

88 Fred E. Beal, *Proletarian Journey* (New York: Hillman-Curl, 1937), pp. 283–85.
89 Burrell, *An American Engineer Looks at Russia*, p. 26.
90 *New York Times*, March 13, 1932, Sec. III, p. 4.
91 *Ibid.*, May 13, 1931, p. 10.
92 *Soviet Union Review*, Nov., 1930, p. 178; *Moscow Daily News*, May 1, 1932, p. 1.
93 Anna Louise Strong, *I Change Worlds* (New York: Henry Holt, 1935), p. 301.
94 *Ibid.*
95 *Ibid.*, p. 303; *Soviet Union Review*, Nov., 1930, p. 178.
96 Strong, *I Change Worlds*, p. 307.
97 *Ibid.*, p. 314.
98 *Ibid.*, p. 338.
99 *Ibid.*, p. 339. Although the original *Moscow News* ended as the result of the merger, a weekly magazine which reprinted some of the items in the *Moscow Daily News* came into existence and took the name *Moscow News*.
100 *Ibid.*, p. 373.
101 Decimal Files, Department of State, 861.5017LC/223, Conversation with Mr. K., assistant to Mr. Walter Duranty, Feb. 21, 1931, pp. 5–6.
102 Burrell, *An American Engineer Looks at Russia*, p. 5.
103 Interview No. 1, March 29, 1963.
104 Kennell and Bennet, "American Immigrants in Russia," p. 466.
105 *Moscow Daily News*, Dec. 30, 1932, p. 1; March 12, 1933, p. 1. For criticism of work among foreigners performed by the foreign language press in the Soviet Union see "O sostoianie raboty s inostrannymi rabochimi i spetsialistami" ("On the state of work with foreign workers and specialists"), Postanovlenie TsK VKP (b) ot 16 Aout 1931 goda (Enactment of the Central Committee of the All-Union Communist Party-Bolshevik, Aug. 16, 1931), *Partiinoe Stroitel'stvo*, No. 18 (Sept., 1931), p. 55, and *Mezhdunarodnoe Rabochee Dvizhenie*, No. 9 (March 30, 1932), p. 15.
106 Chamberlin, *Russia's Iron Age*, pp. 338–39; Eugene Lyons, *The Red Decade* (New York: Bobbs-Merrill, 1941), pp. 332–33.
107 *Moscow News*, Nov. 27, 1931, p. 3.
108 Scott, *Behind the Urals*, p. 138.
109 Beal, *Proletarian Journey*, p. 280.
110 *Ibid.*, p. 281.
111 *Ibid.*, pp. 285–86.

112 A. Rudolf (Raoul Lazlo), *Pourquoi j'ai quitté l'URSS*. La Documentation Anti-Communiste de CILACC, No. 10–11 (1935), p. 8.
113 Decimal Files, Department of State, 861.5017LC/241, memorandum on talk with Mr. H., an American employed at Stalingrad, April 17, 1931, p. 1.
114 Rubiner, "Rabota sredi . . . Partorganizatsii," pp. 17–18.
115 Decimal Files, Department of State, 861.5017LC/677, memorandum on talk with Mr. H., an American employed at Kharkov, June 14, 1933, pp. 5–6.
116 G. Voiloshnikov and Ch. Sommers, "O partinno-massovoi rabote s inostrannymi rabochimi" ("On party-mass work with foreign workers"), *Partiinoe Stroitel'stvo*, No. 3–4 (Feb., 1931), p. 46.
117 Beal, *Proletarian Journey*, p. 282.
118 Voiloshnikov and Sommers, "O partinno-massovoi . . . rabochimi," p. 43.
119 "O rabote sredi inostrannykh rabochikh" ("On work among foreign workers"), Postanovlenie TsK VKP (b) ot 21 Noiabria 1930 goda (Enactment of the Central Committee of the All-Union Communist Party-Bolshevik, Nov. 21, 1930), *Partiinoe Stroitel'stvo*, No. 23–24 (Dec., 1930), p. 67.
120 *Ibid.*
121 Voiloshnikov and Sommers, "O partinno-massovoi . . . rabochimi," p. 45.
122 "O khode vypolneniia direktiv TsK po rabote s inostrannymi rabochimi" ("On the manner in which the directives of the Central Committee pertaining to work with foreign workers are being carried out"), Postanovlenie TsK VKP (b) ot 23 Marta 1931 goda (Enactment of the Central Committee of the All-Union Communist Party-Bolshevik, March 23, 1931), *Partiinoe Stroitel'stvo*, No. 7 (April, 1931), p. 75.
123 "O sostoianie raboty s inostrannymi rabochimi i spetsialistami" ("On the state of work with foreign workers and specialists"), pp. 55–56.
124 Rubiner, "Rabota sredi . . . Partorganizatsii," pp. 17–20.
125 Decimal Files, Department of State, 861.044/68, *Legal Standing of Foreigners in the Soviet Union, 1925*, Jan. 15, 1926, p. 7.
126 *Moscow News*, Dec. 22, 1930, p. 1.
127 Interview No. 7, Feb. 14, 1963.
128 Decimal Files, Department of State, 361.00/4, memorandum on Soviet citizenship laws, Aug. 20, 1934, p. 1.

129 *Ibid.*, 861.012/80, report on the acquisition of Soviet citizenship by American citizens, Oct. 4, 1934, p. 1.
130 *Ibid.*, p. 4.
131 *Ibid.*, p. 13.
132 *Ibid.*
133 *Ibid.*, p. 14.
134 Interview No. 2, Feb. 12, 1963.
135 Decimal Files, Department of State, 861.5017LC/422, memorandum on talk with Mr. K., alien resident of the United States, Feb. 19, 1932, pp. 9–10.
136 *Ibid.*, 861.5017LC/679, memorandum on conversation with Mr. K., Finnish-American, June 10, 1933, p. 5.
137 Interview No. 7, Feb. 14, 1963.
138 M. Yvon, *L'U.S.S.R. telle qu'elle est* (Paris: Gallimard, 1938), pp. 245–46. According to W. G. Krivitsky, *In Stalin's Secret Service* (New York: Harper & Bros., 1939), pp. 26–27, members of one group of émigrés, the Schutzbunder, opted to return to Austria even with the knowledge that long prison terms awaited them. After the Soviet authorities had exploited them for propaganda purposes, they suffered arrest, exile to Siberia, or recruitment for service in the International Brigade which fought in Spain. See also Alexander Evstifeev, *Why I Escaped from Soviet Russia* (Seattle: privately printed, 1937), p. 32; Interview No. 2, Feb. 12, 1963.

CHAPTER 5: PROTECTING THE SOVIET IMAGE

1 See Chapter 3, p. 56.
2 Joseph Douillet, *Moscow Unmasked*, trans. A. W. King (London: Pilot Press, 1930), p. 35.
3 Andrew Smith, *I Was a Soviet Worker* (New York: E. P. Dutton, 1936), p. 25.
4 Although Paul Douglas was assured by the organizers of the group that there were no Communists on the delegation, and more specifically that Robert Dunn was not a Communist (see p. 50), Benjamin Gitlow alleged that Robert Dunn was in fact a secret party member and the real director of the delegation. See Benjamin Gitlow, *I Confess* (New York: E. P. Dutton, 1940), p. 295. An Associated Press correspondent who had interviewed the group in Poland believed that "the Party [i.e., the delegation] had not been able to obtain a correct impression of matters" as long as they "relied principally on the service of Mrs.

Dunn," whom he called "a prejudiced translator." Decimal Files, Department of State, 861.00/11155, memorandum on conversations with American Trade Union Delegation, Sept. 16, 1927, p. 6. The Chargé d'Affairês at the American Embassy in Warsaw appraised the correspondent as a reliable and objective source.

Douglas has commented: "It is true that we were handicapped by not knowing the language. Mrs. Dunn was not my translator nor the official translator for the delegation. I specialized in wage statistics and these were independent of language." In describing his experiences with the delegation, Douglas has reported: "While in Russia, I made it clear that I was opposed to the Russian use of terror to suppress opposition, and at a night meeting outside of Moscow, when the United States was being attacked for the impending execution of Sacco and Vanzetti, I took the floor and said that while I thought that the trial had been unfair, nevertheless Sacco and Vanzetti had been given the full right of appeal for seven long years. I pointed out that in Russia a few months before, a group of bank clerks had been arrested at 2:30 in the morning and shot by 7 AM, and said that this was clear proof that political defendants were not given a fair trial in Russia. I insisted that this be translated. Afterwards I got into a long argument with some of the people about their methods, which I prophesied would be their undoing and would ultimately be turned against each other." Letter to the author, Sept. 29, 1967.

5 Tamara Solonevich, *Zapiski Sovetskoi Perevodchitsy* (*Diary of a Soviet Interpreter*) (Sofia, Bulgaria: Golos Rossii, 1937), p. 52.

6 *Ibid.*, pp. 136–37.

7 Margaret McCarthy, *Generation in Revolt* (London: William Heinemann, 1953), p. 105.

8 Solonevich, *Zapiski Sovetskoi Perevodchitsy*, p. 79.

9 *Ibid.*, p. 65.

10 See Chapter 4, pp. 98–99.

11 Frederick C. Barghoorn, *The Soviet Cultural Offensive* (Princeton, N.J.: Princeton University Press, 1960), p. 39.

12 Interview with Eugene Lyons, Dec. 12, 1962.

13 *Pravda*, Nov. 1, 1927, p. 6.

14 Douillet, *Moscow Unmasked*, p. 35.

15 Silas B. Axtell, "Russia and her Foreign Relations," *Annals of the*

American Academy of Political and Social Sciences, 128 (July, 1928): 86.

16   A. Rudolf (Raoul Lazlo), *Pourquoi j'ai quitté l'URSS*. La Documentation Anti-Communiste du CILACC, No. 10–11 (1935), p. 14.

17   Solonevich, *Zapiski Sovetskoi Perevodchitsy*, p. 58.

18   Douillet, *Moscow Unmasked*, p. 37.

19   Solonevich, *Zapiski Sovetskoi Perevodchitsy*, p. 68.

20   Walter Citrine, *A Trade Unionist Looks at Russia* (London: Trades Union Congress General Council, 1935), pp. 62–65.

21   *Ibid.*, p. 62. (See pp. 151–54 for a discussion of preparations for the visits of delegations and important individuals.)

22   Julian Huxley, *A Scientist among the Soviets* (New York: Harper & Bros., 1932), pp. 85–86.

23   Douillet, *Moscow Unmasked*, p. 36.

24   Theodor Siebert, *Red Russia*, trans. Eden and Cedar Paul (London: Allen & Unwin, 1932), p. 54.

25   E. M. Delafield (Edmé Elizabeth Monica De La Pasture), *I Visit the Soviets* (New York: Harper & Bros., 1937), p. 78. The Seattle Commune was a farm founded in 1922 by American workers from Seattle, the majority of Russian or Ukrainian background, who were dissatisfied with life in the United States.

26   Edmund Wilson, *Red, Black, Blond and Olive* (New York: Oxford University Press, 1956), pp. 308–10.

27   Violet Conolly, *Soviet Tempo* (London: Sheed & Ward, 1937), p. 45. See also David Low and Kingsley Martin, *Low's Russian Sketchbook* (London: Victor Gollancz, 1932), pp. 81–82, for a different experience, and some explanation (p. 81) why opposition to visitors existed in 1932. An American worker at Gorki suggested that one reason for the plant's being closed was the fact that, beginning in 1933, it was being retooled to build tanks in case of a later emergency. Interview No. 2, Feb. 12, 1963.

28   Axtell, *Russia and her Foreign Relations,*" pp. 86–87.

29   Paul V. Harper, ed., *The Russia I Believe In: Memoirs of Samuel N. Harper, 1902–1941* (Chicago: University of Chicago Press, 1945), p. 172.

30   Low and Martin, *Low's Russian Sketchbook*, p. 79.

31   Wilson, *Red, Black, Blond and Olive*, p. 380.

32   Harry Stekoll, *Humanity Made to Order* (New York: L. Furman, 1937), pp. 3–4.

33   Harper, *The Russia I Believe In*, p. 213; interview with John N. Hazard, Dec. 10, 1962; Interview No. 4, March 14, 1963.

34 Interview with Hindus, March 5, 1963.
35 Interview with Mrs. Joseph Kohan, Feb. 26, 1963.
36 Interview with Miss Bigland, March 19, 1963.
37 F. S. Miles, *Changing Russia* (London: Marshall, Morgan & Scott, 1936), p. 13.
38 Eugene Lyons, *Assignment in Utopia* (New York: Harcourt, Brace, 1937), p. 452.
39 Lester Cohen, *Two Worlds* (London: Victor Gollancz, 1936), pp. 80–81.
40 Reply to evaluation, No. 173, in Anglo-American Institute of 1st Moscow University Files, Institute of International Education, New York City.
41 Letter from student, Nov. 9, 1934, *ibid.*
42 Interview with Miss Conolly, April 25, 1963.
43 When this story was published in 1937, the British pound was worth about twenty rubles. In 1926, when the incident happened, the exchange ratio was about nine to one. The author probably substituted by mistake the pound-ruble ratio at the time of writing for that when the incident she described took place. See Solonevich, *Zapiski Sovetskoi Perevodchitsy*, pp. 115–16.
44 Letter from Spencer Williams to Reeve Schley, Nov. 19, 1935, American-Russian Chamber of Commerce Files, in Alexander Gumberg Papers, State Historical Society of Wisconsin Library, Madison.
45 *Ibid.*
46 Barghoorn, *The Soviet Cultural Offensive*, p. 43.
47 Amy S. Jennings, "How to Travel in Soviet Russia," *Nation*, 136, (May 10, 1933): 528.
48 Docteur Maurice Potiron, "A Leningrad avec 500 Francais," *La Tribune de l'Yonne*, Aug. 22, 1932, in Clipping Files, Bibliothèque de Documentation Internationale Contemporaine, University of Paris.
49 Burton Holmes, *The Traveler's Russia* (New York: G. P. Putnam's Sons, 1934), pp. 93–94, 126.
50 Interview No. 4, March 14, 1963.
51 R. A. Simoens, *L'Union Soviétique vue par un travailleur* (Brussels: Impr. "Steenlandt" S.P.R.L., 1941), p. 7.
52 Marc Chadourne, *L'URSS sans passion* (Paris: Libraire Plon, 1932), p. xi.
53 Rudolf, *Pourquoi j'ai quitté l'URSS*, p. 14.

54   Liam O'Flaherty, *I Went to Russia* (New York: Harcourt, Brace, 1931), pp. 267–68.
55   Charlotte Haldane, *Truth Will Out* (New York: Vanguard Press, 1950), p. 46.
56   Fred E. Beal, *Foreign Workers in a Soviet Tractor Plant* (Moscow: Co-operative Publishing Society of Foreign Workers in the U.S.S.R., 1933), p. 46.
57   Sigmund Neumann, "Toward a Comparative Study of Political Parties," *Modern Political Parties*, ed. S. Neumann (Chicago: University of Chicago Press, 1956), pp. 404–5.
58   Anne O'Hare McCormick, *The Hammer and the Scythe* (New York: A. A. Knopf, 1928), p. 49.
59   Rudolf, *Pourquoi j'ai quitté l'URSS*, p. 14.
60   Smith, *I Was a Soviet Worker*, p. 74.
61   Interview No. 12, April 1, 1963.
62   *Ibid.;* André Gide, *Afterthoughts on the U.S.S.R.*, trans. Dorothy Bussy (New York: Dial Press, 1938), p. 102.
63   Interview No. 12, April 1, 1963.
64   Smith, *I Was a Soviet Worker*, p. 186.
65   Douillet, *Moscow Unmasked*, p. 24.
66   Decimal Files, Department of State, 861.00/10993, text of protest sent Central Executive Committee of the Ukraine, Nov., 1926.
67   See p. 159.
68   Heinz Unger, *Hammer, Sickle and Baton: The Soviet Memoirs of a Musician* (London: Cresset Press, 1939), p. 147.
69   See pp. 152–53.
70   Interview No. 2, Feb. 12, 1963.
71   John Scott, *Behind the Urals* (Cambridge, Mass.: Houghton Mifflin, 1942), p. 90.
72   Axtell, "Russia and her Foreign Relations," p. 87.
73   Fernand Corcos, *Une visite à la Russie nouvelle* (Paris: Editions Montaigne, 1930), pp. 23–25.
74   Simoens, *L'Union Soviétique vue par un travailleur*, p. 17.
75   Interview with Andre Lebed, April 1, 1963.
76   Victor Kravchenko, *I Chose Freedom* (New York: Charles Scribner's Sons, 1946), p. 184.
77   Decimal Files, Department of State, 861.5017LC/553, memorandum on conversation with the Russian wife of an American engineer, Nov. 4, 1932, pp. 3–4.
78   Paul Scheffer, *Seven Years in Soviet Russia*, trans. Arthur Livingston (London: Putnam, 1931), p. xiii.

79 Decimal Files, Department of State, 861.5017LC/310, letter from American specialist in Russia to employers in New York, July 19, 1931, p. 2.

80 June Seymour, *In the Moscow Manner* (London: D. Archer, Ltd., 1935), p. 203.

81 George A. Burrell, *An American Engineer Looks at Russia* (Boston: Stratford, 1932), p. 122.

82 Walter A. Rukeyser, *Working for the Soviets* (New York: Covici-Friede, 1932), pp. 29–30. In the early years after the Revolution the regime had to hire for their skills Russian engineers whose politics were suspect, hence the contacts of these technicians with their foreign counterparts were limited.

83 Interview No. 2, Feb. 12, 1963.

84 Interview with Louis Fischer, Jan. 21, 1963.

85 Lyons, *Assignment in Utopia*, p. 80.

86 James E. Abbe, *I Photograph Russia* (New York: Robert M. McBride, 1934), p. 166.

87 Reply to evaluation, No. 170, in Anglo-American Institute of 1st Moscow University Files.

88 Ray Long, *An Editor Looks at Russia* (New York: R. Long & R. R. Smith, 1931), pp. 68–70.

89 McCormick, *The Hammer and the Scythe*, p. 56.

90 E. Ashmead-Bartlett, *The Riddle of Russia* (London: Cassell, 1929), p. 38.

91 "O rabote sredi inostrannykh rabochikh" ("On work among foreign workers"), Postanovlenie TsK VKP (b) ot 21 Noiabria 1930 goda (Enactment of the Central Committee of the All-Union Communist Party-Bolshevik, Nov. 21, 1930), *Partiinoe Stroitel'stvo*, No. 23–24 (Dec., 1930), p. 67

92 Interview with Mosely, Nov. 19, 1962.

93 Interview with Miller, April 21, 1963.

94 Interview with Hindus, March 5, 1963.

95 John D. Littlepage and Demaree Bess, *In Search of Soviet Gold* (New York: Harcourt, Brace, 1938), p. 18.

96 Harry Timbres and Rebecca Timbres, *We Didn't Ask Utopia* (New York: Prentice-Hall, 1939), p. 176.

97 Interview No. 4, March 14, 1963. Kirov's death is usually taken as the beginning of the Great Purge, a period of immense fear and suspicion throughout Russia when relations with foreigners were extremely dangerous.

98 Interviews with Joseph Barnes, Jan. 21, 1963; Louis Fischer, Jan. 21, 1963.

99 McCarthy, *Generation in Revolt*, pp. 197–98.
100 Allan Monkhouse, *Moscow, 1911–1933* (London: Victor Gollancz, 1933), pp. 154–55.
101 Interviews with J. Miller, April 21, 1963; John N. Hazard, Dec. 10, 1962.
102 Wilson, *Red, Black, Blond and Olive*, p. 183; Interview with Fischer, Jan. 21, 1963.
103 Decimal Files, Department of State, 861.00/10978, memorandum on talk with Professor Samuel Harper, Nov. 3, 1926. See also Harper, *The Russia I Believe In*, p. 153.
104 Decimal Files, Department of State, 861.5017LC/168, memorandum given Embassy by Professor Samuel Harper, Aug. 12, 1930, p. 2.
105 *Ibid.*, 861.5017LC/544, statement of Professor Samuel Harper, Oct. 13, 1932, p. 2.
106 Harper, *The Russia I Believe In*, pp. 213–14.
107 John Dewey, *Impressions of Soviet Russia and the Revolutionary World* (New York: New Republic, 1929), p. 20.
108 Burrell, *An American Engineer Looks at Russia*, p. 111.
109 *New York Times*, April 13, 1930, Sec. III, p. 1.
110 Ella Winter, *Red Virtue* (New York: Harcourt, Brace, 1933), p. 77. Soviet authorities hoped that the foreign specialists would do more than the technical job; they hoped that they would also participate in the psychological and sociological aspects of building a new society.
111 Letter from Alexander Gumberg to Hugh Cooper, Aug. 5, 1930, p. 2, in American-Russian Chamber of Commerce Files.
112 Letter from A. Choumak to American-Russian Chamber of Commerce, Jan. 8, 1931, *ibid.*
113 Interview with Williams, Part II, Dec. 6, 1962.
114 *New York Times*, May 13, 1931, p. 10.
115 *Ibid.*
116 As quoted *ibid.*
117 *Ibid.*
118 Interview with Lyons, Dec. 12, 1962.
119 Interviews with Joseph Barnes, Jan. 21, 1963; with Charles Thayer, Feb. 13, 1963.
120 Scheffer, *Seven Years in Soviet Russia*, p. xii.
121 Interviews with Charles Thayer, Feb. 13, 1963; John N. Hazard, Dec. 10, 1962.
122 William Reswick, *I Dreamt Revolution* (Chicago: Henry Regnery, 1952), pp. 214–15.

123 Friedrich Adler, *The Anglo-Russian Report; A Criticism of the Report of the British Trades Union Delegation to Russia, from the Point of View of International Socialism,* trans. H. J. Stenning (London: P. S. King & Son, 1925), p. 16.

124 As described in Scheffer, *Seven Years in Soviet Russia,* p. ix.

125 Lyons, *Assignment in Utopia,* p. 110.

126 William Henry Chamberlin, *Soviet Russia,* rev. ed. (Boston: Little, Brown, 1934), p. 394.

127 William Henry Chamberlin, *Russia's Iron Age* (Boston: Little, Brown, 1931), pp. 147–49.

128 *Ibid.,* pp. 148–49; Lyons, *Assignment in Utopia,* pp. 573–76.

129 See p. 120.

130 Scheffer, *Seven Years in Soviet Russia,* p. viii.

131 Decimal Files, Department of State, 861.5017LC/166, memorandum on interview with Mr. C., Moscow correspondent of *London News Chronicle.*

132 Scheffer, *Seven Years in Soviet Russia,* p. x; Ashmead-Bartlett, *Riddle of Russia,* pp. 8–9; Seibert, *Red Russia,* p. 9.

133 Louis Fischer, *Men and Politics* (New York: Duell, Sloan & Pearce, 1941), p. 233.

134 *Ibid.,* p. 234.

135 Scheffer, *Seven Years in Soviet Russia,* p. x.

136 *Ibid.*

137 *Ibid.,* p. xiv; Chamberlin, *Russia's Iron Age,* p. 149.

138 William Henry Chamberlin, *The Confessions of an Individualist* (New York: Macmillan, 1940), pp. 160–61.

139 Interview with Williams, Part I, Nov. 27, 1962; telegram to Soviet Chamber of Commerce from Reeve Schley, Dec. 21, 1929, in American-Russian Chamber of Commerce Files.

140 Copy of telegram from Soviet Chamber of Commerce to American-Russian Chamber of Commerce, New York, Dec. 20, 1929, *ibid.*

141 Interview with Williams, Part I, Nov. 27, 1962.

142 *Pravda,* 1927: Jan. 29, p. 4; Feb. 2, p.4.

143 Decimal Files, Department of State, 861.602/212, memorandum on German Drusag Concession, Feb. 20, 1930, p. 2.

144 The London *Times,* Feb. 27, 1930, p. 14.

145 Decimal Files, Department of State, 861.602/210, memorandum on Lena Goldfields, Jan. 13, 1930, p. 2.

146 Monkhouse, *Moscow, 1911–1933,* p. 244.

147 *Pravda,* Oct. 16, 1929, p. 4.

148 See Chapter 3, p. 73.

149 Interview with Hazard, Dec. 10, 1962.
150 See p. 132.
151 Hadley Cantril, *Soviet Leaders and Mastery Over Man* (New Brunswick, N.J.: Rutgers University Press, 1960), pp. 65–66.
152 A. G. Kovalev and N. Miasishchev, *The Characteristics of Man* (Leningrad: University of Leningrad Press, 1957), pp. 110–11, as quoted in Cantril, *Soviet Leaders and Mastery Over Man*, p. 66.
153 Solonevich, *Zapiski Sovetskoi Perevodchitsy*, p. 45.
154 *Ibid.*, pp. 45–46.
155 Smith, *I Was a Soviet Worker*, p. 79.
156 Harry Stekoll, *Through the Communist Looking-Glass* (New York: Brewer, Warren & Putnam, 1932), pp. 78–79.
157 Boris Silver, *The Russian Workers' Own Story* (London: G. Allen & Unwin, 1938), pp. 146–47.
158 Solonevich, *Zapiski Sovetskoi Perevodchitsy*, p. 80.
159 Mira Wilkins and Frank E. Hill, *American Business Abroad: Ford on Six Continents* (Detroit: Wayne State University Press, 1964), p. 215.
160 Littlepage and Bess, *In Search of Soviet Gold*, pp. 88–89.
161 *Pravda*, Oct. 16, 1929, p. 2.
162 Rukeyser, *Working for the Soviets*, p. 116; Ruth Kennell and Milly Bennet, "American Immigrants in Russia," *American Mercury*, 34 (April, 1932): 472.
163 Decimal Files, Department of State, 861.5017LC/310, letter from American specialist in Russia to employers in New York, July 21, 1931, p. 6.
164 Interview with Andre Lebed, April 1, 1963.
165 Interview with Mrs. Joseph Kohan, Feb. 26, 1963.
166 Solonevich, *Zapiski Sovetskoi Perevodchitsy*, pp. 131–32.
167 As quoted in Wilkins and Hill, *American Business Abroad*, p. 214.
168 Interview with Spencer Williams, Part I, Nov. 27, 1962.
169 Axtell, "Russia and her Foreign Relations," p. 87.
170 Abbe, *I Photograph Russia*, p. 202.
171 Lyons, *Assignment in Utopia*, p. 107.
172 Decimal Files, Department of State, 861.5017LC/223, memorandum on conversation with Mr. K., assistant to Mr. Walter Duranty, Feb. 21, 1931, p. 10.
173 *Ibid.*
174 *Hamburgher Nachrichten*, Sept. 14, 1927, as quoted in Decimal

Files, Department of State, 861.602/144, Foreign Concessions
in Russia, Sept. 20, 1927, p. 3.
175 *Ibid.*
176 Scheffer, *Seven Years in Soviet Russia*, p. 263.
177 Donald N. Lammers, "The Engineers' Trial (Moscow, 1933)
and Anglo-Soviet Relations," *South Atlantic Quarterly*, 62
(Spring, 1963): 102.
178 Smith, *I Was a Soviet Worker*, p. 38.
179 Decimal Files, Department of State, 861.5017LC/40l, memorandum on interview with Mr. P., bridge engineer, Jan. 6, 1932,
p. 1.
180 *New York Times*, March 14, 1932, p. 8.
181 *Ibid.*, March 18, 1932, p. 9.
182 *Ibid.*
183 Scott, *Behind the Urals*, p. 4.
184 A. Kilinskii, "Ob usloviiakh truda inostrantsev v SSSR" ("On
labor conditions for foreigners in the USSR"), *Voprosy Truda*,
No. 1 (Jan., 1931), p. 78.
185 Decimal Files, Department of State, 361.11Employees/337,
interview with Mr. T., American drilling superintendent at Baku,
Nov. 3, 1934, pp. 2–3.
186 John Vidor, *Spying in Russia* (London: J. Long, 1929), p. 56.
187 Walter Citrine, *I Search for Truth in Russia* (London: G. Routledge & Sons, 1936), p. 214.
188 John A. Armstrong, *The Politics of Totalitarianism* (New York:
Random House, 1961), p. 181, from "Bor'ba bol'shevistskoi
partii za rastsvet sovetskogo iskusstva" ("The struggle of the
Bolshevik Party for the blossoming of Soviet art"), *Bolshevik*,
No. 6 (1949), p. 7.
189 Solonevich, *Zapiski Sovetskoi Perevodchitsy*, p. 70.
190 Stekoll, *Humanity Made to Order*, pp. 99–100.
191 Interview with Hindus, March 5, 1963.
192 Interview with Fischer, Jan. 21, 1963.
193 Cyrille Zaitseff, *Herriot en Russie* (Paris: Nouvelle Éditions-
Latins, 1933), p. 46.
194 While the word *subbotnik* in Russian literally means "Saturday,"
and the original meaning of the word referred to extra work
performed "voluntarily" by Russian workers on that day, *subbotnik* came to mean the performance of so-called voluntary
work performed at any time beyond the ordinary working
hours. See Smith, *I Was a Soviet Worker*, p. 74.

195 Fred E. Beal, *Proletarian Journey* (New York: Hillman-Curl, 1937), p. 313.
196 Judy Acheson, *Young America Looks at Russia* (New York: Frederick A. Stokes, 1932), p. 62.
197 Motus, *A travers de pays des Soviets* (Paris: Les Éditions de France, 1936), pp. 5–6.
198 Beal, *Proletarian Journey*, p. 315; McCormick, *The Hammer and the Scythe*, p. 199.
199 *Ibid.*
200 Vidor, *Spying in Russia*, pp. 54–55.
201 Beal, *Proletarian Journey*, pp. 314–15.
202 Vidor, *Spying in Russia*, pp. 54–55.
203 Arthur Feiler, *The Experiment of Bolshevism*, trans. H. J. Stenning (London: G. Allen & Unwin, 1930), p. 25.
204 *Pravda*, Oct. 27, 1927, p. 4.
205 *Pravda*, Nov. 3, 1928, p. 3.
206 Peter Francis, *I Worked in a Soviet Factory* (London: Jarrolds, 1939), p. 77.
207 Seibert, *Red Russia*, p. 51.
208 Abbe, *I Photograph Russia*, p. 258.
209 John Wynne Hird, *Under Czar and Soviet: My Thirty Years in Russia* (London: Hurst & Blackett, 1932), pp. 208–9.
210 Motus, *A travers de pays des Soviets*, p. 6.
211 *Ibid.*; Ellery Walter, *Russia's Decisive Year* (New York: G. P. Putnam's Sons, 1932), p. 148.
212 Interview No. 7, Feb. 14, 1963.
213 Interview with Lyons, Dec. 12, 1962.
214 Interview with Chamberlin, Jan. 30, 1963.
215 Interview with Thayer, Feb. 13, 1963.
216 *Ibid.*
217 Interview with Fischer, Jan. 21, 1963.
218 As quoted in the *New York Times*, July 30, 1934, p. 5.

CHAPTER 6: UTILIZING FOREIGNERS FOR PROPAGANDA

1 Tamara Solonevich, *Zapiski Sovetskoi Perevodchitsy* (*Diary of a Soviet Interpreter*) (Sofia, Bulgaria: Golos Rossii, 1937), p. 129.
2 Decimal Files, Department of State, 861.5017LC/242, memorandum on information received from the Estonian Foreign Office, April 20, 1931.

3 Fred E. Beal, *Proletarian Journey* (New York: Hillman-Curl, 1937), pp. 285–86.
4 *Ibid.*
5 *Moscow News,* Oct. 5, 1930, p. 1.
6 Interview with Williams, Part I, Nov. 27, 1962.
7 Decimal Files, Department of State, 861.77/4233, memorandum on conversation with Mr. P., American engineer, March 10, 1931, p. 11.
8 Liam O'Flaherty, *I Went to Russia* (New York: Harcourt, Brace, 1931), pp. 216–17.
9 James E. Abbe, *I Photograph Russia* (New York: Robert M. McBride, 1934), p. 315; *New York Times,* Sept. 25, 1933, p. 17.
10 Interview No. 1, March 29, 1963.
11 John E. Waters, *Red Justice* (Madison, Wis.: privately printed, 1933), p. 29.
12 *Ibid.*
13 George A. Burrell, *An American Engineer Looks at Russia* (Boston: Stratford, 1932), pp. 68–69.
14 Decimal Files, Department of State, 861.5017LC/663, memorandum on conversations with American engineer at Chelyabinsk, May 27, 1933, p. 4.
15 Solonevich, *Zapiski Sovetskoi Perevodchitsy,* p. 129.
16 *Ibid.,* pp. 134–35.
17 *Ibid.,* pp. 139–40.
18 Margaret McCarthy, *Generation in Revolt* (London: William Heinemann, 1953), p. 106; John Vidor, *Spying in Russia* (London: J. Long, 1929), p. 20. Miss McCarthy described the partying as "particularly marked among the adult delegation especially at one party during which the men ordered whisky for the toasts. This they diluted from the water decanters on the dining-tables; the decanters, however, contained not water, but vodka, a gift from the crew. The results can be imagined."
19 Vidor, *Spying in Russia,* pp. 20–21.
20 "What British Labor Saw in Soviet Russia," *American Federationist,* 32 (March, 1925): 185.
21 *Ibid.*
22 *Ibid.*
23 Heinz Unger, *Hammer, Sickle and Baton: The Soviet Memoirs of a Musician* (London: Cresset Press, 1939), p. 247.
24 "A Plan of Work of the Agitprop Department of the ECCI for the Next Half Year," in Great Britian, Home Office, *Communist*

Papers—Documents Selected from Those Obtained on the Arrest of Communist Leaders on the 14th and 21st October, 1925, Cmd. 2682 (London, 1926), p. 12.

25 Letter from Agitprop Department of the British Communist Party to the Secretary of the Agitprop Department of the Comintern Executive, May 21, 1925, *ibid.*, p. 14.

26 *La Vie Ouvrière,* Aug. 21, 1925, p. 1.

27 B. Vinogradov, *Desiat' Let Kapitalisticheskogo Okruzheniia SSSR (Ten Years of the Capitalist Encirclement of the USSR)* (Moscow: Kommunisticheskoi Akademii, 1928), pp. 114–15.

28 Friedrich Adler, *The Anglo-Russian Report; A Criticism of the Report of the British Trades Union Delegation to Russia, from the Point of View of International Socialism,* trans. H. J. Stenning (London: P. S. King & Son, 1925), p. 11.

29 *Ibid.*

30 *Ibid.*, p. 13.

31 Benjamin Gitlow, *I Confess,* (New York: E. P. Dutton, 1940), p. 294.

32 *Ibid.*, p. 297.

33 Decimal Files, Department of State, 861.00/11155, memorandum on talk with American Labor Delegation by Associated Press Warsaw correspondent, Sept. 16, 1927, p. 3.

34 *Ibid.*

35 *Ibid.*, p. 4.

36 *New York Times,* Sept. 28, 1927, p. 11.

37 Decimal Files, Department of State, 032/528, memorandum on interview with Professor J. B. Brebner, Sept. 13, 1927, p. 5.

38 Silas B. Axtell, "Russia and her Foreign Relations," *Annals of the American Academy of Political and Social Sciences,* 128 (July, 1928): 86.

39 Since there seems to be considerable difference among the people mentioned above, the question arises: How was such a favorable report produced? Gitlow alleged that Robert Dunn, with the aid of the American Communist party and the Comintern, drafted and put the report of the delegation into final form. Paul Douglas, in discussing the report, has commented that Coyle, initially assigned to write the report, delayed so long that he himself did a first draft of a considerable portion of it, and that Dr. George Counts drafted the chapter on education and Rexford Tugwell the chapter on agriculture. "I wrote a section," Douglas reports, "denouncing the suppression of civil liberties. But I was going back to Chicago and so the draft was put in the hands of

Coyle, who was to see it through the press. Unfortunately, unknown to me and to the others, he softened a great deal of the language, although here and there remains of the earlier criticism were printed. Later in a larger volume [a joint survey by the technical staff of the first American trade union delegation, American Trade Union Delegation to the Soviet Union, *Soviet Russia in the Second Decade*, eds. Stuart Chase, Robert Dunn, and Rexford Guy Tugwell (New York: John Day, 1928)] in the chapter on labor conditions, I refused to approve certain paragraphs by Dunn which I thought were biased and our sections appeared separately. I insisted on identifying his paragraphs and mine to make the distinction between us clear. In my section on wages, I brought out for the first time the extremely low earnings of government employees. It is true that I reported favorably on certain efforts of the Russians, notably in the fields of social insurance, co-operatives, and reducing the wage and salary differentials between groups. It should be remembered that the summer of 1927 showed the new regime at its best. The civil war and the famines were over. The struggle with Trotsky had not culminated in the terror. Stalin was talking about 'socialism in one country,' and saying he wanted to live on good terms with the West. The new economic policy encouraging private farms, handicrafts, and private trade was in effect. Production had risen greatly and so had wages, although they were still low and only about one-third or one-fourth of the American level. It seemed possible that Russia and the West might get along with each other. I thought we should make a try and that we were in no military danger from the Soviet Union, which was then weak. By the time the United States recognized the Soviet Union in 1933, the terror had been reinstated, unknown to the West, and Stalin had adopted Trotsky's program of hostility and permanent revolution. As and when this became clear, I concluded that Russia could not be trusted and that the Communist tactics were full of deception and were basically hostile to the free world and to the United States." (Interview with Douglas, Feb. 5, 1963; letter from Douglas to author, Sept. 29, 1967.) A *New York Times* editorial of Oct. 22, 1927, also noted a difference between the tone of restraint in the comment in the preface that Russia was "as far from a hell of degeneracy and wretchedness as it is from a Utopia," and the details found in the rest of the report.

A former top Communist leader, in an interview, confirmed

Douglas' and Coyle's roles in the production of the report, and revealed that although he went over the report, he altered very little (Interview No. 8, Dec. 18, 1962). These accounts differ greatly from Gitlow's assertion that the delegation gladly entrusted the work of writing the report to Dunn and the Communist party. To confuse the picture still further, Silas Axtell claims that, instead of any procrastination involved with the writing of the report, it was whipped together on the return trip. He further asserts that since he had already expressed negative opinions, he was not invited to participate in any of the discussions that "presumably" took place before the report was issued. He did see the typewritten manuscript for a period of forty minutes on the day before the boat arrived home, and the impression received from reading the report was so different from the one he had received in Russia that he could not subscribe to it. (He could have been talking of the interim report.) (Axtell, "Russia and her Foreign Relations," p. 86.) One final piece of evidence is that the report was published by a Communist-front organization, International Publishers.

40 Interview No. 8, Dec. 18, 1962.
41 See Fred E. Beal, *Foreign Workers in a Soviet Tractor Plant* (Moscow: Co-operative Publishing Society of Foreign Workers in the U.S.S.R., 1933).
42 Interview No. 6, April 23, 1963.
43 Interview with Louis Fischer, Jan. 21, 1963; Eugene Lyons, *Assignment in Utopia* (New York: Harcourt, Brace, 1937), p. 543.
44 Abbe, *I Photograph Russia*, p. 41.
45 William H. Danforth, *Russia Under the Hammer and Sickle* (St. Louis: privately printed, 1927), p. 16.
46 See Chapter 4, p. 83.
47 *Trud*, Aug. 9, 1930, as translated in Decimal Files, Department of State, 361.11/4045, Sept. 4, 1930, p. 2.
48 *Trud*, Aug. 13, 1930, as translated *ibid.*
49 *Trud*, Aug. 29, 30, 1930, as translated *ibid.*, pp. 4–5.
50 Decimal Files, Department of State, 361.11/4046, memorandum on trial of two White southerners, Sept. 11, 1930, p. 1.
51 *Trud*, Sept. 5, 1930 as noted in Decimal Files, Department of State, 361.11/4046, Sept. 11, 1930, p. 4.
52 *Ibid.*
53 Decimal Files, Department of State, 361.11/4046, memorandum on trial of two White southerners, Sept. 11, 1930, p. 1.

Notes to Pages 170–173 253

54 *Ibid.*, p. 7.
55 Decimal Files, Department of State, 661.4116/169, memorandum on conversations with a member of the British Trade Delegation, April 20, 1929, p. 3.
56 Walter Duranty, *USSR* (New York: J. B. Lippincott, 1944), p. 155.
57 Interview with Chamberlin, Jan. 30, 1963.
58 Interview with Fischer, Jan. 21, 1963.
59 Decimal Files, Department of State, 661.6231/84, confirmation of telegram to Department of State, March 19, 1928, p. 2.
60 John D. Littlepage and Demaree Bess, *In Search of Soviet Gold* (New York: Harcourt, Brace, 1937), pp. 104, 203.
61 See USSR Supreme Court, *Hearings Before the Special Session of the Supreme Court of the USSR on Wrecking Activities at Power Stations in the USSR*. Translation of the official verbatim report (Moscow: State Law Publishing House, 1933).
62 Allan Monkhouse, *Moscow, 1911–1933* (London: Victor Gollancz, 1933), p. 285.
63 André Gide, *Return from the U.S.S.R.*, trans. Dorothy Bussy (New York: A. A. Knopf, 1937.)
64 See H. Lartigue, *La vérité sur l'URSS, 1937* (Paris: L'Intersyndical de Services Publics au Profit de ses Oeuvres, 1937).
65 Interview No. 5, April 1, 1963.
66 André Gide, *Afterthoughts on the U.S.S.R.*, trans. Dorothy Bussy (New York: Dial Press, 1938).
67   Stoit Foikhtvanger u dverei
    S antifashistskim vidom
    Smotrite, kak by sei ievrei
    Ne okazalsia Zhidom.

    Here stands Feuchtwanger at the door
    With an anti-Fascist appearance
    Take care, lest this Hebrew
    Turned out to be a Gide.

The Russian word *Zhid* could be translated as either "Jew" or the name "Gide." Interview No. 5, April 1, 1963. For another version see Nathan Leites and Elsa Bernaut, *Ritual of Liquidation* (Glencoe, Ill.: The Free Press for Rand Corp., 1954), p. 405, *n.* 23.

CHAPTER 7: THE REALIZATION OF SOVIET OBJECTIVES

1 Communist Youth International, *The Communist Youth International: Report of Activity between the Fourth and Fifth Congresses, 1924–28* (London: CPGB, 1928), p. 45.

2 Communist Party of Great Britain, "Political Report of the Central Committee," *The New Line: Documents of the Tenth Congress of the Communist Party of Great Britain, January 19–22, 1929* (London: CPGB, 1929), p. 28.

3 "Organizing Report of the Central Committee," *ibid.*, p. 55.

4 Friends of Soviet Russia, *Hands Off Soviet Russia: Report of the Cologne Conference of Friends of Soviet Russia* (London: FOSR, 1928), p. 21.

5 Communist International, *The Communist International Between the Fifth & the Sixth World Congresses, 1924–8* (London: CPGB, 1928), pp. 71–72.

6 CYI, *The Communist Youth International*, p. 43.

7 See pp. 52–55.

8 *Imprecorr*, Oct. 13, 1933, p. 1003.

9 *Soviet Russia Today*, Feb., 1933, p. 13.

10 Labour Party, *The Communist Solar System* (London: Labour Publications Department, 1933), p. 9.

11 Louis Nemzer, "The Soviet Friendship Societies," *Public Opinion Quarterly*, 13 (Summer, 1949): 269–70.

12 O. Piatnitskii, *The Communist Parties in the Fight for the Masses*, 13th Plenum of the Executive Committee of the Communist International (New York: Workers Library, 1933), pp. 74, 78–80; Piatnitskii, *The Work of the Communist Parties of France and Germany and the Tasks of the Communists in the Trade Union Movement*, 12th Plenum of the Executive Committee of the Communist International (New York: Workers Library, 1932), p. 7.

13 CI, *The Communist International Between the Fifth & the Sixth World Congresses*, p. 156.

14 A. Abolin, "The Development of the Soviet Trade Unions," *RILU Magazine*, Nos. 1–2 (Jan. 15–Feb. 1, 1932), p. 98.

15 *Ibid.*, p. 99.

16 Karl Kreibich, "The Delegations to Russia," *Communist International*, 5 (Jan. 1, 1928): 17.

17 Irving Howe and Lewis Coser, *The American Communist Party: A Critical History, 1919–1957* (Boston: Beacon Press, 1957), p. 266.

18 Trades Union Congress, *Russia 1924: Official Report of the British Trades Union Delegation to Russia in November and December, 1924* (London: Trades Union Congress General Council, 1925), p. 162.

19 *Ibid.*, p. 136.

20 American Trade Union Delegation to the Soviet Union, *Russia after Ten Years* (New York: International Publishers, 1927), p. 38.

21 Meno Lovenstein, *American Opinion of Soviet Russia* (Washington, D.C.: American Council on Public Affairs, 1941), p. 162.

22 B. Vinogradov, *Desiat' Let Kapitalisticheskogo Okruzheniia SSSR* (*Ten Years of the Capitalist Encirclement of the USSR*) (Moscow: Kommunisticheskoi Akademii, 1928), p. 114.

23 V. Iarotskii, "Novaia tiaga k Moskve y proletariatov Zapada" ("The new inclination toward Moscow of the Western proletariat"), *Vestnik Truda*, No. 11 (Oct., 1925) p. 30.

24 Walter Citrine, *I Search for Truth in Russia* (London: G. Routledge & Sons, 1936), pp. 205–6; Citrine, *A Trade Unionist Looks at Russia* (London: Trades Union Congress General Council, 1935), p. 18; Max Danish, *The World of David Dubinsky* (New York: World Publishing, 1957), pp. 66–67.

25 Major target groups in this drive were labor leaders and intellectuals interested in the living conditions of Soviet laborers. Rumors of famine would affect the image of a society which supposedly offered to its workers and peasants living conditions superior to those in the West.

26 Eugene Lyons, *Assignment in Utopia* (New York: Harcourt, Brace, 1937), p. 430.

27 The American journalist Eugene Lyons charged the press with aiding the Soviet regime by concealing the presence of the famine. He asserted that the need to stay on good terms with the Soviet censor influenced the press in failing to report honestly the existence of the famine till after the worst of the situation had passed. See *ibid.*, pp. 573–76.

28 See note 138, Chap. 4.

29 G. Voiloshnikov and Ch. Sommers, "O Partiino-massovoi rabote s inostrannymi rabochimi" ("On Party-mass work with foreign workmen"), *Partiinoe Stroitel'stvo*, No. 3–4 (Feb., 1931), p. 43.

30 "O khode vypolneniia direktiv TsK po rabote s inostrannymi rabochimi" ("On the manner in which the directives of the Central Committee pertaining to work with foreign workers are being carried out"), Postanovlenie TsK VKP (b) ot 23 Marta

1931 (Enactment of the Central Committee of the All-Union Communist Party-Bolshevik, March 23, 1931), *Partiinoe Stroitel'stvo*, No. 7 (April, 1931), p. 75.

31 F. Rubiner, "Rabota sredi inostrannykh rabochikh—zadacha vsei Partorganizatsii" ("Work among foreign workers—the task of the whole Party organization"), *Partiinoe Stroitel'stvo*, No. 17–18 (Sept., 1932), p. 18.

32 Decimal Files, Department of State, 861.5017LC/239, memorandum on conversations with two mechanics employed at Stalingrad, April 9, 1931, p. 1.

33 *Ibid.*, 861.5017LC/223, memorandum on conversation with Mr. K., assistant to Mr. Walter Duranty, Feb. 21, 1931, p. 6.

34 *Ibid.*; Voiloshnikov and Sommers, "O Partiino-massovoi rabote s inostrannymi rabochimi," p. 44.

35 See, for example, Howe and Coser, *The American Communist Party*, Chapters VII and VIII.

36 *Ibid.*, p. 280.

37 Raymond Aron, *The Opium of the Intellectuals*, trans. Terence Kilmartin (New York: Doubleday & Co., 1957), p. 291.

38 Marcel Liebman, "The Webbs and the New Civilization," *Survey*, No. 41 (April, 1962), p. 61.

39 Interview with Muggeridge, May 1, 1963.

40 John Dewey, *Impressions of Soviet Russia and the Revolutionary World* (New York: New Republic, 1929), pp. 25–26.

41 Burton Holmes, *The Traveler's Russia* (New York: G. P. Putnam's Sons, 1934), p. 93.

42 Eugene Lyons, *The Red Decade* (New York: Bobbs-Merrill, 1941), p. 94.

43 TUC, *Russia 1924*, p. 3.

44 See Chapter 4, p. 89.

45 Decimal Files, Department of State, 861.797 Austin & Co./5, impressions of Diplomatic Minister of Business Delegation of 1929, Aug. 20, 1929, p. 2.

46 Interview with Douglas, Feb. 5, 1963.

47 Jay N. Darling, *Ding Goes to Russia* (New York: McGraw-Hill, 1932), p. 52.

48 *Soviet Union Review*, March, 1931, p. 69.

49 M. Zhivov, ed., *Glazami Inostrantsev (Through Foreign Eyes)* (Moscow: Gosudarstvennoe Izdatel'stvo Khudozhestvennoi Literatury, 1932), p. xiii.

50 *Britain and the Soviets: Report of the Congress of Peace and Friendship with the USSR, 1935* (London: Martin Laurence,

1936); see also Alfred Sherman, "The Days of the Left Book Club," *Survey*, No. 41 (April, 1962), pp. 75–85.

51 Nathan Glazer, *The Social Basis of American Communism* (New York: Harcourt, Brace & World, 1961), p. 130.

52 George F. Kennan, *Russia and the West under Lenin and Stalin* (New York: Mentor Books, 1962), pp. 279–81, Robert Browder, *The Origins of Soviet-American Diplomacy* (Princeton, N. J.: Princeton University Press, 1953), pp. 108–12.

53 K. A. Jelenski, "The Literature of Disenchantment," *Survey*, No. 41 (April, 1962), pp. 109–19.

54 Statement for Press, April 7, 1954 (not issued) in Files of the Anglo-American Institute of 1st Moscow University, Institute for International Education, New York City.

55 Resume of replies to questionnaires sent to students who attended the Anglo-American Institute, July/August, 1934, p. 3, *ibid.*

56 E. Ashmead-Bartlett, *The Riddle of Russia* (London: Cassell, 1929), p. 38.

57 Decimal Files, Department of State, 861.5017LC/544, memorandum on conversation with Dr. Samuel Harper, Oct. 13, 1932, p. 2.

58 Interview No. 4, March 14, 1963.

59 Walter A. Rukeyser, *Working for the Soviets* (New York: Covici-Friede, 1932), p. 185.

60 Max Beloff, *The Foreign Policy of Soviet Russia, 1929–41*, Vol. 1, *1929–36* (London: Oxford University Press, 1947), pp. 31–32.

61 Browder, *The Origins of Soviet-American Diplomacy*, p. 30.

62 Beloff, *The Foreign Policy of Soviet Russia*, I: 33. Another way the Soviet regime hoped to obtain foreign exchange did not appear very successful until the mid-thirties. The regime periodically expressed dissatisfaction with the amount of money spent in the Soviet Union by foreigners. The authorities didn't feel that the amount spent by foreigners compensated for the cost of rebuilding hotels, organizing special railroad trips, training guides and interpreters, and buying cars and busses for sightseeing trips. One solution found was to require a minimum daily expenditure on the part of the tourist. See *New York Times*, July 5, 1931, Sec. III, p. 4e; Decimal Files, Department of State, 861.111/553. New decrees by Sovnarkom regulating re-exportation of currency and other valuables from that country by foreigners, July 8, 1929, p. 1.

63 *Soviet Union Review,* July–Aug., 1933, p. 172.
64 Browder, *The Origins of Soviet-American Diplomacy,* p. 219.
65 *Ibid.*
66 One group of difficulties resulted from the difference in working habits of foreign and Russian engineers. Foreign specialists often found that the difficulties involved in getting a definite program approved and started were tremendous because of the habit of Russian employees and officials of endlessly discussing each proposal. Engineers also cited the fear of Russian employees of taking any responsibility. Thus, foreigners believed that the Russians were more interested in getting specialists to relieve them of responsibility than in taking their advice. Part of the difficulties faced by foreign specialists stemmed from rivalry between different organs of government and between rival groups in the Soviet administrative hierarchy. Some complaints concerned situations where Communist party supervisors interfered in the work being carried on. Members of the firm of Albert Kahn, Inc., believed that difficulties arose largely from a hostile or critical attitude in which political considerations outweighed professional ones.

   Aside from these problems, friction between Soviet and foreign engineers stemmed from Soviet sensitivity at having to borrow from the West, which resulted in only limited co-operation with the foreign engineers. These attitudes on the part of Soviet engineers were not condoned by the higher Soviet authorities, and Soviet publications continually condemned conditions under which specialists were poorly utilized. However, other articles also criticized foreigners, sometimes with justification, for their refusal to meet Soviet methods half way and to try to understand different concepts of organization and social relations. See Decimal Files, Department of State, 861.602, 861.504, 861.5017LC, and 861.77 for additional material concerning the difficulties faced by foreign engineers, and the Soviet periodical *Ekonomicheskaia Zhizn'* for confirmation of these conditions by Soviet authorities. See also Heinz Unger, *Hammer, Sickle and Baton: The Soviet Memoirs of a Musician* (London: Cresset Press, 1939); Ruth Kennell and Milly Bennett, "American Immigrants in Russia," *American Mercury,* 34 (April, 1932): 463–72; and Rukeyser, *Working for the Soviets.*
67 See Chapter 5, pp. 132, 141–42.
68 Decimal Files, Department of State, 661.6231/86, memorandum on Shakhti Trial, March 27, 1928, pp. 3–4.

69 A. J. Cummings, *The Moscow Trial* (London: Victor Gollancz, 1933), p. 9.

70 Decimal Files, Department of State, 861.5017LC/618, memorandum on conversation with Mr. W., employee of Newport News Shipbuilding and Drydock Co., March 21, 1933, p. 2; 861.602/252, telegram from Berlin Embassy, March 17, 1933.

71 *Ibid.*, 861.5017LC/616, memorandum of conversation with Mr. T., consulting engineer with General Electric, March 15, 1933.

72 *Workers News*, April 18, 1932, p. 3.

73 Decimal Files, Department of State, 861.5017LC/409, memorandum on talk with Mr. P., American engineer in Russia, March 10, 1931, p. 7.

74 *Ibid.*, 861.5017LC/241, memorandum on talk with Mr. W., and Mr. B., former workers with the Soviet grain trust, April 17, 1931, p. 2.

75 *Ibid.*, 861.5017LC/365, memorandum on talk with Mr. G., naturalized American worker at Stalingrad, Nov. 17, 1931, p. 1; 861.5017LC/568, memorandum on conversation with Mr. M., who had been at Kramatorsky, Nov. 22, 1932, p. 6; 861.602/248, memorandum of conversation with an American returning from Russia, Nov. 22, 1932, pp. 1–2.

76 *Ibid.*, 711.61/338, letter from McDonald Engineering Co., Nov. 3, 1933.

77 Peter Filene, *Americans and the Soviet Experiment* (Cambridge, Mass.: Harvard University Press, 1967), p. 190.

78 Kreibich, "The Delegations to Russia," p. 17.

CHAPTER 8: CONTINUITY AND CHANGE, 1925–1965

1 See Frederick C. Barghoorn, *The Soviet Cultural Offensive* (Princeton, N.J.: Princeton University Press, 1960); Edward Crankshaw, "Big Brother Is Still Waiting," *New York Times Magazine*, Dec. 29, 1963, pp. 8, 34–35.

2 Interview with Lyons, Dec. 12, 1962.

3 R. L. Walker, "The Developing Role of Cultural Diplomacy in Asia," *Issues and Conflicts*, George L. Anderson, ed. (Lawrence, Kan.: University of Kansas Press, 1959), p. 45.

4 See Barghoorn, *The Soviet Cultural Offensive.*

5 Nate White, "Prisoners of Intourist: Visitors to U.S.S.R. Face Wall of 'Nyets,' " *Christian Science Monitor*, Aug. 18, 1960, p. 7.

6 Crankshaw, "Big Brother Is Still Waiting," p. 8.

7 Barghoorn, *The Soviet Cultural Offensive*, p. 300.

8   *Ibid.*
9   *Ibid.,* p. 329.
10 See Chapter 3, p. 33.
11 Barghoorn, *The Soviet Cultural Offensive,* pp. 159–60.
12 Crankshaw, "Big Brother Is Still Waiting," p. 36.
13 *Ibid.*
14 Barghoorn, *The Soviet Cultural Offensive,* pp. 201–2.
15 Nate White, "Prisoners of Intourist . . . ," p. 7.
16 Wanda Bronska-Pampuch, "Russia in German Eyes: 1964," *Survey,* No. 51 (April, 1964), p. 95.
17 Barghoorn, *The Soviet Cultural Offensive,* p. 11.

Bibliography

GENERAL WORKS

Armstrong, John A. *The Politics of Totalitarianism*. New York: Random House, 1961.

Aron, Raymond. *The Opium of the Intellectuals*, trans. Terence Kilmartin. New York: Doubleday & Company, Inc., 1957.

Barghoorn, Frederick C. *The Soviet Cultural Offensive*. Princeton, N.J.: Princeton University Press, 1960.

Bell, Tom. *The British Communist Party: A Short History*. London: Lawrence & Wishart, Ltd., 1937.

Beloff, Max. *The Foreign Policy of Soviet Russia, 1929–41*. Vol. I, *1929–36*. London: Oxford University Press, 1947.

Borkenau, Franz. *The Communist International*. London: Faber & Faber, Ltd., 1938.

――――. *European Communism*. London: Faber & Faber, Ltd., 1953.

Browder, Robert. *The Origins of Soviet-American Diplomacy*. Princeton, N.J.: Princeton University Press, 1953.

Cantril, Hadley. *Soviet Leaders and Mastery Over Man*. New Brunswick, N.J.: Rutgers University Press, 1960.

Curtiss, John S. *Church and State in Russia, 1900–1917*. New York: Columbia University Press, 1940.

Deutscher, Isaac. *Stalin: A Political Biography*. New York: Vintage Books, Inc., 1960.

Draper, Theodore. *American Communism and Soviet Russia*. New York: The Viking Press, Inc., 1960.

261

Dulles, Foster Rhea. *The Road to Teheran*. Princeton, N.J.: Princeton University Press, 1944.

Filene, Peter. *Americans and the Soviet Experiment*. Cambridge, Mass.: Harvard University Press, 1967.

Fischer, Louis. *The Soviets in World Affairs*. New York: Vintage Books, Inc., 1960.

Foster, William Z. *History of the Communist Party of the United States*. New York: International Publishers Co., Inc., 1952.

Fraser, Stewart, ed. *Governmental Policy and International Education*. New York: John Wiley & Sons, Inc., 1965.

Friedrich, Carl J., and Zbigniew K. Brzezinski. *Totalitarian Dictatorship and Autocracy*. New York: Frederick A. Praeger, Inc., 1961.

Glazer, Nathan. *The Social Basis of American Communism*. New York: Harcourt, Brace & Company, 1961.

Godden, Gertrude M. *Communist Attack on the People of Great Britain*. London: Burns, Oates & Washbourne, Ltd., 1938.

Hartley, Eugene, and Ruth Hartley. *Fundamentals of Social Psychology*. New York: Alfred A. Knopf, Inc., 1952.

Hovland, Carl I., Irving L. Janis, and Harold H. Kelley. *Communication and Persuasion*. New Haven, Conn.: Yale University Press, 1953.

Howe, Irving, and Lewis Coser. *The American Communist Party: A Critical History, 1919–1957*. Boston: Beacon Press, 1957.

Isaacs, Harold R. *Emergent Americans; A Report on Crossroads Africa*. New York: John Day Co., 1961.

Katz, Elihu, and Paul F. Lazarsfeld. *Personal Influence*. Glencoe, Ill.: The Free Press, 1955.

Keeton, George W. *The Problem of the Moscow Trial*. London: A. & C. Black, Ltd., 1933.

Kempton, Murray. *Part of Our Time*. New York: Simon and Schuster, Inc., 1955.

Kennan, George F. *Russia and the West under Lenin and Stalin*. New York: Mentor Books, 1962.

Leites, Nathan, and Elsa Bernaut. *Ritual of Liquidation*. Glencoe, Ill.: The Free Press for Rand Corporation, 1954.

Lippmann, Walter. *Public Opinion*. New York: The Macmillan Co., 1960.

Lovenstein, Meno. *American Opinion of Soviet Russia*. Washington, D.C.: American Council on Public Affairs, 1941.

McMurry, Ruth Emily, and Muna Lee. *The Cultural Approach*. Chapel Hill, N.C.: University of North Carolina Press, 1947.

Meyer, Alfred G. *Leninism.* New York: Frederick A. Praeger, Inc., 1962.

Moën, Lars. *Are You Going to Russia?* London: Chapman & Hall, Ltd., 1934.

Neumann, Sigmund, ed. *Modern Political Parties.* Chicago: University of Chicago Press, 1956.

Nevins, Allan, and Frank Ernest Hill. *Ford—Expansion and Challenge, 1915–1933.* New York: Charles Scribner's Sons, 1957.

Nollau, Gunther. *International Communism and World Revolution: History and Methods.* London: Hollis & Carter, Ltd., 1961.

Pelling, Henry. *The British Communist Party: A Historical Profile.* New York: The Macmillan Co., 1958.

Robinson, Geroid T. *Rural Russia under the Old Regime.* New York: The Macmillan Co., 1949.

Selltiz, Claire, *et al. Attitudes and Social Relations of Foreign Students in the United States.* Minneapolis, Minn.: University of Minnesota Press, 1963.

Selznick, Philip. *The Organizational Weapon.* Glencoe, Ill.: The Free Press, 1960.

Sherif, Muzafer, and Carolyn W. Sherif. *An Outline of Social Psychology.* Rev. ed. New York: Harper & Brothers, 1956.

Simmons, Ernest J. "Negotiating on Cultural Exchange, 1947," *Negotiating with the Russians,* ed. Raymond Dennett and Joseph E. Johnson. New York: The World Peace Foundation, 1951.

Slonim, Marc. *Modern Russian Literature.* New York: Oxford University Press, 1953.

Taft, Philip. *The AFL from the Death of Gompers to the Merger.* New York: Harper & Brothers, 1959.

Vinogradov, B. *Desiat' Let Kapitalisticheskogo Okruzheniia SSSR (Ten Years of the Capitalist Encirclement of the USSR).* Moscow: Kommunisticheskoi Akademii, 1928.

Vuivovich, V. *Mezhdunarodnoe Rabochee Dvizhenie I. Kommunisticheskii Internatsional (The International Working-Class Movement and the Communist International).* Moscow: Gosudarstvennoe Izdatel'stvo, 1926.

Vutkovskii, V. L. *Inostrannye Kontsessii v Narodnom Khoziaistve (Foreign Concessions in the National Economy of the USSR).* Moscow: Gosudarstvennoe Izdatel'stvo, 1928.

Walker, R. L. "The Developing Role of Cultural Diplomacy in Asia." *Issues and Conflicts,* ed. George L. Anderson. Lawrence, Kan.: University of Kansas Press, 1959.

Wilkins, Mira, and Frank Ernest Hill. *American Business Abroad: Ford on Six Continents.* Detroit: Wayne State University Press, 1964.

Williams, William Appleman. *American-Russian Relations, 1781–1947.* New York: Rinehart & Company, Inc., 1952.

Wolin, Simon, and Robert M. Slusser, eds. *The Soviet Secret Police.* New York: Frederick A. Praeger, Inc., 1958.

Wood, Neal. *Communism and British Intellectuals.* London: Victor Gollancz, Ltd., 1959.

SELECTED MEMOIRS AND BIOGRAPHIES

Abbe, James E. *I Photograph Russia.* New York: Robert M. McBride & Co., 1934.

Acheson, Judy. *Young America Looks at Russia.* New York: Frederick A. Stokes Company, 1932.

Ashmead-Bartlett, E. *The Riddle of Russia.* London: Cassell and Company, Ltd., 1929.

Beal, Fred E. *Proletarian Journey.* New York: Hillman-Curl, Inc., 1937.

Bentley, Elizabeth. *Out of Bondage.* New York: The Devin-Adair Co., 1951.

Bevan, Aneurin, E. J. Strachey, and George Strauss. *What We Saw in Russia.* London: Hogarth Press, 1931.

Bigland, Eileen. *Laughing Odyssey.* New York: The Macmillan Company, 1938.

Bouré, Julien. *Vu et entendu en U.R.S.S.* Paris: Les Éditions des Presses Modernes, 1938.

Bourke-White, Margaret. *Eyes on Russia.* New York: Simon and Schuster, 1931.

Brophy, John. *A Miner's Life.* Madison, Wis.: University of Wisconsin Press, 1964.

Brown, E. T. *This Russian Business.* Boston: Houghton Mifflin Company, 1933.

Buck, Pearl S. *A Talk about Russia with Marsha Scott.* New York: The John Day Co., 1945.

Burrell, George A. *An American Engineer Looks at Russia.* Boston: The Stratford Company, 1932.

Chadourne, Marc. *L'URSS sans passion.* Paris: Libraire Plon, 1932.

Chamberlin, William Henry. *The Confessions of an Individualist.* New York: The Macmillan Company, 1940.

———. *Russia's Iron Age.* Boston: Little, Brown, and Company, 1934.

————. *Soviet Russia*. Rev. ed. Boston: Little, Brown and Company, 1931.

Chardot, Marc. *L'economie soviétique entrevue par un francais moyen*. Paris: Libraire Generale, 1936.

Chesterton, Mrs. Cecil. *My Russian Venture*. Philadelphia: J. B. Lippincott Company, 1931.

Ciliberti, Charles. *Backstairs Mission in Moscow*. New York: Booktab Press, 1947.

Citrine, Walter. *I Search for Truth in Russia*, London: G. Routledge & Sons, Ltd., 1936.

————. *A Trade Unionist Looks at Russia*. London: The Trades Union Congress General Council, 1935.

Cohen, Lester. *Two Worlds*. London: Victor Gollancz, Ltd., 1936.

Conolly, Violet. *Soviet Tempo*. London: Sheed & Ward, 1937.

Corcos, Fernand. *Une visite à la Russie nouvelle*. Paris: Éditions Montaigne, 1930.

Counts, George S. *A Ford Crosses Soviet Russia*. Boston: The Stratford Company, 1930.

Crossman, R. H. S., ed. *The God That Failed: Six Studies in Communism*. London: Hamish Hamilton, 1950.

Crowther, J. G. *Science in Soviet Russia*. London: Williams & Norgate, Ltd., 1930.

Danforth, William H. *Russia Under the Hammer and Sickle*. St. Louis: privately printed, 1927.

Danish, Max. *The World of David Dubinsky*. New York: The World Publishing Company, 1957.

Darling, Jay N. *Ding Goes to Russia*. New York: McGraw-Hill Company, Inc., 1932.

Dawson, Percy M. *Soviet Samples: Diary of an American Physiologist*. Ann Arbor, Mich.: Edwards Brothers, Inc., 1938.

Delafield, E. M. (Edmée Elizabeth Monica De La Pasture). *I Visit the Soviets*. New York: Harper & Brothers, 1937.

Dewey, John. *Impressions of Soviet Russia and the Revolutionary World*. New York: New Republic, Inc., 1929.

Douillet, Joseph. *Moscow Unmasked*, trans. A. W. King. London: The Pilot Press, 1930.

Dreiser, Helen. *My Life with Dreiser*. New York: The World Publishing Company, 1951.

Dreiser, Theodore. *Dreiser Looks at Russia*. New York: H. Liveright, 1928.

Duranty, Walter, *USSR*. New York: J. B. Lippincott Company, 1944.

Eddy, Sherwood. *Eighty Adventurous Years.* New York: Harper & Brothers, 1955.

Edelhertz, Bernard. *The Russian Paradox.* New York: Walton Book Company, 1930.

Evstifeev, Alexander. *Why I Escaped from Soviet Russia.* Seattle: privately printed, 1937.

Feiler, Arthur. *The Experiment of Bolshevism,* trans. H. J. Stenning. London: G. Allen & Unwin, Ltd., 1930.

Feuchtwanger, Lion. *Moscow 1937.* London: Victor Gollancz, Ltd., 1937.

Fischer, Bertha (Mark). *My Lives in Russia.* New York: Harper & Brothers, 1944.

Fischer, Louis. *Men and Politics.* New York: Duell, Sloan and Pearce, 1941.

Francis, Peter. *I Worked in a Soviet Factory.* London: Jarrolds, Publishers, Ltd., 1939.

Frank, Waldo. *Dawn in Russia.* New York: C. Scribner's Sons, 1932.

Gide, André. *Afterthoughts on the U.S.S.R.,* trans. Dorothy Bussy. New York: The Dial Press, 1938.

———. *Return from the U.S.S.R.,* trans. Dorothy Bussy. New York: A. A. Knopf, 1937.

Gitlow, Benjamin. *I Confess.* New York: E. P. Dutton & Co., Inc., 1940.

Greenwall, H. J. *Mirrors of Moscow.* London: G. G. Harrap & Company, Ltd., 1929.

Griffin, Frederick. *Soviet Scene.* Toronto: The Macmillan Company of Canada, Ltd., 1932.

Haldane, Charlotte. *Truth Will Out.* New York: Vanguard Press, 1950.

Harper, Paul V., ed. *The Russia I Believe In: Memoirs of Samuel N. Harper, 1902–1941.* Chicago: University of Chicago Press, 1945.

Hird, John Wynne. *Under Czar and Soviet: My Thirty Years in Russia.* London: Hurst & Blackett, Ltd., 1932.

Holmes, Burton. *The Traveler's Russia.* New York: G. P. Putnam's Sons, 1934.

Howe, Irving. *The CIO and Walter Reuther.* New York: The Devin-Adair Co., 1958.

Huxley, Julian. *A Scientist among the Soviets.* New York: Harper & Brothers, 1932.

Istrati, Panaït. *Russia Unveiled,* trans. R. J. S. Curtis, London: G. Allen & Unwin, Ltd., 1931.

Kaltenborn, H. V. *We Look at the World.* New York: Rae D. Henkle Co., 1930.

Körber, Lili. *Life in a Soviet Factory*, trans. C. W. Sykes. London: John Lane, 1933.

Koestler, Arthur. *The Invisible Writing*. New York: The Macmillan Co., 1954.

Kravchenko, Victor. *I Chose Freedom*. New York: Charles Scribner's Sons, 1946.

Krivitsky, Walter G. *In Stalin's Secret Service*. New York: Harper & Brothers, 1939.

Lansbury, Violet. *An Englishwoman in the U.S.S.R*. London: Putnam, 1940.

Legay, Kleber. *Un mineur francais chez les russes*. Paris: Éditions Pierre Tisné, 1937.

Littlepage, John D., and Demaree Bess. *In Search of Soviet Gold*. New York: Harcourt, Brace and Company, 1938.

Lockhart, H. G. *Babel Visited: A Churchman in Soviet Russia*. Milwaukee, Wis.: Morehouse Publishing Co., 1933.

Loder, John de Vere. *Bolshevism in Perspective*. London: G. Allen & Unwin, Ltd., 1931.

Long, Ray. *An Editor Looks at Russia*. New York: R. Long & R. R. Smith, Inc., 1931.

Low, David, and Kingsley Martin. *Low's Russian Sketchbook*. London: Victor Gollancz, Ltd., 1932.

Luck, Sidney I. *Observation in Russia*. London: The Macmillan Co., Ltd., 1938.

Lyons, Eugene. *Assignment in Utopia*. New York: Harcourt, Brace and Company, 1937.

————. *The Red Decade*. New York: The Bobbs-Merrill Company, 1941.

McCarthy, Margaret. *Generation in Revolt*. London: William Heinemann, Ltd., 1953.

McCormick, Anne O'Hare. *The Hammer and the Scythe*. New York: A. A. Knopf, 1928.

Mannin, Ethel. *Forever Wandering*. New York: E. P. Dutton & Co., Inc., 1935.

————. *South to Samarkand*. London: Jarrolds, Publishers, Ltd., 1936.

Miles, F. S. *Changing Russia*. London: Marshall, Morgen & Scott, Ltd., 1936.

Monkhouse, Allan. *Moscow, 1911–1933*. London: Victor Gollancz, Ltd., 1933.

Motus. *A travers de pays des soviets*. Paris: Les Éditions de France, 1936.

Muggeridge, Malcolm. *Winter in Moscow.* London: Eyre & Spottis-woode, 1934.

O'Flaherty, Liam. *I Went to Russia.* New York: Harcourt, Brace and Company, 1931.

Pares, Bernard. *Moscow Admits a Critic.* London: T. Nelson & Sons, Ltd., 1936.

Pollak, Emmanuil. *SSSR v Obrazakh i Litsakh (The Soviet Union in Images and Pictures).* New York: Russian-American Publishing House, 1935.

Reswick, William. *I Dreamt Revolution.* Chicago: Henry Regnery Co., 1952.

Robinson, William J., M.D. *Soviet Russia as I Saw It.* New York: The International Press, 1932.

Rukeyser, Walter Arnold. *Working for the Soviets.* New York: Covici-Friede, 1932.

Scheffer, Paul. *Seven Years in Soviet Russia,* trans. Arthur Livingston. London: Putnam & Company, 1931.

Scott, John. *Behind the Urals.* [Boston]: Houghton Mifflin Company, 1942.

Seibert, Theodor. *Red Russia,* trans. Eden and Cedar Paul. London: G. Allen & Unwin, Ltd., 1932.

Seymour, June. *In the Moscow Manner.* London: D. Archer, 1935.

Silver, Boris. *The Russian Workers' Own Story.* London: G. Allen & Unwin, Ltd., 1938.

Simoens, R. A. *L'Union Soviétique vue par un travailleur.* Brussels: Impr. "Steenlandt" S.P.R.L., 1941.

Smith, Andrew. *I Was a Soviet Worker.* New York: E. P. Dutton & Co., 1936.

Solonevich, Tamara. *Zapiski Sovetskoi Perevodchitsy (Diary of a Soviet Interpreter).* Sofia, Bulgaria: Golos Rossii, 1937.

Sorenson, Charles E. *My Forty Years with Ford.* New York: W. W. Norton & Company, Inc., 1956.

Stekoll, Harry. *Humanity Made to Order.* New York: L. Furman, Inc., 1937.

——. *Through the Communist Looking-Glass.* New York: Brewer, Warren & Putnam, 1932.

Strong, Anna Louise. *I Change Worlds.* New York: H. Holt and Company, 1935.

Thayer, Charles W. *Bears in the Caviar.* Philadelphia: J. B. Lippincott Company, 1951.

Thompson, Dorothy. *The New Russia.* New York: H. Holt and Company, 1928.

Timbres, Harry, and Rebecca Timbres. *We Didn't Ask Utopia.* New York: Prentice-Hall, Inc., 1939.

Trivanovitch, Vaso. *Crankshafts or Bread.* Ridgfield, Conn.: Acorn Publishing Company, 1940.

Unger, Heinz. *Hammer, Sickle and Baton: The Soviet Memoirs of a Musician.* London: The Cresset Press, Ltd., 1939.

Valtin, Jan (Richard Krebs). *Out of the Night.* New York: Alliance Book Corporation, 1941.

Vidor, John. *Spying in Russia.* London: J. Long, Ltd., 1929.

Walter, Ellery. *Russia's Decisive Year.* New York: G. P. Putnam's Sons, 1932.

Waters, John E. *Red Justice.* Madison, Wis.: privately printed, 1933.

Westgarth, John R. *Russian Engineer.* London: Denis Archer, Ltd., 1934.

Wilson, Edmund. *Red, Black, Blond and Olive.* New York: Oxford University Press, 1956.

Winter, Ella. *Red Virtue.* New York: Harcourt, Brace and Company, 1933.

Yvon, M. *L'U.R.S.S. telle qu'elle est.* Paris: Libraire Gallimard, 1938.

Zaitseff, Cyrille. *Herriot en Russie.* Paris: Nouvelle Éditions-Latins, 1933.

ARTICLES

Aaron, Daniel. "The Three Faces of Lenin." *Survey,* No. 41 (April, 1962), pp. 43–57.

Abolin, A. "The Development of the Soviet Trade Unions." *RILU Magazine,* No. 1–2 (Jan. 15–Feb. 1, 1932), pp. 91–100.

Axtell, Silas B. "Russia and her Foreign Relations." *Annals of the American Academy of Political and Social Sciences,* 128 (July, 1928): 85–92.

Bronska-Pampuch, Wanda. "Russia in German Eyes: 1964." *Survey,* No. 51 (April, 1964), pp. 93–101.

Burns, Emile. "The Congress of Workers Delegations." *Labor Monthly,* 9 (Dec., 1927): 728–33.

Carmody, John M. "American Engineers in Russia." *Engineering News Record,* 107 (Aug. 13, 1931): 262–64.

"Comment by Mathew Woll on an American Trade Unionist's Interview with Stalin." *Current History,* 27 (Feb., 1928): 692.

"Comment fut designé à Vallaures un délegué pour la Russie Soviétique." *Les Cahiers du Bolchevisme,* 5 (Aug., 1930): 796–98.

Communist Party of the United States of America. "Tasks in the Struggle Against Hunger, Repression and War—Resolution of the 13th Plenum of the Central Committee, CPUSA." *The Communist,* 10 (Oct., 1931): 818–37.

Conolly, Violet. "Two Months in Soviet Russia." *Irish Quarterly Review,* 18 (March, 1929): 64–78.

Crankshaw, Edward. "Big Brother Is Still Waiting." *New York Times Magazine,* Dec. 29, 1963, pp. 8, 34–35.

Duranty, Walter. "Moscow Letter." *British-Russian Gazette and Trade Outlook,* 5 (Feb., 1929): 93.

Ercoli, M. "Problems of the United Front." *Communist International,* 12 (Aug. 20, 1935): 1114–27.

"Four Ways to Russia." *Survey Graphic,* May 1, 1929, p. 209.

Furniss, Edgar S. "The Price of Soviet Efficiency." *Current History,* 36 (April, 1932): 123–24.

Gitelman, M. "Foreign Technical Aid." *VOKS,* No. 1–3 (1930), pp. 49–50.

Harris, Lement. "An American Workman in Russia." *Outlook and Independent,* 157 (Feb. 25, 1931): 295–97, 316–17.

"How They Make Cloaks in Soviet Russia." *Justice,* Sept., 1931, p. 5.

Huntington, W. Chapin. "An Uncensored Letter to a Soviet Friend." *Scribners Magazine,* 97 (April, 1935): 209, 224.

Iarotskii, V. "Kongress druzei SSSR" ("Congress of Friends of the USSR"). *Vestnik Truda,* No. 11 (Nov., 1927), pp. 111–23.

————. "Novaia tiaga k Moskve y proletariatov Zapada" ("The new inclination toward Moscow of the Western proletariat"). *Vestnik Truda,* No. 11 (Oct., 1925), pp. 24–33.

"Industry and Engineering in the Union of Soviet Socialist Republics." *Technology Review,* 33 (Nov. 30, 1930): 76–78, 104–6.

Jelenski, K. A. "The Literature of Disenchantment." *Survey,* No. 41 (April, 1962), pp. 109–19.

Jennings, Amy S. "How to Travel in Soviet Russia." *Nation,* 136 (May 10, 1933): 528–30.

"John Dewey in Russia." *Survey,* 61 (Dec. 15, 1928): 348–49.

Kecskemeti, Paul. "The Soviet Approach to International Political Communication." *Public Opinion Quarterly,* 20 (Spring, 1956): 299–308.

Kennell, Ruth, and Milly Bennet. "American Immigrants in Russia." *American Mercury,* 34 (April, 1932): 463–72.

Kilinskii, A. "Ob usloviiakh truda inostrantsev v SSSR" ("On labor conditions for foreigners in the USSR"). *Voprosy Truda,* No. 1 (Jan., 1931), pp. 76–83.

Knox, James. "Diary of a Soviet Guide." *Contemporary Russia,* 2 (Autumn, 1937): 44–55.

Kreibich, Karl. "The Delegations to Russia." *Communist International,* 5 (Jan. 1, 1928): 17–20.

Lammers, Donald N. "The Engineers' Trial (Moscow, 1933) and Anglo-Soviet Relations." *South Atlantic Quarterly,* 62 (Spring, 1963): 256–67.

Laqueur, Walter. "Russia Through Western Eyes." *Survey,* No. 41 (April, 1962), pp. 3–13.

Liebman, Marcel. "The Webbs and the New Civilization." *Survey,* No. 41 (April, 1962), pp. 58–74.

Liss, A. "Novaia volna rabochikh delegatsii v SSSR" ("The new wave of workers' delegations to the USSR"). *Mezhdunarodnoe Rabochee Dvizhenie,* No. 31 (Aug. 5, 1926), pp. 3–4.

Mitford, Captain A. H. "The Russian-British Chamber of Commerce and its Functions." *British-Russian Gazette and Trade Outlook,* 6 (July, 1930): 2.

Morse, Ruth V. "Russia's Four Hundred." *Survey Graphic,* 26 (April, 1937): 209.

Muchnic, Charles M. "A Businessman's View of Russia: Letters from an American Executive." *Harper's Magazine,* 159 (Sept., 1929): 437–53.

Nemzer, Louis. "The Soviet Friendship Societies." *Public Opinion Quarterly,* 13 (Summer, 1949): 265–84.

"Nos prochaines campagnes." *Les Cahiers du Bolchevisme,* 5 (March, 1930): 291–93.

Remnant, Ernest. "The British Industrial Mission to Russia." *English Review,* 49 (July, 1929): 27–41.

Robertson, Ben, Jr. "Our Sailors Sleep in the Palace of the Czar." *Scribner's Magazine,* 91 (May, 1932): 298–99.

Rothstein, Andrew. "Foreign Delegations to the USSR." *RILU Magazine,* No. 13, N.S. (Aug. 1, 1931), pp. 1–6.

Rubiner, F. "Rabota sredi inostrannykh rabochikh—zadacha vsei Part-organizatsii" ("Work among foreign workers—the task of the whole Party organization"). *Partiinoe Stroitel'stvo,* No. 17–18 (Sept., 1932), pp. 17–20.

"Rules for Contracts with Foreign Engineers." *British-Russian Gazette and Trade Outlook,* 6 (Nov., 1929): 38.

"Russia Bids for Tourist Trade." *Review of Reviews,* 84 (Aug., 1931): 94–96.

"The Russian-British Chamber of Commerce and its Functions." *British-Russian Gazette and Trade Outlook,* 6 (July, 1930): 202.

Samoilenko, Z. "The Foreign Workers and Specialists of the Electro Factory." *VOKS*, No. 6 (1931), pp. 49–51.

"Seeing Red; Russia Attracts Students." *Review of Reviews*, 92 (July, 1935): 70–71.

Sherman, Alfred. "The Days of the Left Book Club." *Survey*, No. 41 (April, 1962), pp. 75–86.

Smith, Howard P. "Do Intercultural Experiences Affect Attitudes?" *Journal of Abnormal Social Psychology*, 51 (Nov., 1955): 469–77.

Sollins, I. V. "A New Venture in International Education." *IIE News Bulletin*, 9 (Dec., 1933), 4–5.

"The State Syndicate of Retail Trade (GORT)." *VOKS*, No. 1 (1932), pp. 180–81.

"The USSR as the Shock Brigade of the World Proletariat." *RILU Magazine*, No. 22, N.S. (Dec. 15, 1931), pp. 1–3.

Voiloshnikov, G., and Ch. Sommers. "O Partiino-massovoi rabote s inostrannymi rabochimi" ("On Party-mass work with foreign workmen"). *Partiinoe Stroitel'stvo*, No. 3–4 (Feb., 1931), pp. 42–46.

"What British Labor Saw in Soviet Russia." *American Federationist*, 32 (March, 1925): 184–89.

White, Nate. "Prisoners of Intourist: Visitors to U.S.S.R. Face Wall of 'Nyets.' " *Christian Science Monitor*, Aug. 18, 1960, p. 7.

White, William C. "Americans in Soviet Russia." *Scribner's Magazine*, 89 (Feb., 1931): 171–82.

PERIODICALS

Auto Workers News (Detroit, Michigan). May, 1927—May, 1930; Feb., 1934—Aug., 1934.

Imprecorr (London). 1926–37.

Labor Unity (New York). 1932–34.

La Vie Economique des Soviets (Paris). 1929–30.

Mezhdunarodnoe Rabochee Dvizhenie (Moscow). 1926–32.

Russia Today (London). Dec., 1930—Dec., 1932.

Soviet Culture Review (Moscow). 1933–34.

Soviet Russia Today (New York). Feb., 1932—Dec., 1937.

Soviet Union Review (Washington, D.C.). Jan., 1925—April, 1934.

Weekly News Bulletin of VOKS (Moscow). 1926–29.

NEWSPAPERS

Daily Worker (New York). 1925–37.

Ekonomicheskaia Zhizn' (Moscow). 1925–37.

La Vie Ouvrière (Paris). Jan., 1925—Dec., 1926; Jan.—June, 1928.
Moscow Daily News (Moscow). May, 1932—April, 1933; 1936.
Moscow News (Moscow). 1930–32; 1934–37.
New York Times (New York). 1925–37.
Pravda (Moscow). June, 1925—June, 1937.
Trud (Moscow). Sept. 28, 1927.
The Worker (London). Dec., 1927—June, 1930.
Workers Life (London). April—Sept., 1928; 1929.
Workers News (Moscow). Jan.—April, 1932.
The Young Worker (New York). 1925–36.

REPORTS, PROCEEDINGS AND RESOLUTIONS

American Federation of Labor. *Report of Proceedings of the Forty-Sixth Annual Convention of the American Federation of Labor.* Held at Detroit, Mich., Oct. 4–14, 1926. Washington, D.C.: AFL, 1926.

————. *Report of Proceedings of the Fifty-Fourth Annual Convention of the American Federation of Labor.* Held at San Francisco, Calif., Oct. 1–12, 1934. Washington, D.C.: AFL, 1934.

American-Russian Chamber of Commerce. *Reports.* 1926–30.

American Trade Union Delegation to the Soviet Union. *Russia after Ten Years.* New York: International Publishers, 1927.

American Trade Union Delegation to the Soviet Union. *Soviet Russia in the Second Decade.* Eds. Stuart Chase, Robert Dunn, Rexford Guy Tugwell. New York: John Day, 1928.

Beal, Fred E. *Foreign Workers in a Soviet Tractor Plant.* Moscow: Co-operative Publishing Society of Foreign Workers in the U.S.S.R., 1933.

Britain and the Soviets: Report of the Congress of Peace and Friendship with the USSR, 1935. London: Martin Laurence, 1936.

The Communist International. *The Communist International Between the Fifth & the Sixth World Congresses, 1924–8.* London: Communist Party of Great Britain, 1928.

————. *The Struggle against Imperialist War and the Task of the Communists: Resolution of the Sixth World Congress of the Communist International, 1928.* New York: Workers Library Publishers, 1932.

Communist Party of Great Britain. "Political Report of the Central Committee," *The New Line: Documents of the Tenth Congress of the Communist Party of Great Britain, January 19–22, 1929.* London: Communist Party of Great Britain, 1929.

————. *Reports, Theses and Resolutions of the Eighth Congress of the Communist Party of Great Britain, October 16–17, 1926.* London: Communist Party of Great Britain, 1927.

————. *Resolutions of the Eleventh Congress of the Communist Party of Great Britain, November 30—December 3, 1929.* London: Communist Party of Great Britain, 1930.

————. Central Committee. "The Present Situation in Great Britain and the Tasks of the Party—Resolution of the Central Committee of the Communist Party of Great Britain." *Communist Review,* 2 (May, 1930): 208–34.

Communist Youth International. *The Communist Youth International: Report of Activity between the Fourth and Fifth Congresses, 1924–28.* London: Communist Party of Great Britain, 1928.

Co-op Printing Society. *Report of a Group of Cooperators on a Visit to Russia, August, 1929.* Manchester, 1930.

Co-op Union. *Soviet Russia 1932: Reports of Two Groups of Cooperators on a Visit to the USSR in the Summer of 1932.* Manchester, 1933.

Durham Miners Association. *A Visit to Russia, 1937: Report of Durham Miners on Their Visit to the USSR.* London, 1937.

Friends of Soviet Russia. *Hands Off Soviet Russia: Report of the Cologne Conference of Friends of Soviet Russia.* London: British National Committee of FOSR, 1928.

————. *Russia Today, Britain Tomorrow: Report of British Factory Workers Delegation to Soviet Russia.* London, 1930.

Institute of International Education. *Sixteenth Annual Report of the Director.* 1934/35.

Labour Party. *The Communist Solar System.* London: Labour Publications Department, 1933.

Labour Research Department. *Soviet Russia Today: Report of British Workers Delegation, November, 1927.* London, 1927.

Lartigue, H. *La verité sur l'URSS, 1937.* Paris: L'Intersyndical de Services Publics au Profit de ses Oeuvres, 1937.

Les Femmes pour l'Union Soviétique. *Les Delegations au Xth Anniversaire de la Revolution d'Octobre.* Paris: Bureau d'Éditions, 1928.

Parti Communiste de France. "Resolution du CC sur les dernieres campagnes du Parti." *Les Cahiers du Bolchevisme,* 7 (Oct. 15, 1927), 1061.

————. "Resolution pour le Parti Communiste Francais sur le travail parmi les femmes." *Les Cahiers du Bolchevisme,* 3 (Nov., 1928): 1121–27.

————. "Resolution sur les taches d'organizations." *Les Cahiers du Bolchevisme,* 7 (May, 1932): 44–45.

Piatnitskii, O. *The Communist Parties in the Fight for the Masses.* 13th Plenum of Executive Committee of the Communist International. New York: Workers Library, 1933.

————. *The Work of the Communist Parties of France and Germany and the Tasks of the Communists in the Trade Union Movement.* 12th Plenum of the Executive Committee of the Communist International. New York: Workers Library, 1932.

Report of the Anglo-Russian Committee on the British Trade Delegation to Russia, March–April, 1929. London, 1929.

Roome, W., and J. Crane. *Our Journey Through Russia: Report of Two Kent Miners.* London: National Union of Conservative and Unionist Associations, 1929.

"Sixth Plenum of the Enlarged ECCI of the Communist International, February–March, 1926," *Imprecorr,* March 10, March 25, April 1, 1926.

Society for Cultural Relations (London). *Annual Reports.* 1924–37.

Steiger, Andrew J. *American Engineers in the Soviet Union.* (Pamphlet Series No. 3), Russian Economic Institute-Co-operating Institution of the Research Bureau for Post-war Economics, New York, 1944.

Trades Union Congress. *Russia 1924: Official Report of the British Trades Union Delegation to Russia in November and December, 1924.* London: Trades Union Congress General Council, 1925.

TsK VKP (b) (Central Committee of the All-Union Communist Party-Bolshevik). "O khode vypolneniia direktiv TsK po rabote s inostrannymi rabochimi" ("On the manner in which the directives of the Central Committee pertaining to work with foreign workers are being carried out"). Postanovlenie TsK VKP (b) ot 23 Marta 1931 goda (Enactment of the Central Committee of the All-Union Communist Party-Bolshevik of March 23, 1931). *Partiinoe Stroitel'stvo,* No. 7 (April, 1931), p. 75.

————. "O rabote sredi inostrannykh rabochikh" ("On work among foreign workers"). Postanovlenie TsK VKP (b) ot 21 Noiabria 1930 goda (Enactment of the Central Committee of the All-Union Communist Party-Bolshevik of Nov. 21, 1930), *Partiinoe Stroitel'stvo,* No. 23–24 (Dec., 1930), p. 67.

————. "O sostoianie raboty s inostrannymi rabochimi i spetsialistami" ("On the state of work with foreign workers and specialists"). Postanovlenie TsK VKP (b) ot 16 Aout 1931 goda (Enactment of the Central Committee of the All-Union Communist Party-Bolshevik, Aug. 16, 1931), *Partiinoe Stroitel'stvo*, No. 18 (Sept., 1931), pp. 55–56.

U.S. *Congressional Record*. Vols. 70–74.

U.S. Congress, House of Representatives, Committee on Foreign Affairs, Subcommittee No. 5 on National and International Movements. Supplement 1, "100 Years of Communism, 1848–1948," *The Strategy and Tactics of World Communism*. 80 Cong., 2 sess. (1948).

————, Special Committee on Un-American Activities. *Hearings on Investigation of Un-American Propaganda Activities in the United States*. 76 Cong., 1 sess. (1939).

————, Special Committee to Investigate Communist Activities in the United States. *Hearings*. 71 Cong., 3 sess. (1930).

USSR Supreme Court. *Hearings Before the Special Session of the Supreme Court of the USSR on Wrecking Activities at Power Stations in the USSR*. Translation of the official verbatim report. Moscow: State Law Publishing House, 1933.

MISCELLANEOUS DOCUMENTS AND OTHER PRIMARY SOURCES

Adler, Friedrich. *The Anglo-Russian Report; A Criticism of the Report of the British Trades Union Delegation to Russia, from the Point of View of International Socialism*, trans. H. J. Stenning. London: P. S. King & Son, Ltd., 1925.

Great Britain, Home Office. *Communist Papers—Documents Selected from Those Obtained on the Arrest of Communist Leaders on the 14th and 21st October, 1925*. Cmd. 2682. London, 1926.

International Anti-Communist Entente. *The Red Network*. London: Gerald Duckworth & Co., Ltd., 1939.

Rudolf, A. (Raoul Lazlo). *Pourquoi j'ai quitté l'URSS*. La Documentation Anti-Communiste du CILACC, No. 10–11 (1935).

Russia and the British Labour Delegation's Report: A Reply. London: British Committee for the Defense of Political Prisoners in Russia, 1925.

Spravochnik Profrabotnika: Sbornik Rukovodiashchikh Materialov po Professional'nomi Dvizheniiu (Handbook of Trade Union Work: Collection of Leadership Materials for the Trade Union Movement), ed. G. Mel'nichanskii. Moscow: V.Ts. S.P.S., 1927.

Stalin, I. *Sochineniia (Works)*, Vol. VII. Moscow: Institut Marksa-Engelsa-Lenina, 1947.

Volin, B., ed. *Gosti Proletariata SSSR (Guests of the Proletariat of the USSR)*. Moscow: Profizdat, 1932.

Zhivov, M., ed. *Glazami Inostrantsev (Through Foreign Eyes)*. Moscow: Gosudarstvennoe Izdatel'stvo Khudozhestvennoi Literatury, 1932.

MANUSCRIPT COLLECTIONS

Bibliothèque de Documentation Internationale Contemporaine, University of Paris. Files on Soviet Russia.

Department of State, Washington. Decimal Files, 1925–37.

Institute of International Education, New York. Anglo-American Institute of 1st Moscow University Files.

New York Public Library, Manuscript Division. Frank L. Walsh Files, General Correspondence, 1926–37.

State Historical Society of Wisconsin Library, Madison, Wisconsin, Manuscript Division. Alexander Gumberg Papers, American-Russian Chamber of Commerce Files.

Trades Union Congress Reference Library, London. Files on Soviet Russia.

Index

Abbe, James, 129, 153, 161

Adler, Friedrich, 136, 165

All-Russian Council of Trade Unions. *See* All-Union Central Council of Trade Unions

All-Union Central Council of Trade Unions: mentioned, 33, 44, 45, 47, 52, 57, 123, 160; published *Mezhdunarodnoe Rabochee Dvizhenie* (*The International Working Class Movement*) jointly with Profintern, 36; proposed formation of International Workmen's Information Bureau, 37–38; handled arrangements for Congress of FSU, 1927, 38; behind Cologne meeting of FSU, 43; issued invitations to labor to visit USSR, 44; creation of foreign bureau attached to, for work among foreign workers, 72, 107; ordered to publish materials for foreign workers, 106. *See also* Commission on Foreign Relations; Friends of the Soviet Union; Labor delegations

All-Union Chamber of Commerce for the West: aided business delegations to the USSR, 64; Soviet statement concerning technical assistance at meeting of German section of, 71; invited foreign visitors to address its meetings, 87; objections of manager of American section to idea of American club in Moscow, 134; attempted to influence Moscow representative of American-Russian Chamber of Commerce, 139–40

All-Union Chamber of Commerce for Western Trade. *See* All-Union Chamber of Commerce for the West

All-Union Commissariat for Education, 76

All-Union Commissariat for Foreign Affairs: mentioned, 86; Press Office of, 72, 120, 128, 137–38; planned visit of George Bernard Shaw to state farm, 150; concerned about effect of poor treatment of foreigners on Soviet diplomatic relations, 171. *See also* Journalists (foreign)

All-Union Comissariat for Foreign Trade, 64

All-Union Comissariat for Labor, 67, 71, 147

All-Union Communist Party (b).
See Communist parties, Soviet
All-Union Congress of Soviets, Central Executive Committee of, 63,
108. *See also* Citizenship policy
(Soviet)
All-Union Cooperative Publishing
House of Foreign Workers, 98,
167–68, 183
All-Union Cooperative Publishing
Society of Foreign Workers, 98,
167–68, 183
All-Union Council of People's Commissars, 59, 115–16
All-Union Society for Cultural Relations with Foreign Countries
(VOKS): mentioned, 33; goals
and activities of, with reference
to foreign intellectuals and students, 58, 63, 74, 76, 79, 87;
composition and personnel of, 59,
80; activities of, with reference to
national friendship societies, 60–
63; cultural activities of, among
foreign workers, 72, 99; invited
Dreiser to visit USSR, 83; prevented American editor from contacting Soviet writers directly, 130;
criticism of, 133, 191–92; changed
name to State Committee for Cultural Relations with Foreign Countries, 206. *See also* Front organizations; Intellectuals (foreign)
Amalgamated Bank Travel Service,
73
American business delegation (to
the USSR), 1929: sponsored by
American-Russian Chamber of
Commerce, 64; entertained in
USSR, 84–85; accuracy of statements attributed to, 161; commented on, 189
American Federation of Labor, 49–
50, 182
American League Against War and
Fascism, 190

American League of Professional
Writers, 190
American-Russian Chamber of Commerce; mentioned, 30, 76, 78,
134, 146; activities of, 23, 75; attitude of, toward presence of
forced labor in Russia, 29–30;
questionnaire on forced labor of,
30; sponsored American business
delegation (to the USSR), 1929,
64; relations of, with Mostorg and
Commissariat for Foreign Trade,
64; Soviet attempts to influence
selection of Moscow representative
of, 139–40; U.S. recognition of
USSR and, 194. *See also* American business delegation (to the
USSR), 1929; Business delegations (foreign)
American Society for Cultural Relations with the USSR, 62, 190
American trade union delegation to
the Soviet Union, 1927: Communist control of, 26, 48–52,
238n4; members of, 35; recruitment of, 47–51; opinion toward,
of AFL, 49–50; financing of, 50–
52; instructions on composition of,
53; lack of free choice in itineraries of, criticized, 116; validity
of report of, questioned, 166–67,
250–52n39; Communist inspiration behind report of, 166–67; effects on public opinion of report of,
182; lack of preparation for USSR
of, 189; discrepancy in dates of,
explained, 219n30
Amtorg: mentioned, 31, 76, 140,
153; activities of, with reference
to foreign businessmen, 64, 86;
recruitment of foreign specialists
and workers by, 67, 68, 69, 71, 97;
list of American companies contracting with the USSR, 193; on
need to hire highly qualified foreign specialists, 91–92. *See also*
Employment policy (Soviet); En-